The Films of
Martin Scorsese and Robert De Niro

Andrew J. Rausch

THE SCARECROW PRESS, INC.
Lanham • Toronto • Plymouth, UK
2010

Published by Scarecrow Press, Inc.
A wholly owned subsidiary of The Rowman & Littlefield Publishing Group, Inc.
4501 Forbes Boulevard, Suite 200, Lanham, Maryland 20706
http://www.scarecrowpress.com

Estover Road, Plymouth PL6 7PY, United Kingdom

British Library Cataloguing in Publication Information Available

Library of Congress Cataloging-in-Publication Data
Rausch, Andrew J.
 The films of Martin Scorsese and Robert De Niro / Andrew J.
Rausch.
    p. cm.
 Includes bibliographical references and index.
 Includes collaborative filmography.
 ISBN 978-0-8108-7413-8 (cloth : alk. paper) — ISBN 978-0-8108-7414-5
(ebook)
 1. Scorsese, Martin—Criticism and interpretation. 2. De Niro,
Robert—Criticism and interpretation. I. Title.
 PN1998.3.S39R38 2010
 791.4302'33092—dc22   2009049523

Printed in the United States of America

For Kerri

Sometimes I say, "Look, I'm gonna do this," and somehow he knows that's right to do, to make that choice. Marty is very good at picking up on things. He gives people more latitude to come up with ideas, because he's not afraid to experiment with things or accept ideas from other people. And even if they seem a little off-the-wall, sometimes an idea that's so out in left field is actually more appropriate than you would imagine. And he's able to see that and orchestrate it in the scene—maybe bring it down a notch if it's too much but still keep the basic idea intact. We have a kind of shorthand understanding about a lot of things. It's a lot more complicated than "alter ego."

—Robert De Niro

Bob De Niro, when he shows me something, or when he has an idea, when something comes right from that visceral part of him, it just comes right out of his soul. You know, I'm surprised that it's always extremely valid and quite good—I usually find it to be pretty much according to what I feel. We're always finishing each other's sentences creatively. We'll put it that way. If we're struggling for words, creatively, he can find them. And that's a pretty rare thing.

—Martin Scorsese

Contents

Foreword

There's no real way to gauge the greatest films of all time. Sure, you can look at things like box office receipts and the number of awards won, but none of that stuff really tells you anything. If you used the formula of dollars earned plus awards won, *Titanic* would come out as one of the greatest films of all time, which proves that the equation doesn't work. And that's not to knock *Titanic*, because in the opinion of many people, it is a great film. But we all know what opinions are like. . . .

The reason I bring up the whole question of determining the greatest films of all time is because it is something that has fascinated me for many years—films that are universally loved and appreciated by a significant number of the movie-watching public. And of course, the concept of universally loved movies in and of itself is subjective and dictated by the tastes of individuals. As someone who doesn't care for *Titanic* but is endlessly amused by *D.C. Cab*, I serve as the perfect example of the bizarre nature of subjectivity.

By now, most of you are wondering what any of this has to do with the cinematic collaborations of director Martin Scorsese and actor Robert De Niro. It's actually pretty simple—when Andy Rausch asked me to write the foreword to this book, I jumped at the opportunity, in part because I know and like Andy, but also because I love and appreciate the films of Scorsese and De Niro. And in my humble opinion, the collaborations of Scorsese and De Niro rank among some of the greatest films of all time.

The problem, of course, is that there is no way to prove that any of the eight films directed by Scorsese that have starred De Niro are all that great. Certainly the dollars-plus-awards equation is not an effective measure, because although some of these films have done well at the box office, none were blockbusters by any stretch of the imagination. The top grossing film of 1990, the year *GoodFellas* was released, was *Home Alone*. In fact, *GoodFellas*, which was number twenty-six in terms of top earners for the year, was beat out by such movies as *Kindergarten Cop*, *Teenage Mutant Ninja Turtles*, and the Steven Seagal pinnacle of cinematic quality, *Hard to Kill*. All of which proves that dollars earned is not an adequate gauge of a film's greatness.

The same is true, to a lesser extent, of awards won. While De Niro took home an Oscar for his performance in *Raging Bull* (and was nominated for *Taxi Driver* and *Cape Fear*), Scorsese never won an Academy Award for any of his films starring De Niro (only *GoodFellas* and *Raging Bull* earned him Best Director nominations). The year that Scorsese was nominated for *Raging Bull*, both director and film lost to Robert Redford and *Ordinary People*. A decade later, Scorsese and *GoodFellas* lost to Kevin Costner and *Dances with Wolves*. And while both *Ordinary People* and *Dances with Wolves* have their cinematic merit, how many people have been clamoring for a deluxe, double-disc special edition DVD of *Ordinary People*? When was the last time you were at a party and someone started spitting out quotes from *Dances with Wolves*?

In the history of film, there has never been a relationship quite like that of Martin Scorsese and Robert De Niro. Yes, there have been special partnerships between directors and actors that have resulted in work that defines the careers of both. Director Akira Kurosawa's best films almost always starred Toshiro Mifune, and John Wayne was never better than when he was working with director John Ford. But Kurosawa had directed more than a half-dozen movies before collaborating with Mifune. Ford had directed more than ninety movies and Wayne had appeared in more than seventy before the two collaborated on *Rio Bravo* (which wasn't even their first time working together). Anthony Mann and Alfred Hitchcock were both seasoned professionals before working with Jimmy Stewart, turning out some of their best work. By comparison, Scorsese had directed only two features before making *Mean Streets* with De Niro, who was still struggling to make a name for himself after a handful of screen performances.

Scorsese was part of a new generation of filmmakers that stormed the motion picture industry in the late 1960s and early 1970s. Educated in the first real film schools and nurtured on movies during the early days of television when movies were delivered into the living rooms of America, this new generation quickly set itself apart from the directors who had come before them. Before the arrival of Francis Ford Coppola, Brian De Palma, Hal Ashby, and the other mavericks that made up the last great era of American cinema, the rules of filmmaking were clearly defined by the studio system of Hollywood. But this new generation rewrote the rulebook in an effort to make film more reflective of the changing times of America's sociopolitical landscape.

There were so many amazing films made between the late 1960s and the mid-1970s that it would be difficult if not impossible to list them all. But of all those films, one that stands out for a variety of reasons is 1973's *Mean Streets*, the first collaboration between Scorsese and De Niro.

Scorsese was barely thirty at the time, and De Niro was still in his twenties. And both were eager to prove themselves in an industry that was not slowing down for anyone who was playing it safe. There was no room for directors or actors who wanted to continue doing things the way they had been done for decades. Film had become the place where the volatile emotions of the decaying American Dream could not only be explored, but exposed with a cinematic truth that was brutal and real. It was a truth that was ugly, but within its ugliness was a profound beauty of uncompromising honesty. And any director or actor who was not willing to shove an audience's face into the stinky reality of the steaming pile of crap that had been deposited on the carpet of Vietnam War–era America was risking irrelevance.

Mean Streets was the beginning of a prolific, beautiful, and dangerous relationship that would result in some of the most influential films of the last four decades. I know that may sound a bit hyperbolic. But the importance of Scorsese and De Niro's collaborations are as close to fact as you can get in the subjective world of film criticism.

Think about it. To date, Martin Scorsese and Robert De Niro have done eight films together. Among those movies were *Mean Streets*, *Taxi*

Driver, *Raging Bull*, and *GoodFellas*. I'll say that again, for those not paying attention—among the cinematic collaborations of Scorsese and De Niro are the films *Mean Streets*, *Taxi Driver*, *Raging Bull*, and *GoodFellas*. And that only represents half of the films they did together. The only other dynamic duo of film to mine more gold than Scorsese and De Niro would be Kurosawa and Mifune.

Having marveled at the films discussed in this book, I realize now that despite my devotion to the Scorsese/De Niro team, I didn't know much about the history of the two or their films for that matter. For all the times I've seen *Raging Bull*, I never knew the story behind the making of the movie. And now, having read about the trials and tribulations of bringing such a landmark picture to fruition, I appreciate it and those who made it even more.

One of the things that makes the collaborations of Scorsese and De Niro such incredible works of cinema is that as individuals and collaborators, they make the process look natural and effortless. You watch *Taxi Driver* and see nothing but the pure genius that unfolds on the screen, never once questioning how it got there or how difficult it was to capture. But in chronicling all that went into *Taxi Driver* and the other seven films of Marty and Bobby, this book creates a new level of appreciation for their incredible body of work by explaining that it didn't all come naturally. It wasn't all effortless. There were difficulties and setbacks that threatened the very existence of these films—and yet here they are today, to entertain and inspire, to be appreciated and analyzed.

The Films of Martin Scorsese and Robert De Niro is filled with great information, entertaining anecdotes, and a wealth of insight into eight movies and two men who worked closely together to make the films. But there is something else within the pages that I hope is not lost on anyone reading this book, be they film buffs or aspiring filmmakers. This book serves as a vital reminder of the essential nature of collaboration in an industry driven by ego. Great films are not made by one person or even two. Even *GoodFellas* and *Taxi Driver*—my two favorite Scorsese/De Niro films—are not the product of two men, but the cumulative result of a team that pulled together to make great movies.

If there is in fact an aspiring filmmaker reading this book, looking to glean some secret of success from the history that unfolds in these pages, never lose sight of the fact that no one person can do it alone. To become the next Scorsese, you must find your De Niro, as well as the others that will challenge you to be your best, just as you challenge them. Truly great cinema comes from nothing less.

—David Walker, film journalist, motion picture director,
editor of *Bad Azz Mofo* magazine, and
coauthor of *Reflections on Blaxploitation*
(with Andrew J. Rausch and Chris Watson)

Acknowledgments

I am indebted to a number of people who have assisted me on this project, but none more so than Melissa Prophet. Melissa not only allowed me to interview her, but she was also instrumental in coordinating several other interviews for this book. I would also like to thank the following individuals: my editor, Stephen Ryan, for allowing me to write this book, which I had dreamed of for more than a decade; my wife and assistant/editor Kerri Rausch, without whose help no book would ever get finished; my friend and literary agent Marilyn Allen; David Walker, who came through in the clutch; each and every person who allowed me to interview them for this book; and Martin Scorsese and Robert De Niro, without whose films this book would not exist.

Additional thanks goes to the following individuals for listening to me drone on for hours on end about this project: Ron Riley, Charles Pratt Jr., Chris Watson, and Michael Dequina.

Introduction

It would be difficult to overstate the importance of the collaborations of Martin Scorsese and Robert De Niro. Four of these eight films—*Mean Streets, Taxi Driver, Raging Bull,* and *GoodFellas*—are bona fide masterpieces. Each of these films has raised the bar for cinematic artistry and forever changed the landscape of American cinema. The latter three of these four have each been labeled by many critics as the defining films of the decades in which they were released. Even the so-called failures of this collaborative duo are remarkably well-crafted films that pushed the boundaries of their respective genres. Say what you will about the excesses of *New York, New York,* but surely we can all agree that this dark film is one of the most fascinating and superbly acted musicals ever produced. And as film historians and cineastes, how can we fail to recognize and appreciate the deliberately subdued work of both men on *The King of Comedy?*

Scorsese and De Niro's less-appreciated works are ripe for reappraisal. Upon closer inspection I believe these films will ultimately become recognized as minor masterpieces. Perhaps *Casino* and *The King of Comedy* aren't in the league of *Taxi Driver* and *Raging Bull,* but what is? *Casino* may not be as great a film as *GoodFellas* but does it have to be? The problem with appraising the films of these two artists is that critics and film journalists tend to compare each new entry to the masterpieces that preceded it. It is my contention that if one compares these "lesser" Scorsese/De Niro collaborations to other films made within the same genres or within the same time frame, one quickly finds that these films are immensely better than most. I would contend that, save for a lagging third act, much of *Casino* is every bit as good as Scorsese's Best Picture–winner *The Departed*. Obviously *Casino* is not in league with *The Departed*, but I daresay it's close.

Each of the eight films made by the team of Scorsese and De Niro is significant, even if to a lesser extent. If *New York, New York* is the least qualitative film these men have made together, it's also their most ambitious. Many cineastes thumb their noses at *Cape Fear* and dismiss it as being popcorn fare, but it's difficult to dismiss the effort that De Niro put into his role, once again transforming his body. I would contend that another factor making it difficult to immediately rank the films of these men is that they frequently defy expectations and deliver films that aren't exactly what critics and audiences expect or want. Who would have envisioned Scorsese and De Niro following up the gritty *Taxi Driver* with a musical? Who among us could have anticipated that odd little film *The King of Comedy*? How about a big-budget Hitchcockian thriller in which De Niro plays the villain?

What is it about the collaborative process of these two men that pushes each of them to reach levels of artistry well beyond their normal boundaries? Both Scorsese and De Niro are gifted artists when left to their own devices, and each has an extraordinary résumé filled with superlative work. Despite this, it can easily enough be argued that Martin Scorsese and Robert De Niro do their finest work when collaborating with one another.

The initial idea behind this book was to investigate the processes that created these films and uncover what exactly it is about this partnership that enables these men to produce such magnificent works of art. However, this turned out to be quite difficult. Anecdotal tidbits, production minutiae, and details of their methodology provide us with clues, but definitive answers remain elusive. The two men are very private about their collaborative working habits, which likely explains the fact that neither of them would agree to sit down with me for this book. Both Scorsese and De Niro have touched upon the subject of their partnership in interviews, but they are both extremely guarded about the dynamics of this most celebrated collaborative union. The secrecy remains even when they are making a film together; rather than including other actors or crew members in their discussions, the two men prefer to exchange ideas regarding set-ups and character motivations in private.

The truth, I suspect, is that even Scorsese and De Niro don't know exactly what it is about these collaborations that produces such cinematic magic. I would also venture that their discomfort in talking about this union is much like in baseball when no one talks about a no-hitter while a pitcher is in the midst of tossing one; the thought is that if you talk about it, that magic just might disappear. And who can blame these artists for not looking the proverbial gift horse in the mouth? Surely these men are as much a gift to one another from the gods of cinema as are their individual talents. Perhaps it's enough simply to know that this artistic alliance yields incredible results. Why ask why?

The secretive nature of this union only serves to add to the mythos surrounding these already legendary productions. So if this book is incapable of fully explaining the dynamics of the Scorsese/De Niro collaboration, then let it serve as both a record of and tribute to these eight fantastic films.

CHAPTER ONE

Mean Streets (1973)

I was raised with them, the gangsters and the priests. And now, as an artist, in a way, I'm both a gangster and a priest.

—Martin Scorsese

The Backstory

The story behind *Mean Streets* began way back in 1966, some six years before Martin Scorsese and Robert De Niro met for the first time. Scorsese, along with film school classmate Mardik Martin, began hammering out early drafts of the screenplay, which was at that time titled *Season of the Witch*. First Scorsese wrote an outline. Then Martin "worked out the structure" while Scorsese worked to add depth and dimension to his characters, as well as further detail to a number of the incidents in the story line. Scorsese and Martin did much of the work on these early drafts while driving around Manhattan in Martin's beat-up old red Valiant. "We were used to that," Scorsese says. "We were film students. Film students write anywhere."[1]

The screenplay, a tale about petty Italian American thugs in New York's Little Italy, was steeped in religion. The screenplay reflected Scorsese's love of cinema as it drew its inspirations from John Cassavetes'

1

1959 film *Shadows* and Italian neorealism. And like the films of French auteur Francois Truffaut, *Season of the Witch* was drawn from the life experiences of its director. Growing up a small, sickly asthmatic, Scorsese hadn't been a hood like the characters in his script, but he'd run with friends who were. Scorsese and Martin envisioned the project as the third installment in a trilogy of films about religious conflict that had begun with the unfilmed screenplay *Jerusalem, Jerusalem* and had continued with the student film *Who's That Knocking at My Door?*

However, the screenplay proved to be a difficult sell. "The first place I took [the screenplay] was the AFI [American Film Institute] in New York," Scorsese explains.

> At that time, they were just starting a feature program. I went over and gave them about a fifty-page outline. It was ridiculous. The girl was nothing and it had no character but it had all the basic elements. They told me they couldn't do it. They said, "We should be doing this kind of thing, but we can't do it." Then I took it to Joe Brenner, who's a sex film distributor who distributed *Who's That Knocking?* with the sex scene in it. I was trying anything. I said, "I'll shoot it in 16, anything." He said no, so we put it away. . . . In 1968, I thought I had access to some money, and I got it out and rewrote it again. Another rejection. So I put it away totally.[2]

The screenplay for *Season of the Witch* remained on the shelf until after the completion of Scorsese's first "real" film, *Boxcar Bertha*, which he'd made for exploitation impresario Roger Corman. After the completion of that film, Scorsese planned to direct a second film for Corman—either a gladiator picture called *The Arena* or a *Papillon* rip-off titled *I Escaped from Devil's Island*. However, two painful responses to *Boxcar Bertha* helped to change his mind. The first blow to Scorsese's pride came when American International Pictures chieftain Sam Arkoff commented that the film was "almost good." The second blow—the one that finally nudged Scorsese to return to *Season of the Witch*—was delivered by Scorsese's mentor, John Cassavetes. Cassavetes informed Scorsese that he had just wasted a year of his life making a "piece of shit." He told the younger director that *Boxcar Bertha* was good for what it was—exploitation—but that Scorsese was capable of much more. Having seen *Who's That Knocking at My Door?* Cassavetes asked Scorsese if he had any other ideas for projects that would be as personal and important as that one had been. Remembering the script he and Mardik Martin had penned half a decade earlier, Scorsese said yes, but added that he needed to rewrite it. To this Cassavetes urged him, "Rewrite it then!"[3]

Scorsese then began reworking the material. His girlfriend, Sandy Weintraub—the daughter of producer Fred Weintraub, with whom he had worked as an editor on *Woodstock*—heavily influenced the rewrite. She convinced Scorsese to remove some of the religious symbolism and dialogue in favor of more personal anecdotes about growing up in Little Italy. This led to the firecrackers incident and the "mook" scene, among other new additions. When it was advised that he change the title of the screenplay, Scorsese changed it to *Mean Streets*. Scorsese never really liked this title, which had been suggested by his friend, *Time* critic Jay Cocks, and planned to change it when a better title came along. But, as often happens, the title grew on him over time and ultimately stuck.

Once the screenplay was rewritten, Scorsese pitched it first to Roger Corman. Being the savvy businessman that he is, Corman agreed to finance the picture for $150,000 if Scorsese agreed to make all of the characters black. "He came to me with the idea and I liked it, but at that time the black films were really very successful," Corman explains. "I'd been thinking that I wanted to make a black film and I thought, this film would really work as a black film."[4] At first Scorsese was prepared to make this compromise but then had a change of heart and declined. In his mind, this film was to be more about the characters than the plot, and he couldn't envision African Americans struggling with the tenants of Catholicism. (As a nod to Corman, the first man to hire him for a studio film, Scorsese included a scene from *The Tomb of Ligeia* in the film.) Scorsese also gave a copy of the screenplay to Francis Ford Coppola, who passed it along to actor Al Pacino, but nothing ever came of this.

Scorsese's continuing search for funding led to an introduction to would-be producer Jonathan Taplin by Jay Cocks and his wife, Verna Bloom. The twenty-six-year-old Taplin had previously been the road manager for Bob Dylan and The Band, and was now interested in producing movies. "Jay said, 'When you're in LA, look up this young editor named Marty Scorsese,'" Taplin recalls.

"He's a big music fan and he cut some of *Woodstock*." And of course The Band was at Woodstock, so we had a connection there. So I came out to Los Angeles and I called Marty up. We met and he showed me some of his student films, and I loved them; particularly a short called *It's Not Just You, Murray*. That's the one that really caught my eye. I just thought it was really original. Then he gave me the script for *Mean Streets* and I decided to finance it. I didn't know enough not to go forward and put my own money into this.[5]

Taplin also convinced a childhood friend, twenty-three-year-old E. Lee Perry, to invest his $175,000 inheritance in the project.

The weeks following were hectic ones. Scorsese and Martin were furiously rewriting the screenplay (there were approximately twenty-seven drafts of the script in all), and Scorsese was working as editor on two different films, *The Unholy Rollers* and *Elvis on Tour*. Despite all of this, things seemed to be going great for Scorsese. Then, about three weeks after Perry had signed on as a financier, the deal fell through. According to Scorsese, Perry's family had telephoned Taplin's family and accused Taplin of swindling their son. "I don't know how it happened but this guy Perry came back into town and we had dinner with him," Scorsese says. "It was him and his wife and Taplin and his girlfriend and me and Sandy. It was very relaxed because I knew that the guy wasn't giving us any money so I didn't have to worry. We just told a lot of funny stories and had a good time and the next thing I know we've got the money back."[6] Taplin then secured a deferment from CFI (Consolidated Film Industries) labs, who rated scripts and then granted monies based on the quality of the screenplay. CFI was so taken with the project that they rated it somewhere around ninety and gave Scorsese and company complete facilities, from screening to processing, under the condition that the expenses be paid back within a year of the film's completion. After contributions by Taplin, Perry, and CFI, the working budget was $300,000.

With the money now in hand, Scorsese knew he needed someone with filmmaking experience to aid and oversee the operation. For this he turned to Paul Rapp and Peter Fain, both veterans of the Corman camp. Rapp, his first assistant director on *Boxcar Bertha*, had helped Scorsese bring the film in on time and under budget. (The film, shot in twenty-four days, had been made for $600,000.) Rapp, now working as line producer, told Scorsese that *Mean Streets* could be shot for $300,000. However, Rapp informed him, it would have to be filmed at least partly in Los Angeles as shooting in New York would be too costly. Scorsese objected, but Rapp set him straight, telling him that it was the only way the film could be made on such a shoestring budget. Rapp was able to budget four days for shooting exteriors (and a few interiors) in New York. With some creative juggling, Scorsese then stretched these four days into six days and six nights, shooting with a skeleton crew of New York University students under the guise that they were making a thesis film. The six days in New York proved to be problematic, however, from problems with the wireless microphones to a vehicle running over an electrical distribution box to cold and wet weather. The rest of the film was shot in seedy Los Angeles neighborhoods utilizing the crew from *Boxcar Bertha*.

Scorsese had written the lead role of Charlie Cappa with Harvey Keitel in mind. He had worked with Keitel previously on *Who's That Knocking at My Door?* and since *Mean Streets* was to revisit many of the same themes, Keitel seemed like the logical choice. However, box office considerations caused Scorsese to instead cast Jon Voight in the role. Voight, who had been passed the screenplay by two of his acting students, Richard Romanus and David Proval, was still hot from his Oscar-nominated performance in *Midnight Cowboy*. However, as Scorsese was gearing up to shoot footage of Charlie at the October festival of San Gennaro in New York City, Voight dropped out of the picture in favor of playing an idealistic teacher in *Conrack*. This led Scorsese to beg Keitel to come and work on the film on short notice. Keitel accepted.

"Perhaps I got the part of Charlie because Marty sensed that I came from a similar background," Keitel explains. "I was new, I was raw, I hadn't much experience. I don't think it was my experience at acting that landed me that work, but the experience Marty saw in me. Our neighborhoods said to a young man, 'You have a place and you will not go beyond this place because you do not belong anywhere beyond this place.' Marty and I rebelled against it."[7]

Then, at a 1972 Christmas party held by Jay Cocks and Verna Bloom, Scorsese would, in a historic meeting, come face to face with the actor who would assume the second most important role in *Mean*

Streets. Scorsese recognized the young actor, Robert De Niro, who had grown up near him in New York City and had been known there by such names as "Bobby Milk" and "Bobby Irish." De Niro recognized Scorsese, as well.

"I know you," De Niro said. "You used to hang out with Joe Morali and Kurdy on Elizabeth Street."

"And you used to hang out in Kenmare Street and Grand," Scorsese answered.[8]

"He'd heard that I had made a film about his neighborhood—*Who's That Knocking at My Door?*—though he used to hang out with a different group of people, on Broome Street, while we were on Prince Street," Scorsese recalls. "We had seen each other at dances and said hello. He recognized me first at the dinner and mentioned several names of people I used to hang out with."[9] De Niro remembers things similarly: "Sometimes when we were kids we'd meet at the dances at a place on Fourteenth Street. It was just an Italian-American dance place. I saw Marty around there and we knew each other. Friends of his, from his group, would sometimes change over into our group. We had like a crossover of friends."[10]

The two soon found themselves deep in conversation about the old days and what they were both up to now. "De Niro found in Martin the one person who would talk for fifteen minutes on the way a character would tie a knot," explains Julia Cameron, Scorsese's second wife. "That's what drew them together, and since then I have seen them go at it for ten hours virtually non-stop."[11]

Scorsese soon offered De Niro his choice of roles in *Mean Streets*—anything but Charlie. After all, Scorsese had already filmed the San Gennaro footage with Keitel in the role. As he was mulling over which role to take, De Niro met Harvey Keitel. "We looked at each other and we just laughed," Keitel recalls. "That was it, we just kept laughing. Looking back I see that we recognized each other. I knew he was a great actor."[12] As De Niro was more established than Keitel and had just given a spectacular turn in *Bang the Drum Slowly* that he was sure would change his career forever, De Niro felt that he should play Charlie. He even managed to convince Keitel of this, but Scorsese put his foot down as he was not about to lose his precious San Gennaro footage.

According to Scorsese, when De Niro showed up at an audition wearing the pork pie hat that he eventually wore in the film, he knew which role he wanted De Niro to play—Johnny Boy. "I didn't tell him that, I just told him [the audition] was good," Scorsese says. "But when I saw the hat I knew it was Johnny Boy."[13] Keitel saw things the same way and eventually suggested to De Niro that he take the role of Johnny Boy. "I hadn't thought of playing him at all," De Niro explains.

> But Harvey somehow made me see it in another way. I couldn't see Johnny Boy at first, but in a way, it was a good thing. When you play a role you don't see yourself doing at first, you can get good things from yourself that you ordinarily wouldn't get. I didn't see myself as Johnny Boy as written, but we improvised in rehearsal and the part evolved. We would find structure for the improvisations and figure out how to pace it. It's not just freewheeling, it has to have a structure. Then we'd tape what we'd do. It had to build. Working this way takes a lot of personal stuff.[14]

Once filming began, Scorsese was so nervous that he had to wear white gloves on the set to keep from chewing his fingernails. His frayed nerves revealed themselves when he blew his top and attacked one of his actors. "Marty got really pissed off at David Proval while we were filming a scene around a pool table," recalls second assistant director Ron Satlof, who also appears in the film. "David couldn't remember when he struck the ball. So after the master shot, during the close-up, he was hitting the ball at all the wrong times. Marty was trying to tell him, 'No, no, it's on this word,' and David could not get it right. And Marty literally charged over the table and attacked him. I had to grab him and carry him away."[15]

Satlof, now a director himself, remembers Scorsese as being one of the most well-prepared directors he's ever encountered. "He's a shining example of being extremely well-prepared and thought-through," Satlof explains. "He knew exactly what he was looking for in scenes, not just visually, but also in terms of emotion and dramatic structure."[16] Taplin agrees with this assessment. "The cool thing about Marty was that he was so organized," Taplin says. "He'd wanted to make the movie for so long that he had literally drawn every single shot in the storyboard. He

had five books of storyboards. Every single shot, every pan, every movement, the thing where Harvey Keitel is moving through the bar, all of
it. He'd already figured it all out. So he was able to be efficient—he
would have like thirty set-ups a day—that it was just scary. He was so
prepared that he could spend time with the actors."[17]

Although Scorsese had never taken any acting classes, the actors
found that he was able to relate to them well. A true collaborator, he
would listen to their ideas about the characters, scenes, and dialogue.
If the suggestions made sense to him and he thought it felt true to the
piece, he would allow them to experiment with different things. "Marty
and I always discussed a scene and, usually, he trusted me to do what I
had in mind to do," Keitel recalls.[18] As Keitel and De Niro were both
open to experimentation, they thrived in this type of collaborative
environment. From this experimentation came a fully improvised conversation scene (the nonsensical "Joey Scala–Joey Clams" discussion)
between Keitel and De Niro. This new scene, suggested by De Niro,
was inspired by the comic banter of comedians Abbott and Costello.
"When I shot it, it was about fifteen minutes long, hilarious, and clari-

fied everything totally," says Scorsese. "It's like the betrayals of trust, one character taking advantage of another, that I enjoyed so much in the Hope and Crosby movies."[19]

Such suggestions by De Niro were typical. According to Mardik Martin, De Niro would say, "Can I talk to you about this scene? I have some ideas."[20] Then the director and actor would go off to some private corner and discuss what they were about to do. Even in the beginning it was clear that Scorsese and De Niro were on the same wavelength. "They can shorthand stuff," explains Jonathan Taplin. "They know each other so well that they can say just two or three words or just one sentence, and the other will understand it. They've worked out the way to communicate with each other."[21]

Other new scenes were added at the last minute, as well. "I kept adding scenes," Scorsese says. "I added a scene in front of the gun shop in New York. I added the scene where they steal the bread in front of his [Charlie's] uncle's shop. All that stuff. I added a lot of stuff like that. I kept pushing the limits of the budget and drove everybody crazy."[22]

As filming progressed, De Niro, consumed with the idea of fully realizing his character, became more and more isolated from the rest of the cast and crew. "He was extremely serious, extremely involved in his role and preparation," recalls Satlof. "He was not at all social, not at all one of the boys. Very internal. Not at all kidding around—just totally focused on the part."[23] Eventually De Niro became so focused that he remained in character at all times. "Bobby was really into the character, and he didn't really come out of the character at any time in the little trailer we had," Taplin recalls. "And it really messed with Richard Romanus' head."[24]

On the second to last day of shooting, Scorsese filmed the confrontation between Romanus and De Niro in which De Niro's character pulls a gun on him. De Niro, ever the method actor, sought to invoke actual anger in Romanus by screaming unscripted insults at him in take after take. "Something had happened between Bobby and Richard because the animosity between them in that scene was real, and I played on it," Scorsese says. "They had got on each other's nerves to the point where I think they really wanted to kill each other."[25]

The following day the film wrapped production, coming in on budget in a Corman-like twenty-seven days. Scorsese then went into the editing bay with editor Sid Levin. Although Levin was ultimately credited with cutting the film due to Directors Guild rules, Scorsese edited the film himself. With help from Sandy Weintraub and Brian De Palma, Scorsese seamlessly wove together halves of scenes shot on opposite coasts. When Johnny Boy shoots a rifle from a rooftop in New York, the bullet strikes a window in Los Angeles. In another scene, a man shot in a bar in Los Angeles staggers out into a New York street. So masterfully did Scorsese cut these scenes that most critics ultimately believed the whole thing had been filmed in New York. It was only when it came time to cut the final scene that Scorsese found difficulty and had to turn to Levin for advice.

However, the film went over budget in postproduction due to the incredible amount of music Scorsese put in the film. Depending on whom you ask, the budget soared to somewhere between $460,000 and $600,000. "Marty had all this music he wanted in the movie," Taplin explains. "And literally no one had ever licensed that much music in a movie before. When we were budgeting at the beginning, we had no idea that Marty was going to put all this music in the rough cut. The music was brilliant though, and once you heard it and saw it that way, you realized you couldn't make the film without those songs."[26] Some of the bands, like the Rolling Stones, raised their rates. When the Stones' fee doubled from $7,500 per song to $15,000, Taplin had to go to Mick Jagger and convince him to scale the fee back.

When *Mean Streets* was completed, Scorsese and Taplin set out to find a distributor. Scorsese believed Paramount would be a lock. After all, his pal Francis Ford Coppola's *The Godfather* had done quite well for them. Surely, Scorsese thought, Paramount would be interested in snatching up another film about hot-blooded Italian thugs. When Taplin set up a screening at Warner Bros. the same day as the screening at Paramount, Scorsese suggested that maybe they should cancel the Warner Bros. meeting altogether. After all, he considered Paramount a sure thing. Taplin suggested that they keep both appointments just to be on the safe side, and Scorsese agreed. This turned out to be a wise decision as Paramount was anything but a sure thing. Peter Bart, who was at that time head of production at Paramount, arrived at the screening in a bad mood. He watched only ten minutes of *Mean Streets* before instructing the projectionist to the turn off the film. Bart then told Scorsese that the film was a waste of his time and that he wasn't interested. He then stood and walked out, leaving Scorsese stunned.

Later that day Scorsese and Taplin screened the film for Warner Bros. president John Calley and head of distribution Leo Greenfield. As the film ran, Scorsese nervously watched the two men for a visible reaction, but there was none. Then, just as everyone's favorite scene featuring the improvisation between De Niro and Keitel came on, a waiter walked in and stood in front of the screen loudly announcing Calley and Greenfield's lunch. The men told the waiter to be quiet, and Scorsese began to breathe a little easier. Soon he noticed that the two men were laughing at the right places and even reminiscing happily about locations used in the film. This screening turned out to be quite different from the earlier screening with Peter Bart. Warner Bros. bought the film for $750,000, which pleased Scorsese since he considered the film an homage to the classic Warner Bros. gangster films.

When *Mean Streets* screened at Cannes in May 1973, Scorsese, De Niro, and Taplin were introduced to Federico Fellini. Scorsese and Fellini were soon knee-deep in conversation about cinema. During their conversation, a representative of Fellini's distributor walked into the room. Fellini, who hadn't even seen *Mean Streets*, told the distributor that Scorsese's film was the finest American picture he'd seen in a decade. Based on Fellini's glowing endorsement, the company purchased the film's foreign distribution rights immediately.

Mean Streets debuted at the New York Film Festival the first week of October 1973, closing the festival. Most of the critics were kind to Scorsese, commenting on the seediness and truthfulness of *Mean Streets*. And while the critics liked Keitel's subtle turn, they loved De Niro's scene-stealing performance as Johnny Boy. When writing about De Niro, some even compared his work to that of Marlon Brando. *New Yorker* critic Pauline Kael, who would later dub *Mean Streets* the best American movie of 1973, raved that the film was "a true original of our period, a triumph of personal filmmaking." She went on to say of De Niro's performance: "De Niro here hits the far-out, flamboyant and makes his own truth. He's a bravura actor, and those who have registered him only as the grinning, tobacco-chewing dolt of that hunk of inept whimsy *Bang the Drum Slowly* will be unprepared for his volatile performance. De Niro does something like what Dustin Hoffman was doing in *Midnight Cowboy*, but wilder; the kid doesn't just act—he takes off into the vapors."[27] *Chicago Sun-Times* critic Roger Ebert, who had first taken notice of Scorsese after viewing his student film *I Call First*, commented on the director's "fiercely driven visual style." Ebert went on to say that De Niro's turn was a "marvelous performance, filled with urgency and restless desperation."[28]

A few reviewers were less kind. Stanley Kauffmann of the *New Republic* labeled the film "theatrical in the wrong way," and even gave De Niro backhanded praise. "It's a flash part, and every actor who sees it will gnash his teeth because he'll know that anyone with any talent at all could score in it."[29]

According to Scorsese, the only reviews he had worried about with *Mean Streets* were the judgments of his old friends whom the film was based upon. If they thought the film felt true to their experiences, then Scorsese would consider the film a success. Luckily, his old friends loved the film. However, not everyone from the old neighborhood shared their feelings, as *Mean Streets* received some criticism regarding its depiction of Italian Americans. For this Scorsese makes no apologies. "People complained about my depiction of Italian-Americans, and I must say, finally, that I can't help them with that," Scorsese says. "I'm sorry. It's just that it's my perception of what I know. You know, there are guys who, as I say, are upstanding members of the community. They're doing fine. [Then there are] guys who are out of town—who can't come back. There are guys who are dead."[30]

Because of the positive word the film had received at the New York Film Festival, it was initially suggested that the film open in twenty-five cities just as *The Last Picture Show* and *Five Easy Pieces* had. Instead Taplin and Scorsese convinced the studio to roll the film out a bit more slowly. It opened on October 13, 1973, in five more cities. Unfortunately, it was far less successful in these cities than it had been in New York. Many audiences found the picture to be too New York for their tastes, and Warner Bros. had no idea how to sufficiently market the film. Because Warner Bros. had spent $14 million on *The Exorcist*, which was still two months away, the studio's promotional department chose to focus on that film instead. Making matters worse, the hit film *The Way We Were* opened the week after *Mean Streets*, helping to drive Scorsese's little film right out of theaters.

Mean Streets continued a long run in New York. Scorsese and Mardik Martin received a Writers Guild Award nomination for Best Drama, and De Niro took home the National Society of Film Critics Awards' Best Supporting Actor prize. The film, which has gained recognition over time, was listed to the National Film Registry in 1997.

The Film

There are a number of clues in the film that Charlie Cappa (Harvey Keitel) is the onscreen representation of Scorsese himself. Both Charlie's first and last names were derived from the names of Scorsese's parents. (Charles was his father's name and Cappa was his mother's maiden name.) Another clue is that Scorsese himself gives voice to Charlie's conscience through voice-over. There is also a single hidden frame in the home movie sequence of Harvey Keitel and Scorsese together. Then, later in the film, a scene from *The Searchers* is played, depicting a battle between characters named Marty and Charlie, representing the inner conflict of Charlie Cappa (and presumably of Scorsese himself).

The film begins with Charlie's conscience speaking over a black screen. Here he explains that a person must make up for his or her sins in the streets rather than in church. Everything else, he explains, is "bullshit."

Charlie wakes up. He stands and walks to the mirror hanging on the wall. A crucifix is visible on the wall behind him. He stares at his face, contemplating his own struggle between what he perceives to be good and evil. Inspired by Alfred Hitchcock's 1963 film *The Birds*, Scorsese uses three quick cuts that zoom in on Charlie's face. In the middle of these three cuts the classic Ronettes tune "Be My Baby" starts to play, and the main title sequence begins.

The music in the film—from "Be My Baby" to the Giuseppe Di Stefano recordings—is important. Scorsese has said that there was always a variety of music playing at all times when he was growing up in Little Italy. To represent this, the characters of *Mean Streets* move from song to song (and musical genre to musical genre) as they make their way from one scene to the next.

The unorthodox main title sequence is shown as a home movie running through a projector. Interestingly, the Kodak leader identifies the home movie as the property of one C. Cappa. The title of this home movie is then identified as *Season of the Witch*, which was the initial title of *Mean Streets*. When one looks at these two curious inclusions together, this can be seen as yet another indication that Scorsese and Charlie are in fact one and the same. As the film makes its way through the credits, we see a montage comprised of footage of Charlie and his friends. This gives us our first glimpse at the characters, providing us with clues as to how they will interact with one another and just what their place in Charlie's life is. The footage also gives us our first glimpse, though only a microcosm, of the Italian American culture that defines Charlie's world. Opening shots of flashing police lights and later footage of Charlie shaking hands with his priest are representative of the duality of these "mean streets" of Little Italy and of Charlie himself.

The movie-within-a-movie wraps up with the footage of Charlie walking through the streets during the San Gennaro festival. After this, the main characters are introduced in sequences that will provide us with some insight into each of them. The first sequence introduces us to Tony (David Proval), who owns Volpe's Bar & Grill. Tony walks into the men's room, discovering a junkie shooting heroin. Tony becomes enraged and drags the junkie out of the bar. He then throws out a second man whom he suspects of having sold smack to the junkie. This scene reveals a sort of moral code present in the criminal underworld in which the film takes place.

The second introductory sequence focuses on Michael (Richard Romanus), an up-and-coming hoodlum. Michael is snappily dressed and clearly has higher aspirations within the realm of the criminal underworld. However, this scene in which Michael attempts to fence a truckload of stolen "Jap adaptors" he has mistaken for German lenses indicates that he's not yet ready to ascend to the levels of criminal management to which he aspires. His later dealings with Johnny Boy, which have been mishandled from the start, will serve as further testament to this.

The third sequence introduces us to Johnny Boy (Robert De Niro), who is approaching a U.S. mailbox in midday. As pedestrians walk past, he nonchalantly drops a package into the mailbox. He then begins to move away from the mailbox, finally breaking into a sprint. Just as he dives into a doorway, the mailbox explodes violently. In this scene, shot by Scorsese's second unit cameraman David Osterhout, De Niro makes the grandest entrance in a film since Orson Welles' arrival in *The Third Man*. In a short thirty seconds this scene conveys to us that Johnny Boy is a volatile, unpredictable maniac.

It should be noted that Mardik Martin has stated that he sees Johnny Boy as also being representative of Scorsese. In Martin's view, Charlie (good) and Johnny Boy (evil) represent the duality of Scorsese. According to Scorsese, Johnny Boy was inspired by one of his uncles, who refused to pay his debtors. "My father comes from a family of eight or nine kids, and he had a number of brothers," Scorsese explains. "One of them was just a wild man. . . . My father was constantly in the middle of negotiating peace for him."[31]

The fourth and final introductory sequence takes us back to Charlie, who is in church, internally questioning the practices of his religion. He once again concludes that the teachings of the church are all bullshit. Believing that pain is the only true penance, he holds his hand over the flickering flame of a candle for as long as he can bear to do so. This scene once again alludes to the conflict of duality within Charlie as it features internal monologues voiced by both Scorsese and Keitel.

The next scene finds Charlie in Tony's bar, which looks quite similar to the bar that will play a significant role in a later Scorsese/De Niro collaboration, *GoodFellas*. The bar, lit as red as the fires of hell, stands in sharp contrast to the church where we just saw Charlie. Mick Jagger is just starting to sing "Tell Me." With help from a dolly beneath Keitel's feet, Charlie seems to float through the crowd in a long uninterrupted shot, concluding with his jumping on stage and dancing with an African American stripper. In the next shot we see Charlie once again practicing his ritual of penance, holding his hand over a candle at his table in the bar. Michael arrives and sits with him. First, he sells Charlie two cartons of cigarettes, which have presumably "fallen off the back of a truck" (again similar to the later *GoodFellas*), and second, he informs him that Johnny Boy hasn't been paying him back on a debt he owes. But Charlie vouches for his irresponsible friend, insisting that he will make Johnny Boy see the error of his ways.

Mere seconds later Johnny Boy shows up at the bar with two women in tow. Always outrageous and always the center of attention, Johnny Boy checks his pants with the checkroom girl instead of his coat. As he makes his way through the bar toward Charlie, there is another internal monologue performed by Scorsese, and we learn that Charlie sees Johnny Boy as a penance of sorts. If he can take care of Johnny Boy and make him see the light, Charlie will be redeemed. The burden this places on Charlie is apparent from his reaction, as he is seemingly the only person in the bar who isn't amused by Johnny Boy's checkroom antics. As the Rolling Stones' "Jumpin' Jack Flash" plays, Johnny Boy introduces Tony and Charlie to the two women. When Johnny Boy pulls out money and attempts to buy the girls a drink, Charlie takes exception and leads him to the back room for a talk.

This leads to the improvised scene suggested by De Niro. Trimmed down to a taut four minutes, the Abbott and Costello–inspired scene is performed terrifically by De Niro and Keitel, who both display uncanny comic timing. In the scene Charlie asks Johnny Boy why he didn't make his weekly payment to Michael on Tuesday, to which Johnny Boy lies and says he paid him. The two then have a comical back-and-forth discussion about which Tuesday it was, and finally Johnny Boy admits that he didn't pay Michael after all. He then breaks into a long-winded spiel about various characters whom he owes—such as Joey Scala and Joey Clams, who then turn out to be the same person—and tells an unbelievable story about how he lost a substantial amount of money gambling. The story ends with Johnny Boy explaining that he has just purchased new clothing. Finally Charlie takes most of Johnny Boy's money to put toward the following week's payment, and the two return to the front of the bar.

The open contempt that Charlie shows for the two Jewish girls must be seen as a product of the neighborhood's exclusion of outsiders. Charlie refers to the girls first as "bohemian" and second as "matta christos"—Christ killers. It might also be noted that the two Jewish girls—one of whom is referred to as "the Weintraub girl"—are played by Scorsese's then real-life girlfriend (and editorial assistant) Sandy Weintraub and one of her sisters.

Once again in the front of the bar, Johnny Boy orders a round of drinks and puts it on his tab. Michael then approaches Johnny Boy to inquire about the debt he's owed, to which Johnny Boy swears to pay the following Tuesday. Because Charlie signals to him that everything will be all right, Michael lets Johnny Boy go with a friendly warning.

The next scene finds Charlie collecting on a debt for his Uncle Giovanni, the neighborhood crime boss. Oscar (Murray Moston), a hardworking restaurateur, informs Charlie that he doesn't have enough money to make his weekly payment. He concedes to Charlie that one day Giovanni will end up owning the restaurant as the debt is getting more and more difficult for Oscar to pay. He then explains that his business partner, Groppe, has disappeared. The fact that Charlie is a debt collector himself tells us that he knows all too well what the consequences will be if Johnny Boy doesn't pay off his debt to Michael. In the next scene, Charlie relays to his Uncle Giovanni (Cesare Danova) the information regarding Oscar's inability to pay his debt and the disappearance of his partner Groppe. Giovanni shows compassion regarding Oscar's situation but still hints at the fact that one day he will own the man's business when he asks Charlie if he likes restaurants. This is also intended as a thinly veiled message to Charlie that he may one day be given the restaurant if he continues to climb the ranks in the criminal hierarchy and do what is instructed of him.

We then witness two long-haired hippies from Riverdale looking for black market fireworks on the streets of Little Italy. Their search leads them to Michael and Tony, who are more than happy to scam the men out of their money. Michael advises the hippies not to buy fireworks from the "Chinks" as their product is inferior. All four of them then drive in Tony's car to a spot where the hippies are instructed to get out and wait. Michael tells them that he cannot allow anyone to see where he keeps his stash of fireworks but that he will return. However, he needs the cash up front. Once the hippies are out of the car, Michael counts the money and finds that the hippies have shorted him twenty dollars. He and Tony then go get Charlie, and the three of them go to the movies with their newfound cash. They go to Times Square and watch *The Searchers*, a Scorsese favorite that is discussed in *Who's That Knocking at My Door?* and will later serve as the primary inspiration for *Taxi Driver*.

The next scene finds Charlie, Johnny Boy, and Tony going to a pool hall to meet their friend Jimmy (Lenny Scaletta). The dark underground pool hall is operated by a numbers runner named Joey Catucci (George Memmoli) who refuses to pay Jimmy for hitting the weekly combination. The always calm Charlie is there to serve as a mediator and to try to persuade Joey to pay Jimmy what he is owed. Things are going well until Johnny Boy inevitably calls Joey a "scumbag" and refers to his female patrons as "skanks." The tension escalates with each insult until Joey says he will not pay Jimmy. When asked why he won't pay Jimmy, Joey says it is because Jimmy is a "mook." None of them has ever heard this word before, but they still take it as an insult. This results in a brawl set to the tune of the Marvelettes' "Mr. Postman." This scene feels so spontaneous that many critics assumed it was improvised. However, this was not the case. "The mook scene was in the script," Mardik Martin says, recalling a debate he had with one film critic who insisted the scene was improvised. "I said, 'If you want to see the script, I'll send it to you.' So he read it and he said, 'You're right, it is in the script.'"[32]

The brawl continues until two police officers arrive and break it up. The two officers soon reveal that they are on the take, refusing to go until they shake Joey down for "car fare" to Philadelphia. Once the police officers leave, Joey offers everyone a drink and agrees to pay Jimmy the money he is owed. However, once again Johnny Boy insults Joey and a second brawl breaks out.

Back at Volpe's, Tony shares a story with Johnny Boy concerning Charlie's faith. Tony explains that a priest told Charlie a story about a young couple who decided to have premarital sex and ended up dying in an automobile collision as a result of this sin. Tony then explains that a different priest had told him the exact same story only with different characters. As a result, Tony now sees religion as being nothing more than a business with the priests working as salesmen. Charlie says that he is angry, not because the story has done anything to diminish his faith, but because the priest lied to him.

A suspicious-looking man (Robert Carradine) enters the bar and sits waiting for some time. When a drunk (David Carradine) announces that he has to go to the restroom, the man follows him into the men's room and shoots him four times. The dying drunk attacks the gunman and the two struggle, eventually finding their way back out into the bar. The gunman shoots the drunk again, and everyone inside the bar turns and runs. The drunk staggers outside and dies. At first this appears to be a random shooting, but we will later learn that this was a hit carried out by an ambitious young "climber." Tony quickly closes up shop before the police can show up asking questions, and Charlie and Johnny Boy catch a ride with Michael. When they are leaving, two flamboyantly homosexual men (Robert Wilder and Ken Sinclair) talk Michael into giving them a ride away from the scene of the crime, as well. Johnny Boy repeatedly insults the men, calling them faggots, while one of them flirts with Charlie and yells catcalls from Michael's car. Finally Michael forces the two men out of the car. Charlie and Johnny Boy also exit.

While standing in front of a gun shop, Charlie and Johnny Boy reminisce about an incident in which Johnny Boy was beaten by police officers. As they talk, Johnny Boy hides behind a car. He tells Charlie that he has seen yet another person he owes money to down the street. Once the man is gone, Charlie and Johnny Boy break into a heavily improvised skirmish with trashcan lids. While making their way to Charlie's mother's apartment, the two steal some bread from outside a grocery store owned by one of Charlie's uncles.

Once they arrive at the apartment—empty because Charlie's mother is staying with his sickly grandmother—Johnny Boy complains that there is no food. He then suggests breaking into his aunt's apartment across the alley and stealing some food. Charlie suggests that Johnny Boy might frighten his cousin Teresa, to which Johnny Boy coldly jokes that she might have an epileptic fit and they could watch. This remark establishes the relationship between Johnny Boy and Teresa and further serves as a testament to Johnny Boy's lack of respect for anyone or anything. The remark also angers Charlie, who verbally reprimands him for being a "jerk off." Charlie then goes to the window and watches Teresa undress, and the scene cuts to Charlie and Teresa naked in a hotel bed. Charlie reveals to her that he had a dream about having sex with her in which he ejaculated blood. Despite Charlie's insistence that he does not love Teresa, his anger toward Johnny Boy and his guilt-ridden dream both hint that Charlie does love Teresa but doesn't want to admit it to either himself or her.

In the next scene Charlie goes to visit his Uncle Giovanni, who is talking with the father of the climber who gunned down the drunk at Tony's bar. The man asks Giovanni for forgiveness for an unwarranted hit and asks him to protect his son. Giovanni tells the man to send his son to Miami for six months to a year until things have died down and then he will see what he can do to help him. Scorsese then cuts to Charlie and Teresa walking down the beach. While Charlie still refuses to say that he loves Teresa, he does affectionately tell her that he likes her. They then discuss his friendship with her cousin Johnny Boy, which she discourages. Charlie stands his ground, asking who will help Johnny Boy if he doesn't. Charlie then compares himself to St. Francis, prompting Teresa to remind Charlie of his occupation, which is at odds with his vision of himself. St. Francis, she reminds him, did not run numbers.

We then see Charlie at the bar hitting on Diane (Jeannie Bell), an African American stripper. Charlie suggests to her that one day when he opens his restaurant/nightclub, she can work there as a hostess. The two agree to go out together for Chinese food to discuss this offer. Charlie takes a cab to pick up Diane but ends up instructing the cabbie to take him home. After all, he reasons, it wouldn't do to be seen with a black girl. This is yet another example of the racism and restrictive traditional mind-set that permeates Charlie's neighborhood. Diane, just like Teresa, could potentially make Charlie happy, but he once again chooses to forgo his own happiness in favor of what the neighborhood deems appropriate. In Charlie's conflicted mind, if he does what is expected of him, then he can one day take over Oscar's restaurant and be happy.

We next see Charlie meeting with Uncle Giovanni, who is holding court at Oscar's restaurant. Giovanni instructs Charlie to stay away from Johnny Boy. He then brings up Teresa, saying that she's sick in the head because of her epilepsy. He then instructs Charlie to stay away from both of them as he considers them both to be trouble. After subtly giving this command, Giovanni and his associate Mario (Vic Argo) advise Charlie to look around the restaurant so they can talk in private. As Charlie inspects the kitchen, he once again performs his own act of penance by holding his hand over an open flame.

Charlie goes to see Teresa to tell her that he can't see her anymore, telling her that she and her cousin are making life difficult for him. He explains that his uncle is going to give him Oscar's restaurant in due time if he follows his commands. Charlie cannot sever the ties with Teresa, however, and ends up kissing her. When she tells him that she loves him, he says he doesn't want to say that, implying that he does in fact love her.

In the next scene Charlie once again meets with Giovanni, who informs him that Oscar's missing partner has killed himself. The subtext here is that Oscar will not be able to keep his restaurant much longer without his partner, so Charlie's time may be coming soon. Michael arrives while Charlie and Giovanni are talking, and Charlie asks him to wait outside until after the conversation has concluded. Charlie then goes outside and talks to Michael, who informs him that Johnny Boy has quit his job. As a courtesy, Michael agrees to one last sit down at a private party later that night, but it is clear that Michael has almost reached his breaking point where Johnny Boy is concerned.

That night at the party Michael shows Tony a photograph of his new girlfriend. Tony then informs him that he saw the girl kissing a "nigger." This fact, coupled with the fact that Johnny Boy is two hours late for their meeting, has Michael irritated. Here Scorsese employs a brief montage to the tune of the Chips' "Rubber Biscuit" showing the partygoers drinking and having a good time. We then see a long uninterrupted shot of an inebriated Charlie gliding jerkily through the bar. This stylistic effect was created by fitting Keitel with an Arriflex body harness that was covered by his jacket. A camera was then attached, giving Keitel's movements an unusually stylistic appearance and making it look as though the room is moving rather than Charlie himself. Charlie is soon sobered up when Michael comes to tell him that Johnny Boy is late. Ever the peacemaker, Charlie attempts to stall Michael. He then negotiates a deal with Michael, convincing him to lower the vig (slang for interest owed) from $3,000 to $2,000. Michael warns that if Johnny Boy is trying to make him look like a jerk he will break his legs, reminding Charlie that this is business. He then tells Charlie that he should have had sense enough not to have gotten involved. Once it is apparent that Johnny Boy isn't coming, Michael promises that if he isn't paid the following Tuesday he will personally break Johnny Boy's legs.

Violence once again erupts in the bar when a man's girlfriend dances with another man. Once the dust has settled, Teresa arrives, telling Charlie that Johnny Boy is shooting a handgun on the roof. As Johnny Boy attempts to shoot the lights out on the Empire State Building, Charlie shows up and tries to talk some sense into him. But even as Charlie is talking to him, the mischievous Johnny Boy tosses a lit firecracker off the building in the hopes of waking up the neighborhood. The two then make their way to a cemetery, where they sit and talk. Charlie tells Johnny Boy to go back to his job, but Johnny thinks loading trucks is beneath him. Johnny then tells Charlie that he's figured out a way out of the situation—he wants Charlie to talk to his Uncle Giovanni on his behalf. Not wanting his uncle to know about Johnny Boy's outstanding debts or Charlie's continued involvement with him, Charlie says no.

The next scene skips to the following Tuesday. Michael warns Charlie that Johnny Boy had better show up this time, threatening to inflict bodily harm upon him if he doesn't. Michael then seeks out Teresa and instructs her to remind Johnny Boy of their meeting later that night. Charlie and Teresa then meet, and Charlie asks Teresa where her cousin is, but she doesn't know. Meanwhile, we see Johnny Boy on the street senselessly beating a man for no reason whatsoever. Back at Charlie's mother's apartment Charlie and Teresa are arguing because of Johnny Boy. As Charlie tries to calm Teresa, Johnny Boy shows up at the window. As Charlie attempts to talk some sense into him,

Johnny Boy mocks him. He threatens to tell Giovanni about Charlie's secret relationship with Teresa. Johnny Boy then makes a joke about Teresa having a seizure when having an orgasm, causing Charlie to slap him. The stress proves to be too much for Teresa, and she has a seizure. Charlie asks Johnny Boy to help him with Teresa, but he runs out of the building. When a woman, played by Catherine Scorsese, the director's mother, comes to the rescue, Charlie runs after Johnny Boy. The two talk about the meeting with Michael, and Johnny Boy tells Charlie that he doesn't have the money. Charlie then gives Johnny Boy some money to pay Michael, and they go to the bar.

When Charlie and Johnny Boy arrive at Volpe's, they are told that Michael has left, but will return soon. As they wait, Charlie causes a scene with a "Jew bastard" when he holds his girlfriend, inviting him to try and pull her away. Michael shows up shortly after. When Charlie informs him that Johnny Boy has only thirty dollars to pay him, Michael is offended. Johnny Boy then gives him ten dollars, explaining that he has spent the other twenty dollars on drinks. Johnny Boy then insults Michael repeatedly, saying that he borrows money from him because he's the only person he could borrow money from without paying him back. When Michael jumps over the bar to get at him, Johnny Boy pulls a gun on him. Michael leaves the bar, and Charlie and Tony take the gun away from Johnny Boy. Charlie borrows Tony's car, and he and Johnny Boy go to a movie to hide out for a while. The movie is Roger Corman's *The Tomb of Ligeia*.

After the movie, Charlie telephones Teresa and asks to borrow some money. Teresa then insists that she go along with them. Charlie drives them all to Brooklyn, where Johnny Boy will be safer. As they are driving, a car swerves around them. At first they assume the car is simply a reckless driver, but then they see that Michael is driving. Upon Michael's order, a man in the backseat (Martin Scorsese) starts firing a pistol into their car. Johnny Boy is struck in the neck, and both Charlie and Teresa are injured. Charlie's car then crashes, and we see Teresa's hand sticking out of the windshield. As all of this is happening, we see brief shots of Tony washing his hands, Giovanni watching television, and Diane the stripper sitting in a diner as though she were still waiting for Charlie. These shots are meant to imply that life will continue in Little Italy whether Charlie and company live or die.

At the end of the film, we don't know whether or not Charlie, Johnny Boy, and Teresa will survive. However, Scorsese has stated, "people think that at the end of *Mean Streets*, Johnny Boy and Charlie die. They don't die, they live, they go on. That's the really hard part, going on."[33] Scorsese has also said that each of the three survivors is now damned. Charlie will have to face his uncle again, Johnny Boy will still have to face his unpaid debts, and Teresa will continue fighting, to no avail, for Charlie's affections.

Notes

1. Biskind, Peter, *Easy Riders, Raging Bulls* (New York: Simon & Schuster, 1998), 229.

2. Scorsese, Martin, *Martin Scorsese: Interviews*, ed. Peter Brunette (Jackson: University Press of Mississippi, 1999), 21.

3. Kelly, Mary Pat, *Martin Scorsese: A Journey* (New York: Thunder's Mouth Press, 1991), 68.

4. Rausch, Andrew J., *Fifty Filmmakers: Conversations with Directors from Roger Avary to Steven Zaillian* (Jefferson, NC: McFarland, 2007), 59.

5. Taplin, Jonathan, interview by the author, January 11, 2007.

6. Scorsese, *Martin Scorsese*, 22.

7. Fine, Marshall, *Harvey Keitel: The Art of Darkness* (New York: Fromm International, 1997), 59.

8. Baxter, John, *De Niro: A Biography* (New York: HarperCollins, 2002), 96.

9. Thompson, David, and Christie, Ian, eds., *Scorsese on Scorsese* (Boston: Faber and Faber, 1989), 42.

10. Dougan, Andy, *Untouchable: A Biography of Robert De Niro* (New York: Thunder's Mouth Press, 1996), 52.

11. Baxter, *De Niro*, 96.

12. Fine, *Harvey Keitel*, 61.

13. Dougan, Andy, *Martin Scorsese: Close Up* (New York: Thunder's Mouth Press, 1998), 37.

14. Dougan, *Untouchable*, 54.

15. Satlof, Ron, interview by the author, October 20, 2008.

16. Satlof, interview.

17. Taplin, interview.

18. Fine, *Harvey Keitel*, 63.

19. Dougan, *Martin Scorsese*, 37.

20. Martin, Mardik, interview by the author, October 10, 2008.

21. Taplin, interview.

22. Scorsese, *Martin Scorsese*, 22.

23. Satlof, interview.

24. Taplin, interview.

25. Dougan, *Untouchable*, 57.

26. Taplin, interview.

27. Kael, Pauline, "The Current Cinema," *New Yorker*, October 8, 1973, 157.

28. Ebert, Roger, *Scorsese by Ebert* (Chicago: University of Chicago Press, 2008), 34.

29. Kauffmann, Stanley, "Stanley Kauffmann on Films: Young Americans," *New Republic*, October 27, 1973, 22.

30. Schickel, Richard, *Scorsese on Scorsese*, documentary (TCM, 2004).

31. Schickel, *Scorsese on Scorsese*.

32. Martin, interview.

33. Jacobson, Mark, "Pictures of Marty," *Rolling Stone*, April 14, 1983, 108.

CHAPTER TWO

 ›

Taxi Driver (1976)

I felt all those feelings in the story at that time. I was thirty-two-years old. I really felt that way at times and so really felt it was special to express. De Niro felt very strongly about it too. I thought at the time we were making a sort of labor of love; a picture that wouldn't necessarily speak to many people.

—Martin Scorsese

The Backstory

The story behind *Taxi Driver* began in the summer of 1972. Screenwriter Paul Schrader was down on his luck and living out of his car. He'd recently been forced out of his position at the American Film Institute, his wife had left him, and he was having great difficulty getting his first screenplay, *Pipeline*, sold. "I was enamored of guns, I was very suicidal, I was drinking heavily, I was obsessed with pornography the way a lonely person is," Schrader recalls.[1] And out of this darkness came a bleak new script about "self-imposed loneliness" titled *Taxi Driver*. Schrader wrote furiously, completing his first draft in seven days, and finishing the rewrite in three. Schrader's script, which was presented in chapter form, was inspired by Jean-Paul Sartre's existential novel *Nausea*, the diaries of would-be assassin Arthur Bremer, and John Ford's film *The Searchers*. The screenplay told the story of lonely Vietnam vet, Travis Bickle, who works as a taxi driver on the midnight shift in the most degenerate sections of New York. Eventually Travis seeks redemption through two women. The first is Betsy, an attractive political campaign worker whom he attempts to impress by assassinating the politician for whom she works. After his assassination attempt is derailed, he then focuses his attention on Iris, a child prostitute whom he seeks to set free by murdering her pimp.

Once he was finished with the screenplay, Schrader gave it to his agent, who began shopping it. One day Schrader was playing chess with director Brian De Palma, and he mentioned that he had a script called *Taxi Driver*. De Palma then read the script and loved the writing, but couldn't imagine how to direct it or just who would pay to see it. De Palma then showed the screenplay to another of his chess partners, his neighbor, producer Michael Phillips. Phillips loved the screenplay and told his production partners—Tony Bill and Phillips' wife, Julia—that they had to make this film. Although she ultimately agreed to produce the film, Julia Phillips was somewhat less impressed with the screenplay than her husband was. "I had found nothing really attractive about *Taxi Driver* when I first read it, except for its sociology," she would later write in her memoir *You'll Never Eat Lunch in This Town Again*. "Travis was a nut case, a valid nut case but a nut case. I thought Schrader was, too."[2] Nevertheless, the three producers optioned *Taxi Driver* for $1,000 and offered De Palma a point as a finder's fee. Shortly after optioning the script, the production team split up. Tony Bill took several of the projects they had optioned with him, and the Phillipses kept the rest (including *Taxi Driver*).

Michael and Julia Phillips talked with a number of directors about attaching their names to the project. These included Irvin Kershner, John Milius, Lamont Johnson, and Robert Mulligan. A number of actors' names were bandied about for the role of Travis Bickle, including Jeff Bridges and singer Neil Diamond.

Brian De Palma later introduced Schrader to Martin Scorsese in San Diego while Scorsese was there to meet the film critic Manny Farber. Scorsese, De Palma, and Schrader were to meet at a restaurant and have dinner together. By this time Schrader had sold his third screenplay, *The Yakuza*, for a record $325,000, and Scorsese wanted him to adapt Fyodor Dostoevsky's *The Gambler* for him. However, Scorsese got lost and could not locate the restaurant. By the time he arrived three hours later, De Palma and Schrader had conceived what eventually became *Obsession*. De Palma then told Scorsese about *Taxi Driver*, which was still in limbo with the Phillipses. Scorsese read the script and loved it. "I know this guy Travis," he would later say. "I've had the feelings that he has, and those feelings have to be explored, taken out and examined. I know the feeling of rejection that Travis feels, of not being able to make relationships survive. I know the killing feeling, the feeling of really being angry."[3]

However, Schrader was not so taken with Scorsese. He wanted a "Tiffany" director with more credentials than Scorsese had. "Paul was never really gracious to me at all," Scorsese remembers. "He was abrasive."[4] The Phillipses didn't see Scorsese as a legitimate contender to direct *Taxi Driver* either. They told him to come back after he'd directed more than just *Boxcar Bertha*, which they saw little value in. Nevertheless, Scorsese made a point to be at every party where either Schrader or the Phillipses were. And each time he saw them he reminded them that he wanted to direct *Taxi Driver*. He also told them that he was editing a film called *Mean Streets*. Scorsese's agent, Harry Ufland, eventually convinced Schrader and the Phillipses to screen *Mean Streets*, and their opinions of Scorsese changed. They not only wanted Scorsese for *Taxi Driver*, but they also wanted Robert De Niro, whom they believed was perfect for the role of Travis Bickle. De Niro then read the script and found that he too could relate to Travis and his situation. In fact, De Niro was actually in the midst of developing his own script about a political assassin. Recognizing the quality of Schrader's screenplay, De Niro abandoned his own script and signed on to appear in the film.

But even with the director and actor attached, the Phillipses found *Taxi Driver* to be a difficult sell. Most studios believed the project wasn't commercial enough. Warner Bros. showed some interest, but studio head John Calley couldn't make up his mind. Calley finally agreed to make the film, but only if it could be made for a meager $750,000. However, everyone involved was working on other projects. By the time all of the principals were available again, Warner Bros. had backed out because they didn't believe the film could be made for less than $1 million. Luckily, most of the projects the *Taxi Driver* team had worked on during the interim had proven to be successes. Given that Schrader had written *Obsession*, the Phillipses had produced *The Sting*, Scorsese had directed *Alice Doesn't Live Here Anymore*, and De Niro had won an Oscar for his turn in *The Godfather Part II*, the project was now much more enticing to the studios. David Begelman at Columbia Pictures agreed to finance *Taxi Driver* for $1.5 million. Because *Taxi Driver* meant so much to each of the principals, they agreed to work for lower fees than they were receiving for other projects. De Niro was paid $35,000; Schrader $30,000; and Scorsese $65,000.

Now Scorsese had to cast the rest of the film. For the part of Betsy, the political campaign worker, they envisioned someone who looked like Cybill Shepherd, only with less baggage. Both Julia Phillips and the studio wanted television star Farrah Fawcett. When Scorsese was auditioning he telephoned agent Sue Mengers, telling her he was looking for a "Cybill Shepherd type." Since Mengers represented Shepherd, she urged Scorsese to take a look at the real thing. Scorsese agreed to audition her, and he liked what he saw. Shepherd, on the other hand, was not as excited about *Taxi Driver*. When she first read the script, she angrily threw it across the room, wondering why she was being offered such a small role. Then there was the money; Shepherd would only receive $35,000 for her work on the film. However, Mengers reminded her of the string of flops behind her and advised her that she needed to work with a director of Scorsese's growing stature. Then another problem presented itself—*Nickelodeon*, a project in which Shepherd was involved with her boyfriend, Peter Bogdanovich, was now moving forward at the same time as *Taxi Driver*. Since both projects were at Columbia, David Begelman told her she had to choose between them. Shepherd chose *Taxi Driver*.

Next Scorsese had to find an actress to play Iris, the child prostitute. Scorsese wanted twelve-year-old Jodie Foster, with whom he'd just worked on *Alice Doesn't Live Here Anymore*. So he called her in for an audition. "Jodie walked into our office on the Burbank lot, and she had total command," Scorsese recalls. "A total professional, especially at the age of twelve, is very reassuring. You can rely on their instincts, and their ability to show up on the set and do the work and be ready and willing for anything and be in a good mood about it. That's terrific, and extremely rare."[5] The only problem was that her mother, Brandy

Foster, didn't want her daughter playing a prostitute. However, she soon recognized what an opportunity this was for her daughter, and she relented. The Los Angeles Welfare Board, on the other hand, did not agree that the role was suitable for a child. Eventually a compromise was made that allowed Foster to make the film with her older sister Connie standing in for the more explicit scenes. In addition to this, a child welfare worker was present throughout the shoot.

Scorsese then offered the role of Betsy's coworker at the campaign office to Harvey Keitel, who turned it down. Instead Keitel asked to play the role of Iris' pimp, Sport. "Why?" Scorsese asked. "The other role is bigger." To this Keitel answered, "I have no idea."[6] Keitel would later explain the aspects of the role that had interested him: "There is great humanity in a pimp. I don't mean humanity in the benevolent sense. I mean humanity in its suffering sense. They come out of a place of great need, usually of poverty, of broken homes, of never having opportunity. What comes out of an environment like that is often a pimp, a thief, a drug addict, a mugger. What the hell does someone like that know about giving love, caring for, supporting, being the most you can be? They're trying to eat, keep the rats out of their food."[7] Scorsese agreed that Keitel was right for the role and cast him.

He then rounded out the cast with comedian Albert Brooks, who took on the role of the campaign worker. Brooks would later say he believed he was cast because he was quick on his feet and could come up with dialogue for the character, which was underdeveloped in the script. Once shooting wrapped, Schrader approached Brooks and thanked him for fleshing out the character, saying this was the only character he didn't know when he wrote the script. This amazed Brooks, who wondered how Schrader could "know" pimps, prostitutes, and assassins, but not an everyday working man.

As usual, De Niro's preparation for the film was meticulous. While in Italy working on Bernardo Bertolucci's *1900*, De Niro traveled to a nearby U.S. Army base. There he studied a group of techs with the Midwestern accent he sought for the character of Travis Bickle. He made friends with them, studying the way they dressed and their mannerisms. He then practiced reproducing their movements and speech patterns until he could mimic them perfectly. He returned stateside and secured a hack license, landing himself a weekend job as a cabbie.

Once while he was driving the cab, he was recognized by a passenger who asked him if he was Robert De Niro. The passenger was an actor himself. "Well, that's acting," the actor lamented. "One year, the Oscar—the next, you're driving a cab!" De Niro also took pistol lessons and spent many an hour in taxi garages and cabbie hangouts, closely studying the behavior of the drivers. He listened repeatedly to tapes of Schrader reading from Arthur Bremer's diaries. De Niro lost thirty pounds for the role and met with Schrader frequently to pick his brain about the dark period during which he had written the screenplay. Realizing that De Niro wanted to incorporate elements of him into the character of Travis Bickle, Schrader gave him a pair of his jeans and his boots, which De Niro wore in the film. One day De Niro asked Scorsese what type of animal Travis would be. To this Scorsese answered that he would probably be a tiger. "No," De Niro said, "I think I'd be more like a wolf."[8] De Niro then went to a nearby zoo and studied the movements of caged wolves.

Keitel, equally serious about his craft, also conducted painstaking research into the background of his character. He took to the streets, locating a real pimp, whom he convinced to work with him prior to filming. The two would meet at the Actors Studio, where they would role-play for hours on end. Keitel and the pimp would alternate in the roles of pimp and prostitute, improvising entire exchanges. The actor also convinced the pimp to talk at length about his upbringing, his day-to-day operation, and his aspirations. As he did, Keitel recorded the conversations so he could analyze them later. Keitel also conceived Sport's look himself, including the shoulder-length hairpiece. The Phillipses didn't want to spend money on the wig, but Scorsese trusted Keitel's instincts and finally managed to convince them.

Interestingly, the pimp in Schrader's original screenplay was black, as are all of the characters that Travis kills. Scorsese, Schrader, and the Phillipses all decided that this element of the screenplay would have to be changed. Certainly the character Travis Bickle was racist, but the film itself didn't have to be. "When Marty and I started working together, we got to the scene where Travis shoots Sport and we just looked at each other and we knew we couldn't do it the way it was written," Schrader recalls. "We would have had fights in the theater. It would have been an incitement to riot. There wasn't even a discussion about it."[9] Scorsese then sent Schrader out into the streets to find a white pimp, but Schrader never found one. During his search, he did, however, meet a child prostitute named Billie Perkins who later served as inspiration for Jodie Foster's portrayal of Iris.

While scouting locations for *Taxi Driver*, Scorsese witnessed an act of random violence that seemed to reaffirm the validity of the violent film he was about to make. "The ballet had just let out and a number of women were crossing to catch a bus," Scorsese recalls. "Suddenly a big guy walked over to a very old lady and punched her in the mouth, and a young lady began screaming and crying. The guy just walked away. Senseless violence. Yet if you got into that guy's head—into his character—who knows?"[10]

While preparing for the film, Scorsese met composer Bernard Herrmann and asked him to score *Taxi Driver*. Scorsese was a huge fan of the legendary composer, whose film credits included such classics as *Citizen Kane*, *Vertigo*, and *Psycho*. But Herrmann was very dismissive of the project, saying that he had no interest in scoring a film about a taxi driver. Scorsese then convinced Herrmann to read the screenplay, and Herrmann changed his mind because he liked the scene in which Travis pours peach brandy on his cornflakes. "I like that," Herrmann said. "I'll do it."

Scorsese and crew ultimately faced a number of problems on this "forty day, forty night" shoot in the summer of 1975. The weather was a huge factor; it was constantly raining, and when it wasn't, it was steamy hot. Potholes on the streets continually caused the cameras mounted on the taxi to jar loose, ruining shot after shot and darkening the mood of the crew. As the problems continued to occur, tempers started to rise. One day Scorsese got into a heated argument with his mother, Catherine Scorsese, after she walked into the frame, ruining a shot. Shooting almost always lasted well into the night, and much of the crew reportedly turned to cocaine to keep themselves revived. While the crew filmed the scene in which Travis plays hero by shooting a stickup man in a bodega, a real-life murder occurred just around the corner. Fact and fiction soon became blurred when real-life police officers arrived at the location where the crew was shooting, inadvertently intermingling with the movie cops. Scorsese and crew couldn't tell them apart and simply filmed whatever police officers were there.

With the crew constantly surrounded by the crime-ridden nightlife of New York, a feeling of gloomy despair began to permeate the shoot. "We shot the film during a very hot summer and there's an atmosphere at night that's like a seeping kind of virus," Scorsese says. "You can smell it in the air and taste in your mouth."[11]

Perhaps the biggest problem during the making of *Taxi Driver* was Cybill Shepherd, whom Julia Phillips has said Scorsese cast merely because he liked her "big ass." Scorsese grew frustrated with her performance, Julia Phillips questioned her acting ability, and De Niro apparently disliked her immensely, even mocking her. "[De Niro] treated Cybill like a pile of dogshit," says one source. "It was really hot. One of the grips or somebody gave her a little electric fan because she was in this really hot dress. De Niro would kind of like go—'the princess' kind of thing. It was horrendous to watch. The truth is, Bobby treated people badly if he decided they were not up to snuff."[12]

Shepherd herself was unhappy, and at one point seriously believed Scorsese was purposely torturing her by making her watch an adult movie during the porno theater scene. "I'm overwhelmingly repulsed by pornography anyway," Shepherd says, "and for five or ten minutes I was sure, I *knew*, that asking me to make the picture was another way of humiliating me."[13]

De Niro's relationship with Jodie Foster was much smoother than his relationship with Shepherd. Seeing serious potential in the young actress, he took her under his wing and taught her how to get more out of her performance. The two would sit in diners in the Bronx and Spanish Harlem and rehearse their scenes until Foster was bored. She later acknowledged that De Niro taught her that true improvisation comes from knowing a scene so well that one eventually becomes bored with the dialogue.

Victor Magnotta, who appears in the film as a Secret Service photographer, shared valuable information about his tour in Vietnam with Scorsese and De Niro. "During dinner Bob was asking him about Special Forces," Scorsese recalls. "He told us that, in Saigon, if you saw a guy with his head shaved—like a little Mohawk—that usually meant that those people were ready to go into a certain Special Forces situation. You didn't even go near them. They were ready to kill."[14] This story simultaneously gave both Scorsese and De Niro the idea to incorporate the Mohawk into the film. "It was one of those things that started to happen with the two of us," Scorsese explains. "We'd both get the same idea—literally."[15]

The Mohawk—a fake—was part of a bald-cap created by special effects make-up artist Dick Smith, whom De Niro had just collaborated with on *The Godfather: Part II*. Because the latex cap was quite thin, a new cap was applied each day. Smith, known for his attention to detail, would paint on the stubble each day before attaching the centerpiece. Smith was also responsible for such effects as Travis' blood-spurting neck and the bloodied hand that was shot by Travis.

When actor George Memmoli was injured while performing a stunt on another film, Scorsese was forced to stand in for him as a vengeful husband who considers shooting his unfaithful wife in the vagina. De Niro, who shared the scene with Scorsese, managed to coax a better performance out of the director. "I learned a lot from Bob in that scene," Scorsese explains. "I remember saying the line 'Put down the flag, put down the flag.' De Niro said, 'No, make me put it down.' And Bobby wasn't going to put that flag down until he was convinced that I meant it. And then I understood. His move had to be a certain way and if he didn't feel it the move wasn't going to be right. For me, it was a pretty terrifying scene to do."[16]

Other scenes came together at the last minute as well. During the shoot a journalist named Julia Cameron arrived on set to interview Paul Schrader for *Oui* magazine. While there, she met Scorsese, who ultimately allowed her to rewrite all of the political speeches and the campaign office dialogue. Shortly thereafter Scorsese began dating Cameron, and within the year they were married.

Scorsese employed less improvisation in *Taxi Driver* than he had in *Mean Streets*, but he still allowed De Niro and Keitel some freedom to experiment within the parameters of the scenes as Schrader had scripted them. Perhaps the most notable instance of this came in the film's most famous scene. The original screenplay said only, "Travis talks to himself in the mirror." Recalling instances growing up when he himself would imitate heroes like Marlon Brando and James Dean in the mirror, Scorsese allowed De Niro to riff a bit here—and out came the film's most famous line: "You talkin' to me?" There has since been some debate as to the origins of this line. Some credit a concert call and response by Bruce Springsteen, while others point to an improvisational acting exercise taught by acting coach Stella Adler.

Once the shoot had wrapped, Scorsese then went into the editing bay with editors Tom Rolf, Melvin Shapiro, and Marcia Lucas. Rolf was especially intrigued by Scorsese's unconventional method of cutting the film. According to Rolf, Scorsese insisted on some shots being longer than instinct would normally allow in order to build tension. Julia Phillips would later write in her memoir that Scorsese spent an inordinate amount of time focusing on his own scene in the film. He would play several takes of the scene over and over again. In one take he had inadvertently implied that a woman's brains are located in her vagina. All of the editors and producers agreed that this take worked the best, but Scorsese was worried about seeing himself saying such a thing on film. In the end, despite his own admission that this take worked the best, Scorsese decided to cut it from the film. During editing, Scorsese also received news that Bernard Herrmann had passed away only hours after completing the film's score.

The first cut of *Taxi Driver* adhered perfectly to Schrader's original screenplay but didn't gel right. When Scorsese and the Phillipses screened it privately for a group of friends that included filmmakers

Steven Spielberg and Brian De Palma, the results were disastrous. The laughter was unintentional and uncontrollable. Julia Phillips would later point to the final scene between De Niro and Shepherd as being the scene that brought forth the most laughter. Scorsese and company then returned to the editing bay to recut the film. This time, rather than adhering so closely to Schrader's script, Scorsese reassembled the scenes in a slightly different way to give the film the dreamlike quality of being all in Travis' head. These changes did not sit well with Schrader. However, when he finally got to see this cut of the film he was immensely pleased, as was everyone else involved.

However, Columbia Pictures was not pleased. Fearing that *Taxi Driver* would receive an X rating from the Motion Picture Association of America (MPAA), the studio wanted another recut that removed most of the violence. Scorsese and Julia Phillips met with David Begelman and executive vice president Stanley Jaffe, who insinuated that the studio would make the cuts if Scorsese didn't. This infuriated Scorsese, who called an impromptu meeting at his Mulholland home with his old friends Brian De Palma, Steven Spielberg, and John Milius. The friends tried to calm their enraged host but to no avail. Scorsese then began to talk about purchasing a gun and shooting Stanley Jaffe. "He wasn't serious about it," Spielberg recalls. "But he was relishing the rage, and he wanted us to share his anger."[17] Then late that night Scorsese telephoned Julia Phillips, essentially telling her the same thing. Phillips then convinced Scorsese that this was silly, to which Scorsese replied, "You're right, I can't shoot him . . . maybe just threaten him."[18] Jaffe would later record detailed notes regarding which scenes to trim, but Julia Phillips kept the tape from Scorsese for fear that he would attack Jaffe.

Instead of making all the cuts that the studio suggested, Scorsese experimented with the colors of the film in sixty-five cuts at the end of the film. By saturating the color of the blood in the massacre scene, thus making it look less realistic, Scorsese was able to obtain an R rating from the MPAA, making everyone happy. Perhaps most happy was Scorsese himself, who reveled in the fact that the change actually managed to make the scene even darker by making the blood look more pronounced. "Look at what it does to Murray's brains," Scorsese would chirp gleefully. "Isn't that great?"[19]

Taxi Driver opened on February 8, 1976, at the Coronet Theater, shattering their first and second day box office records, raking in $58,000 the first weekend. The film ultimately made more than $25 million at the box office. *Taxi Driver* proved to be divisive for review-ers, and even those who praised it denounced its violent tendencies. *New Yorker* critic Pauline Kael once again gave Scorsese a rave review and praised De Niro for yet another brilliant turn. *Newsweek* critic Jack Kroll wrote that "first and last, *Taxi Driver* belongs to Robert De Niro, the most remarkable young actor of the American screen. What the film comes down to is a grotesque *pas de deux* between Travis and the city, and De Niro has the dance quality that most great film actors have had, whether it's allegro like Cagney or largo like Brando. De Niro controls his body like a moving sculpture."[20]

In May 1976, *Taxi Driver* was awarded the *Palme d'Or* at Cannes. However, festival jury president Tennessee Williams read a statement on behalf of the jury that seemed to be aimed primarily at Scorsese's film. The statement denounced the upswing of cinematic violence and

the recent trend toward bleakness. "We are well aware that this violence and hopelessness reflect the image of our society," Williams said. "However, we fear that violence breeds violence and that, instead of being a denunciation, it leads our society to an escalation of violence. The jury . . . expresses its wish that the cinema not become a source of hatred."[21]

Taxi Driver received many accolades, including Best Actor honors for De Niro from the National Society of Film Critics, the Los Angeles Film Critics Association, and the New York Film Critics Circle Awards. The film also received four Oscar nominations in the categories of Best Actor (De Niro), Best Supporting Actress (Foster), Best Original Score (Herrmann), and Best Picture. The night of the Academy Awards ceremony, March 28, 1977, was ultimately bittersweet for Scorsese. Not only did *Taxi Driver* lose in all four categories, but Scorsese received a death threat (for casting Foster as a prostitute) and had to be escorted from the ceremony by armed FBI agents.

The controversy surrounding the film did not end there. Five years later a gunman named John Warnock Hinckley Jr. attempted to assassinate President Ronald Reagan outside the Washington Hilton. Hinckley told police that he'd attempted to kill the president in the hopes of impressing actress Jodie Foster. Hinckley later stated that his fifteen viewings of *Taxi Driver* had caused him to shoot the president, once again opening up debates regarding the validity and effects of the film's violence. Hinckley was later acquitted on grounds of insanity.

Today *Taxi Driver* is widely considered one of the finest films produced in the 1970s. In the 2007 version of the American Film Institute's "100 Years . . . 100 Movies" list, *Taxi Driver* is ranked as the fifty-second greatest film in the history of American cinema.

The Film

The film begins with a stylish credit sequence in which a taxi emerges slowly from steam vapors on the streets of New York. The credits are presented in blood red against a backdrop of seedy New York streets at night as a haunting Bernard Herrmann piece fills the soundtrack. The perspective then changes and we are shown these same dirty streets through the eyes of the cabbie, Travis Bickle (Robert De Niro).

The story begins with Travis, a lonely twenty-six-year-old Vietnam veteran, entering the personnel office of a cab company to apply for a job as a cabbie. Travis explains to the personnel officer (Joe Spinell) that he cannot sleep at night, so he figures he might as well get paid for being awake. He says that he will work anytime, including holidays, and will work in the seediest neighborhoods. The personnel officer seems skeptical at first, but eventually hires Travis after the revelation that they both served in the Marines.

We then see (and hear through voice-over) Travis writing in his journal inside his tiny rattrap apartment. He is now working long hours as a cabbie, keeping him busy. He makes between $300 and $350 a week and can make more if he works "off the meter." We see hookers, pimps, and passersby through the rainy windshield of Travis' cab. The animals come out at night, Travis explains in a voice-over. He laments that someday a rain will come and wash all of this scum from the streets. Here Travis reveals himself as a racist, referring to blacks as "spooks." As we see the New York night through Travis' eyes, we see that he is completely voyeuristic—he comes into contact with dozens of people each night, but forms no bonds and has no true interaction with any of them. When Travis returns to the station the following morning, he engages in the daily routine of cleaning blood and semen from the backseat of the cab.

After the conclusion of his shift, Travis goes to a porn theater. Here we witness Travis' inability to relate with others as he awkwardly attempts to make conversation with a female concession stand worker (Diahnne Abbott). As Travis watches the X-rated film, we once again hear another entry in his journal. Here he states that all he needs is a sense of purpose in his mundane life. In his journal entry, Travis reveals that, although he has no friends and finds difficulty in making connections with other people, he longs to be a part of normal society.

Travis' desire to fit in and be a part of society leads him to develop a crush on a beautiful woman in white named Betsy (Cybill Shepherd), whom he views as angelic. He places her on a pedestal above the rest of New York, which he deplores. "Out of this filthy mess, she is alone," he says. Travis watches her enter the New York headquarters for presidential candidate Charles Palantine (Leonard Harris), where she is a campaign worker. Proving once again that he is socially inept, Travis sits in his parked cab and stares at her. Finally Betsy becomes so uncomfortable that she sends her coworker Tom (Albert Brooks) out to ask him to leave. Seeing Tom approaching, Travis speeds away.

In the next scene, we see Travis working late at night. He enters a diner that is inhabited by other cabbies. When one of the cabbies, Wizard (Peter Boyle), tries to talk to him, Travis becomes uneasy and avoids conversation. This is our first indication that Travis' loneliness is self-imposed. Another cabbie tells Travis that he can get him a gun if he ever needs one.

The next day, Travis enters the Palantine campaign headquarters and approaches Betsy. At first he pretends that he wants to assist with the campaign, but then tells Betsy she's the most beautiful woman he's ever seen and asks her out. She tells him that she has a break at four o'clock and that if he's there at that time, she will go around the corner to have pie and coffee with him. Travis returns at four, and the two of them go out for coffee. During the conversation, which covers topics from Betsy's background to Travis' dislike for Tom, her coworker, it is once again apparent that Travis is unable to relate with others. The conversation is awkward, and at times it appears that Travis has no idea what Betsy is talking about. Nevertheless, he manages to appear normal enough that she agrees to go out on a date with him and see a movie sometime.

It is night once again, and Travis is driving his cab. While doing so he has a chance encounter with Senator Charles Palantine, for whom Betsy works. Travis tells Palantine that he's one of his biggest supporters. This encounter once again becomes awkward when Travis curses in front of the senator and goes on a rant about New York being a cesspool. After dropping the senator off at his destination, Travis encounters a child prostitute named Iris (Jodie Foster). Iris climbs into the cab, but her pimp, Sport (Harvey Keitel), violently drags her from the car, paying Travis twenty dollars to forget the incident.

The following day, Travis meets Betsy outside the campaign office for their date. Things seem to be going well until Travis—apparently ignorant to social mores—takes Betsy to a porn theater. Betsy is obviously uncomfortable but enters the theater anyway. The two of them sit and watch an X-rated film, *Swedish Sex Manual*, until Betsy cannot take it any longer and storms out. Travis follows her out, and Betsy expresses her displeasure outside the theater. Travis isn't sure exactly what he's done wrong, saying in earnest that he doesn't know much about movies. He tries to talk her into going somewhere else, but it's too late—the damage has been done. Betsy hails a taxi and leaves. Later we see Travis desperately pleading with Betsy on a pay phone in his apartment building. As Travis begs futilely, the camera slowly pans away from him, focusing instead on an empty hallway. Interestingly, this shot, which signifies the emptiness in Travis' life, was the first shot of the film conceived by director Martin Scorsese when he went to work on this project.

The following scene finds Travis going once again to the Palantine campaign headquarters. There he confronts Betsy, telling her that he knows she's there, avoiding his calls. He tells her that he has decided that she's just like everyone else in New York and that she will burn in hell with the rest of them.

Now that Travis has lost his hope of connecting with Betsy, the tone of the film changes, becoming much darker. We see Travis driving a passenger (Martin Scorsese) who asks him to park outside an apartment building. The passenger then watches the silhouette of his wife and another man—a "nigger"—through a window. Travis listens quietly as the passenger heatedly rants about shooting his wife in the vagina with a .44 magnum pistol. Travis then goes to the all-night diner, where he sits with the other cabbies. Realizing that he's descending into madness, Travis tries to reach out to Wizard, telling him that he has some bad ideas in his head. But Wizard doesn't understand what Travis is trying to say, and he dismissively tells him not to worry so much.

In the next scene, the score becomes much more foreboding as Travis watches Senator Palantine speak on television. This is foreshadowing of what is to come later in the film. We then see several images of Travis driving his cab through the city, picking up passengers here and there. Later that night Travis once again encounters Iris when she walks out in front of his moving cab. He then follows her down the street in his cab until she meets a john, walking away with him.

In a voice-over, Travis talks of being lonely. He says that his days have been indistinguishable from one another, but now "there is a change." Finally Travis has found a sense of purpose in his life. We see him purchasing black-market guns in a motel from a man named Easy Andy (Steven Prince). We next see Travis getting into shape by doing push-ups and pull-ups and lifting weights. He then holds his fist over a flame, just as Charlie did in *Mean Streets*. We see him firing pistols at a gun range. An idea has been growing inside his mind, Travis explains in a voice-over, as we see campaign posters of Palantine. Travis then prepares by practicing drawing his pistol and making dumdum bullets, designed to expand on contact, making a larger wound.

In the next scene, we see Travis walking around at a rally where Senator Palantine will soon be speaking. He approaches a Secret Service agent and asks him questions about his occupation. In doing so, Travis becomes a suspect, and the Secret Service agent orders a photographer to take pictures of him. Travis is spooked and leaves the rally.

We next see Travis in his apartment, practicing drawing his gun in the mirror in the famed "You talkin' to me?" scene. He stares at some posters of Palantine. In a voice-over Travis explains that he was now a man who would not take it any longer—a man who "stood up against the scum." Now a transformation has officially taken place. Travis walks into a bodega and foils a robbery, gunning down the robber. Travis then slips away into the night as the shop owner (Vic Argo) pummels the corpse with a crowbar. In the next scene, we see Travis pointing a pistol at a black man dancing on television on *American Bandstand*. Travis then sits in his cab at the edge of a Palantine rally. In a voice-over we hear a letter Travis has written to his parents. Delusional, Travis tells them that he is working for the government and that he has a girlfriend named Betsy. All of this serves to tell us that Travis is now very unstable. After a policeman orders Travis to move his cab, he once again leaves the Palantine rally.

With Travis now completely past the tipping point and well into the land of irrationality, we are presented with an emblematic scene in which Travis tips his television over, breaking it. As Travis sits hunkered down, battling his own inner demons, a brooding Herrmann score fills the soundtrack. Travis now shifts his focus back to Iris, the child prostitute. He attempts to befriend her, but she mistakes his intentions; thinking he wants to have sex with her, she starts to undress. Travis tells her he wants to save her but is discouraged to learn that she doesn't want to be saved. Travis then has breakfast with her, again encouraging her to leave the world of prostitution but to no avail.

As Travis prepares for battle, polishing his boots and sharpening his knife, he tells us that he now sees things clearly for the first time.

He explains that his entire life has pointed toward what he is about to do now and that he never had a choice. Herrmann's score once again becomes menacing, and we see Travis at yet another Palantine rally. Just as Palantine says, "We have reached the turning point," we see that Travis has shaved his head and now has a Mohawk, just as some Special Forces soldiers do when they are preparing to kill. As Palantine is led from the stage after his speech, Travis moves toward him through the crowd, his grin falling away. He reaches into his jacket for his gun, but this move is spotted by Secret Service agents, who attempt to chase him. However, the crowd is too dense, and the agents are unable to catch Travis.

Travis once again shifts his focus, this time from Palantine to Iris' pimp, Sport. In a scene that plays like a surreal nightmare, Travis enters the pimp's lair, grinning like a madman. He then guns down Sport and several of his henchmen. Travis is shot in the arm and the neck, but continues moving forward as if inhuman. Once Travis has dispatched all of Sport's men, he attempts to commit suicide but finds that he has no bullets left. As Travis sits among the carnage, awaiting the police, Iris weeps. Once the police arrive, Travis raises his finger like a gun and motions as if he were shooting himself in the temple.

At the conclusion of the film, which many people mistake for Travis' dying fantasy, we see Travis in a hospital. Through newspaper clippings and a voice-over by Iris' father, we learn that Travis is seen as a hero of sorts. In the film's final scene, we see Travis once again driving a cab. He picks up Betsy, who says she read about him in the newspaper. Travis downplays all of this, hardly speaking to her. After arriving at her destination, Betsy asks how much she owes Travis, but he will not accept her money. He then drives off into the New York night.

It should be noted that *Taxi Driver*, like many of Scorsese's other films, focuses on the Madonna-whore complex. In fact, here it is more apparent and more central to the theme of the film than in any of Scorsese's other works. When Travis first meets Betsy, he envisions her as being pure and wholesome. After she scorns him, however, his vision is distorted and he begins to see her as something impure and dirty. In Iris, who actually is a whore, Travis sees something impure that he can save, thus transforming her into something virginal.

Notes

1. Jackson, Kevin, *Schrader on Schrader* (Boston: Faber and Faber, 1990), 117.

2. Phillips, Julia, *You'll Never Eat Lunch in This Town Again* (New York: Random House, 1991), 214.

3. Flatley, Guy, "Martin Scorsese's Gamble," *New York Times*, February 8, 1976, 56.

4. Biskind, Peter, *Easy Riders, Raging Bulls* (New York: Simon & Schuster, 1998), 246.

5. Foster, Buddy, and Wagener, Leon, *Foster Child: A Biography of Jodie Foster* (New York: Dutton, 1997), 91.

6. Fine, Marshall, *Harvey Keitel: The Art of Darkness* (New York: Fromm International, 1997), 78.

7. Fine, *Harvey Keitel*, 79.

8. Powell, Elfreda, *The Unofficial Robert De Niro* (Bristol: Parragon Books, 1996), 27

9. Taubin, Amy, *Taxi Driver* (London: British Film Institute, 2000), 18.

10. Goodman, Mark, "Tripping with Martin Scorsese," *Penthouse*, May 1977, 102.

11. Thompson, David, and Christie, Ian, eds., *Scorsese on Scorsese* (Boston: Faber and Faber, 1989), 54

12. Biskind, *Easy Riders, Raging Bulls*, 300.

13. Baxter, John, *De Niro: A Biography* (New York: HarperCollins, 2002), 134.

14. Dougan, Andy, *Martin Scorsese: Close Up* (New York: Thunder's Mouth Press, 1998), 51.

15. Dougan, *Martin Scorsese*, 51.

16. Dougan, Andy, *Untouchable: A Biography of Robert De Niro* (New York: Thunder's Mouth Press, 1996), 77.

17. Biskind, *Easy Riders, Raging Bulls*, 307.

18. Phillips, *You'll Never Eat Lunch in This Town Again*, 219.

19. Phillips, *You'll Never Eat Lunch in This Town Again*, 220.

20. Kroll, Jack, "Hackie in Hell," *Newsweek*, March 1, 1976, 82.

21. Tennessee Williams is quoted in Brode, Douglas, *The Films of Robert De Niro* (Secaucus, NJ: Citadel Press, 1996).

CHAPTER THREE

New York, New York (1977)

It's about the difficulties of maintaining relationships while you're making it. It takes in that period of your life when your first marriage breaks up, when people who are crazy in love with each other can't live with each other. Since that happened to me, I can say that this film is just as personal in its own way as Mean Streets and Taxi Driver.

—Martin Scorsese

The Backstory

With the success of *Taxi Driver*, Martin Scorsese was now recognized as one of the most talented and stylish young filmmakers working in Hollywood. This type of overnight success frequently leads to excess and self-indulgence, and Scorsese would be no exception. It was Scorsese's *Taxi Driver* collaborator Paul Schrader who first predicted his downfall in 1976: "It will finally reach a point where Scorsese can get enough power that he won't have to deal with other people; then he'll be so cut off he'll make a big flop. It's a familiar pattern."[1] True to Schrader's words, Scorsese would soon produce his first flop, *New York, New York*.

Scorsese was making *Alice Doesn't Live Here Anymore* when he first read about *New York, New York* in the *Hollywood Reporter*. The article announced that producer Irwin Winkler had purchased a screenplay from Earl Mac Rauch about a romance between two musicians in the big band era but had yet to find a suitable director for the project. A huge fan of the musicals of the forties and fifties, Scorsese telephoned his agent Harry Ufland, informing him that he wanted to make the picture. Scorsese then convinced both Robert De Niro and singer Liza Minnelli—the daughter of Scorsese's hero Vincente Minnelli—to star in the film. Ufland then presented the package deal of Scorsese, De Niro, and Minnelli to Winkler, who jumped at the chance to work with the talented trio. "This is a love story, and Marty is a very passionate man," Winkler explains. "He also grew up on musicals, especially the Vincente Minnelli musicals at MGM. Besides, I loved *Mean Streets*, and, despite the violence, I thought it had a great humanity. We were looking for someone who could tell a story that on the surface was very simplistic and yet had an undertone of reality. We want the people to look real and human."[2]

Both Scorsese and De Niro wanted to work on the film because they sought a thematic change of material. With the public's dismissal of De Niro's more sensitive portrayal in *The Last Tycoon*, many believed that he would forever be seen as the star of violent films like *Mean Streets*, *The Godfather: Part II*, and *Taxi Driver*; he might appear in other types of films, but the public would only accept him as a tough guy in violent films. *New York, New York* gave De Niro the opportunity to do something completely different before the mold had set, while once again teaming him with Scorsese. For Scorsese, *New York, New York* would be an escape from the violence. "I wanted to have some fun for a change," Scorsese says. "Doing *Taxi Driver*, I found it a little tough going on location every morning, with blood splattered all over the walls. We laughed about it, but it was an emotional strain. This is the kind of movie I always wanted to make."[3]

Scorsese envisioned *New York, New York* as a nod to vintage MGM musicals. Remembering films of his childhood that featured a New York City that was very foreign to him, Scorsese planned to make a film about the Big Apple that would be shot entirely in the back lots of Hollywood. The sets on the film would be designed to look just like those of the musicals of the forties and fifties. Scorsese saw the film as being a film noir musical, a combination of Raoul Walsh's *The Man I*

Love and the Richard Widmark vehicle *Road House*. "I wanted to do a valentine to Hollywood," Scorsese recalls. "But update it, update it to the point where you have the look and feel of an old Hollywood film that grows in time, and each time, each date, it would look like a film of that period."[4] Scorsese vowed that he would not use handheld cameras on this film, and he would not use close-ups except for love scenes. He also planned to use old-school methods of photography and editing, as well as the archaic hues associated with Technicolor.

Since most of the old sets had long since been destroyed, Scorsese hired set designer Boris Leven, a veteran of such musicals as *West Side Story*, to create his vision of New York City. Songwriters Fred Ebb and John Kander, who had previously collaborated with Liza Minnelli on *Cabaret*, were hired to write the songs for the film. The rest of the songs in the film were rounded out with standards, such as "You Brought a New Kind of Love to Me" and "You Are My Lucky Star" (from *Singin' in the Rain*).

In order to give *New York, New York* the feeling of those films of yesteryear, Scorsese hired crew members and used sets and props from classic films. For instance, script girl Hannah Scheel had worked on Orson Welles' *Touch of Evil*. Assistant director Melvin Dellar had performed the same function on Alfred Hitchcock's *Dial M for Murder*. Liza Minnelli's hair stylist, Sydney Guilaroff, had previously worked with her mother, Judy Garland, on *The Wizard of Oz*. Barry Primus donned a suit in the film that had once been worn by John Garfield. Portions of the film were filmed on Stage 29, where Vincente Minnelli's *An American in Paris* had been shot. De Niro's dressing room once belonged to Greta Garbo. In addition to these things was the presence of veteran actors Lionel Stander and Jack Haley.

Scorsese felt he could relate to certain aspects of *New York, New York*. The screenplay told the story of a rising saxophonist and a vocalist who have a stormy love affair that ultimately fails. In Scorsese's mind, the film could just as easily have been the story of a film director and a writer—any two creative people—and he saw in it the opportunity to tell a personal story that would ring just as true as *Mean Streets* had. Subsequent rewrites of the film reflected elements of both Scorsese's and De Niro's offscreen relationships. Scorsese would later joke that neither he nor De Niro knew whether or not the couple portrayed in the film would make it because they didn't know whether or not their own relationships would survive. (Ultimately none of the relationships worked out.) Because of these additions to the film, Scorsese would later lament that his "light, frothy musical" had turned into his most personal film to date.

As Scorsese sought to make the film more personal, he was continually coming up with new scenes and questioning old ones. Suddenly Earl Mac Rauch's screenplay wasn't big enough, and Scorsese commissioned him to rewrite it. However, Scorsese found the rewrites to be unsatisfactory. According to Scorsese, each suggestion would lead to Mac Rauch's adding ten or twelve more pages. Eventually the screenplay became unmanageable, and Scorsese hired his wife, Julia Cameron, to assist Mac Rauch with the rewrites. The two of them collaborated for some time, churning out several drafts of the screenplay. Finally, after working on the screenplay for some two years, Mac Rauch concluded that he had nothing left to add to the project and walked away. Scorsese then turned to his old friend and collaborator Mardik Martin and asked him to rewrite the screenplay further. Martin obliged, and several more drafts were written.

Finally, due to Liza Minnelli's scheduling obligations in Las Vegas, Scorsese was forced to begin shooting before the screenplay was completed. Then, in a move that Scorsese chalks up to having oversized egos, he, De Niro, and Minnelli decided to throw out the screenplay altogether and begin improvising their scenes. The three of them began rehearsing on the set for six to seven hours a day, improvising and completely reworking the existing scenes.

"There was so much improvisation that we had to stay locked in the characters," Minnelli recalls. "He'd give us a starting point, where we had to go through, and where we had to finish. And we would find our way there."[5]

Scorsese would record these improvisations on videotape, and then go home each night and analyze them, cherry-picking the best lines. Then he and Mardik Martin would write that day's scenes based on those improvisations. "So it's all on tape, the different scenes we've rehearsed, and we usually spend two or three hours on one scene," Minnelli explains. "You know, because we go crazy, we take it every possible way we can take it. From those tapes he takes the very best

moments. And builds the scene. . . . And from five hours, it's suddenly like two pages. But it's all there, all the beats are there."[6]

Mardik Martin remembers some confusion at the studio regarding the differences between the screenplay and the rushes. "The script itself, a lot of it wasn't used the way I wrote it," Martin says. "And the people at UA [United Artists] when they saw what was shot, they were saying, 'Gee, what happened to the Mardik script?'"[7]

Not surprisingly, all of this improvisation led to some problems. "We were trying to keep the technique of improvisation and documentary approach in the foreground, with the artifice of the fake sets in the background," Scorsese explains. "But you have to build the sets in advance, which means you're not being practical, because once you start improvising in one set you soon improvise your way out of that set into another situation. In the meantime, they're building a different set because it's in the script! So you have to go back and shoot some more to get yourself back in line to use that second set—and that's one of the reasons the scenes are so long."[8]

This improvisation also led to some problems in the editing room. "Directors love improv," editor Tom Rolf explains. "Actors love it.

Editors hate it, basically, because to try to make it smooth—to make a dialogue scene, especially, smooth . . . and realistic with the certain punctuation and certain rhythms and voice tonal quality, etcetera etcetera. . . . You want it to be a constant attack, if you will. Well, with improv that doesn't happen. People come in and say essentially the same thing using different words, different timing, different body positions, different accents. So you try to put those together, and it's a nightmare."[9] Because of this, Rolf and the other editors would frequently find themselves in a position where they were forced to use one long uninterrupted take.

With the improvisation that Scorsese allowed him, De Niro was in his element. It has been rumored that one of the actor's inspirations for the character Jimmy Doyle was Scorsese himself. De Niro also found inspiration in Georgie Auld, the fifty-eight-year-old big band veteran hired to teach him to play the saxophone. Like Doyle, Auld had worked as a sideman for the big bands of 1930s, playing alongside such icons as Benny Goodman, Bunny Berrigan, and Count Basie. Armed with the most expensive tenor sax available at the time, De Niro set out to learn the instrument. "He has a talent for grasping things like nobody I've ever seen," Auld initially said of De Niro. "I couldn't believe he could do that great."[10] By all accounts De Niro trained like a madman, spending his nights on the set, practicing. However, De Niro soon became so obsessed with this training that he drove Auld crazy with his desire to learn. Auld began to feel like he was De Niro's "slave." "He asked me ten million questions a day," Auld explains. "He got to be a pain in the ass."[11] Things eventually got so bad that Auld's wife, Diane, said, "We thought he was going to climb into bed with us with the horn."[12]

While De Niro was unable to fully master the instrument, he was ultimately able to create the illusion that he was playing. In reality, Doyle's sax solos were performed by Auld himself. "I play the same stuff that's in the movie," De Niro explains. "I have to synch to what George plays. It took awhile to learn; I can't read music, but I got a horn and George taught me how to play phonetically, and I've learned phrasing and breathing, the way Georgie does it."[13]

De Niro spent the first two weeks of shooting locked away in his dressing room, relentlessly searching to find his character and practicing the sax. Then one day, he showed up on the sound stage, and everyone noticed something different about him. His hair was slicked back, and he was wearing a loud novelty shirt, chewing gum, and making smart-ass remarks. His agent saw him and remarked that the actor had just "locked in" to the part of Jimmy Doyle. The agent turned to a bystander and said, "There he goes. He's off. A metamorphosis right in front of us."[14]

De Niro's hard work certainly impressed costar Minnelli. "Bobby is *so* dedicated," she says. "Bobby is just . . . just fabulous. I think he's addicted to film itself. In rehearsals, man, he opens up and he's terribly funny. People think that he's introverted. Whereas, in fact, he's quiet. He's intense and he's very shy. Introverted always somehow means a flaw in one's character. When somebody's introverted, that usually means something is wrong with them. I don't think there's anything wrong with Bobby. A great, great deal of talent."[15] Minnelli also saw a similarity between De Niro and herself. "Bobby and I have one thing in common," she says. "We're listening actors. Nothing throws either of us. The ceiling could fall through and we'd keep right on."[16]

Other actors and crew members soon noticed another similarity between De Niro and Minnelli; both of them required enormous amounts of time with Scorsese on the set. This would often lead to them going off with the director to one of their trailers, as extras and crew members stood around waiting for long periods of time. "People still tell horror stories about the filming of *New York, New York*," costume designer Theodora van Runkle explains. "We would get our first call at 7 A.M., and often they wouldn't get their first shot until after dark. The crew were treated like peasants . . . totally ignored. Meanwhile, Marty and Liza would be closeted in her trailer. Going over the script, presumably."[17]

The reasons why De Niro and Minnelli required so much of the director's time were quite different. De Niro was constantly searching to find truth in the work and to discover more and more regarding his character's motivations. Meanwhile, Minnelli and Scorsese were having an affair. Things became even more interesting when Scorsese dressed Minnelli down in front of her husband, Jack Haley Jr., for having a second affair with dancer Mikhail Baryshnikov. Scorsese's wife, Julia Cameron, would later cite the director's affair with Minnelli as one of the reasons for her filing for divorce.

De Niro and Scorsese became closer while working on *New York, New York,* and other actors grew tired of seeing the two leaving the set to confer about character motivations. "Bobby hogs Marty on the set," one actor observed. "Marty gives Bobby anything he wants. And what Bobby wants is constant attention—constant talk about his character."[18] Hearing the whispers of disgruntled actors, Scorsese said, "The real stuff between me and Bob is private. Bob talks to me in private. He needs a lot of time. We both need a lot of time."[19] In an interview with George Hickenlooper, Scorsese later explained the nature of his deliberations with De Niro:

> Bob would say something to me like, "Can I try one thing?" or "I have an idea, just let me show you," it was great. Of course, other actors have done that too, but when they showed me, I couldn't find anything new. I wondered what they were trying to show me. Well, Bob De Niro, when he shows me something, or when he has an idea, when something comes right from that visceral part of him, it just comes out of his soul. You know, I'm surprised that it's always extremely valid and quite good—I usually find it to be pretty much according to what I feel. We're always finishing each other's sentences creatively. We'll put it that way. If we're struggling for words, creatively, he can find them. And that's a pretty rare thing.[20]

Under pressure to make a coherent film out of *New York, New York,* which was still being written, Scorsese turned to cocaine. "I didn't know how to get these feelings," Scorsese explains. "I kept pushing and shoving and twisting and turning myself in different ways, and I started taking drugs to explore, and got sidetracked a lot of the time. We put ourselves through a lot of pain."[21] In one of the most famous instances of his getting sidetracked, Scorsese kept more than 150 extras standing around waiting as he talked to his psychiatrist on the phone in his trailer.

The grueling shoot proved to be tough for everyone. "I don't know how any of us survived it," Minnelli says. "It was like a whirlwind—it's the only film where I can't remember sitting down."[22]

The all-out style of filmmaking employed by Scorsese and company also led to some injuries. "There was a scene with Liza where we had to have a fight in the car," De Niro recalls. "I thought it was funny to

be so hopping mad that my head was sort of banging on the ceiling and I'd hit my hand somehow. I didn't get out of control, I just went a smidgen over, which can happen. Liza got hurt and I think I hurt my hand too. But we would try anything. So sometimes you can't predict the outcome."[23]

A number of high-profile distractions caused the production to slow down further. Milos Forman, Bernardo Bertolucci, Sylvester Stallone, Jeanne Moreau, Ingmar Bergman, Jack Nicholson, and Scorsese's hero Vincente Minnelli all made visits to the set during filming. Watching Scorsese and crew working on an elaborate set-up for the film's opening scene, Minnelli commented that he frequently worked on films that required several days to set up, but only a few minutes to shoot. This, however, was not the case with Scorsese's elaborate V-J (Victory over Japan) Day scene. Due largely to the improvisational techniques Scorsese was utilizing, the scene took several more days to film.

Scorsese was also shooting an exorbitant amount of film. Producer Irwin Winkler recalls Scorsese routinely shooting twenty or more takes. "All the problems started multiplying," Winkler says. "And I said to

Marty, 'Listen, you know, at twenty-two takes, how do you feel, don't you think we have it?' He said, 'You know, Irwin, on the last take I think I saw a tear coming out of the corner of Liza's eye. I think if I go two more takes, maybe three, I can get the tear. Do you want me to go for the tear, or do you want me to stop?' And I said, 'Go for the tear.'"[24]

Scorsese even asked songwriters Kander and Ebb to rewrite songs. Feeling that "New York, New York" wasn't "punchy enough," the director ordered the songwriters to rewrite the song three times before he was satisfied with it.

By the time filming was completed, Scorsese's runaway production nearly doubled the eleven weeks allotted for filming, dragging on for another nine. In addition, the $7 million budget ballooned to $9 million. Scorsese, in public, blamed this extra time and money on Winkler's mistakenly underscheduling the film. While there may be some truth to this, the constant rewriting, the improvisation, the on-set rehearsals, the drugs, the affairs, and the excessive shooting could not have helped matters.

Once shooting was completed and the film was in postproduction, a burned-out Scorsese received a call from *Mean Streets* producer Jonathan Taplin asking him to make a concert movie about The Band's final concert on Thanksgiving Day 1976. Despite all of the pressure he was under with *New York, New York*, Scorsese agreed to shoot the film behind producer Irwin Winkler's back. This project, which was ultimately titled *The Last Waltz*, took three weeks to prepare and film. "At a certain point you have to leave it," Scorsese says of *New York, New York*.

> I left it for about three weeks. I left in a way that was not leaving it. I mean, nobody knew I left it. They sensed I wasn't around as much. "What's Scorsese doing? What's he playing the fuck around? What is this? Isn't he serious about the picture?" I mean when they got to that point, I just said, "Leave me alone for a goddamn three days. Let me goddamn think about the goddamn movie. Everybody's given ideas, ideas, ideas. I appreciate it all, but at this point, it's total clutter. I can't see the picture and I don't know what the hell anybody is talking about anymore."[25]

Simultaneously editing both *New York, New York* and *The Last Waltz*, Scorsese was becoming more and more fatigued. When it appeared that there was no end in sight for either film, Scorsese asked Marcia Lucas to come and assist him in the editing room. Lucas was assisting her husband, George Lucas, in editing *Star Wars*—a film that she had little faith in. She then left her husband's film to work with Scorsese. Confused by the bleak tone of Scorsese's musical, a visiting George Lucas suggested that an upbeat ending could add perhaps $10 million to the film's box office receipts. Scorsese agreed with this assessment but chose to ignore the advice.

The editors on *New York, New York* began working in round-the-clock shifts, with Scorsese running back and forth from room to room. Before the first cut was completed, Scorsese prepared a forty-minute segment to screen for friends and crew members. This footage contained the opening V-J Day sequence, the lavish "Happy Endings" number, and several scenes that were ultimately cut from the film. The screening crowd, which included George Cukor and Vincente Minnelli, applauded thunderously. The positive reactions to this material helped shape Scorsese's first cut of the film, which clocked in at an astounding four and a half hours. Scorsese was extremely happy with this cut, as it was a fair representation of his vision of what the film should be.

Editor Tom Rolf also felt that this cut was perfect. "I remember running the first cut," recalls Rolf. "We ran it at Metro in the Cary Grant Theater at 8 o'clock on a Thursday night. . . . At 12:30, when the lights came back up, I remember standing up and walking back to the very last row and saying, 'Marty, you're a bleeping genius.' And I felt that."[26]

The studio then ordered a recut, as this first cut was way too long for U.S. theatrical audiences. Scorsese and his band of editors then labored over the material, eventually producing a second cut, which was 163 minutes long. This version contained the "Happy Endings" number, which had cost $350,000 and had taken some ten days to film. The film was still deemed to be too long, and the studio strongly advised Scorsese to cut the number altogether, saying that it was non sequitur and brought the film's dramatic story to a halt. Although the scene was

Scorsese's favorite, he was now exhausted and unable to see the film objectively. So he agreed to cut the scene. The theatrical cut of the film was 153 minutes, with another seventeen minutes being trimmed for a European release.

"When Marty Scorsese had to cut out the small 'Happy Endings' number it just killed him," Liza Minnelli recalls. "I've never seen a director so destroyed."[27] Scorsese would later comment on the theatrical version of the film: "At times I think it became brilliant, but for the sake of the little brilliant pieces we lost too much of the whole [by cutting what we cut]."[28]

The film was previewed before its release in San Francisco. Large groups of people surrounded the theater, and the police had to be called. The film was met with wildly enthusiastic applause, and both De Niro and Minnelli were mobbed by fans. "The only way we could appease them was by agreeing to have two separate shows—to have two sneak previews in that one theater that one night," recalls producer Robert Chartoff. Based on this reaction, everyone involved with the film was convinced it would be a smash hit.

The film was released in the United States on June 21, 1977, and Scorsese soon realized that the San Francisco screening had been an anomaly. The film was met with lukewarm box office sales and tepid reviews. Audiences and critics alike were unsure what to make of the film's dark tone. Most critics were kind to De Niro and Minnelli, but bashed the director. The *Variety* review read, "Using many of the same team from *Cabaret* . . . director Martin Scorsese has taken exactly 30 minutes longer to accomplish far less. He deserves his share of the credit for the best of the musical and dramatic moments, but must also bear the blame for many of the pic's schizophrenic shifts between excellence and amateurism."[29] In his book *TV Movies* (1981–1982 edition), Leonard Maltin called *New York, New York* a milestone—"the first sick Hollywood musical," giving the film a Bomb rating.[30]

In addition, the film did not receive a single Academy Award nomination. Scorsese was so upset by the critical and box office failure of *New York, New York* that he gave serious consideration to moving to Italy to make documentary films about the saints for the rest of his life.

"Eventually I understood the picture," Scorsese says. "Jean-Luc Godard came over for lunch one day and he was talking about how much he liked *New York, New York*. He said it was basically about the impossibility of two creative people in a relationship—the jealousies, the envy, the temperament. I began to realize that it was so close to home that I wasn't able to articulate it while I was making the film."[31]

In 1981, the film was rereleased in a restored two-hour-and-forty-three-minute version that included the entire "Happy Endings" sequence. This time the film received positive reviews and did much better box office. *New York, New York* has since become a cult favorite and eventually broke even. "I was extremely disappointed when the movie was finished because I had had a really bad experience making it," Scorsese explains. "But over the years I've been able to see that it has truth to it. I still don't really like it, yet in a way I love it."[32]

"We all thought it was going to be a huge hit, but it wasn't," Minnelli explains. "But the funny thing is that people still watch it and talk about it, and love it. It's the movie that won't die."[33]

The Film

Author's note: The following examination refers to the 163-minute thirtieth anniversary edition, which is now considered the definitive version of the film.

New York, New York opens with a credit sequence set against an artificial-looking backdrop depicting the New York City skyline at night. The style of the letters and the backdrop look very much like an opening credits sequence from the musicals of the 1940s.

The film opens on August 15, 1945, also known as V-J Day, or Victory over Japan Day. (This was the date on which the announcement of Japan's World War II surrender was announced.) Under film noir lighting we see Jimmy Doyle's (Robert De Niro) shoes step on a rain-soaked newspaper announcing the end of the war in the Pacific. Jimmy makes his way through a cheering crowd in an intentionally artificial-looking Times Square.

We go to an interior shot of a stylized nightclub where Tommy Dorsey (William Tole) and his orchestra are performing. Jimmy reveals himself to be somewhat of a heel, moving from woman to woman, and spewing corny pick-up lines to each of them. He runs into some of his army buddies, to whom he says that he has thrown his uniform away. He explains that he obtained the gaudy blue Hawaiian shirt he's now wearing in a card game.

Jimmy continues making his way around the room and finally meets up with Francine Evans (Liza Minnelli). Jimmy naturally attempts to pick up Francine with one of his lines, but she sees through this and shoots him down. Francine repeatedly asks Jimmy to leave, but he refuses to take no for an answer and continues to pester her. Jimmy finally excuses himself, but promptly returns to try a fresh angle, even going so far as to try kissing her. After continuously being told no, Jimmy says, "I can take a hint," to which Francine asks him if he can also take a walk. Jimmy finally leaves, making his way around the room again. After striking out repeatedly, Jimmy runs into his pal Eddie (Frank Sivero), who invites Jimmy to sit with him and some friends, one of whom turns out to be Francine. Once Jimmy sits down at the table, Eddie and his gal pal Ellen (Kathi McGinnis) return to the dance floor, again leaving Jimmy and Francine alone. Francine again dismisses Jimmy, standing up to walk away. However, the strap on her purse is caught on Jimmy's arm and she is forced to untangle it before leaving.

Since Eddie and his newfound female friend are occupying his hotel room, Jimmy walks the dark early morning streets. As he does, he stops to watch a man and a woman dancing beneath the L train.

When Jimmy finally returns to the swanky hotel where he's staying under false pretenses, he attempts to sneak past the desk clerk (Norman Palmer). Francine is talking with him. When she calls out to Jimmy, the desk clerk learns that he has been staying at the hotel under a pseudonym ("M. Powell," a nod to *The Red Shoes* director Michael Powell). The desk clerk then calls the manager and confronts Jimmy, who begins screaming that he lost his leg in Anzio. After selling Jimmy out and telling the desk clerk that the signatures on several unpaid bills from other hotels do in fact belong to him, Francine agrees to go to Jimmy's room to warn their friends that they've been discovered and to retrieve his saxophone.

While Francine is upstairs warning Eddie and Ellen, Jimmy attempts to run out of the hotel lobby. However, the desk clerk chases him and ultimately catches him. Here Scorsese utilizes a sweeping wipe such as those used in the films of the forties to transition into the next scene, in which Jimmy and Francine flee the hotel for the safety of a cab. Inside the cab, Jimmy and Francine quibble over their destination. Since Jimmy has an audition at a Brooklyn club on Flatbush Avenue, he directs the cabbie to take them there. While en route to the club, Jimmy tries to get fresh with Francine, but his ploys are once again thwarted. Francine does, however, warm to Jimmy somewhat during the drive.

Once they arrive at the Palm Club, Jimmy auditions for the club owner (Dick Miller) but fails to impress him. Francine takes Jimmy aside to advise him to play a little more smoothly, and the two of them get into an argument. When the nightclub owner suggests that Jimmy play a different style of music, he and Jimmy start to argue. This argument is broken up, however, by the melodic sounds of Francine singing "You Brought a New Kind of Love to Me." (The 1930 standard had appeared previously in the films The Big Pond and Monkey Business.) Jimmy begins to accompany her vocals, and the club owner changes his mind, booking them two to three shows nightly with Sundays off.

We are shown a brief montage in which Jimmy and Francine dance while various nightclub signs (such as Cumberly Tavern and Halo Bar & Grill) flash on screen. By the end of the montage, it is clear that Jimmy and Francine are now lovers. Once the montage ends, we see Francine attempting to climb out of a parked cab in the rain, as Jimmy kisses her and asks her not to go. The two continue to kiss with Francine half out of the cab, and she finally manages to pull herself away. When Francine gets inside her hotel, she finds a call from her agent awaiting her. As she talks with her agent, Jimmy enters the hotel and checks in—again under the pseudonym M. Powell. Francine tries to convince Jimmy to go to another hotel, but he refuses, suggesting that he come to her room to work on new material. Jimmy finally relents, however, and tells the desk clerk that he will not be staying. He grabs Francine, and the two of them engage in a long passionate kiss. Once Jimmy has left the hotel, Francine returns to her phone call, during which her agent informs her that she has to go on the road to play with Frankie Hart's (Georgie Auld) band.

We next see Jimmy having a jam session with several other musicians at the Palm Club. Tony (Lionel Stander), Francine's agent, shows up with a message from Francine. The letter says that Francine will be playing with Frankie Hart and that there may be an open spot for Jimmy.

In the next scene, Francine is singing "Once in a While" (a standard that had appeared previously in the films *Throw a Saddle on a Star* and *I'll Get By*) with Frankie Hart's orchestra. During the song, we see Jimmy attempting to hitchhike to follow the band. We see Jimmy attempting to board a stylized artificial-looking train in a scene played for comedic value. We see Francine singing "You Are My Lucky Star" (a song that previously appeared in several films, most notably *Singin' in the Rain*) at the Meadows. As Francine wraps up the standard, Jimmy enters the club. Once the song is over, Jimmy applauds so obnoxiously that Frankie Hart becomes annoyed. Francine takes a momentary break from the set to talk with Jimmy, but Jimmy will not allow her to return to the stage.

Jimmy and Francine are now outside, walking through a snowy forest (a purposefully artificial-looking painted backdrop). This scene reveals Jimmy to be even more of an arrogant and controlling person than any scene prior to this. Jimmy says things like, "You don't say goodbye to *me*; *I* say goodbye to *you*!" Jimmy also says such romantic things as "I don't love you . . . but I like you." Despite all of this, Francine once again warms to Jimmy.

Although he refuses to call it "auditioning"—he says he will *play* for him, but not *audition*—the challenging Jimmy auditions for bandleader Frankie Hart. Jimmy lands the gig and takes to the road with Frankie, Francine, and the orchestra. We see Jimmy performing with the orchestra, attempting to hog the spotlight as he does. This is followed by several scenes depicting life on the road, and we see that Jimmy and Francine are growing closer with each passing day.

Jimmy and Francine are in a hotel room, and she allows him to read a poem she's written about him. He then urges her to get dressed, and he drags her out into the night toward an unknown destination. Francine is surprised when the cab arrives at the home of the justice of the peace (Bernie Kuby). Jimmy wants to get married, but Francine balks because he hasn't even taken the time to propose. Standing outside in front of the justice of the peace and his wife, the two "lovebirds" get into an argument (complete with Jimmy screaming). After asking the cab driver to run him over, Jimmy finally brings Francine around to his way of thinking, and they get hitched.

Frankie Hart soon decides to retire from touring, and Jimmy takes over his position in front of the orchestra. Jimmy and the band audition for a gig at the Gold Room at the Hotel Sherman in Chicago, but the club owner has no interest in them—until he hears Francine sing "The Man I Love," that is. (This Gershwin number previously appeared in the films *Rhapsody in Blue* and *The Man I Love*.) The band lands the gig based on the strength of her performance, and soon the newspapers are filled with rave reviews mentioning only Francine. This makes Jimmy jealous, but he manages to keep his cool until one day at rehearsal when he blows his top and throws a tantrum. He overturns tables, belittles the band, and reprimands Francine for trying to lead them.

Shortly after this, Francine informs Jimmy that she's pregnant. Jimmy acts happy, but he becomes irritated when Francine tells him she wants to leave the show to have the baby in New York. "The doctor said I could lose this kid if I travel," she explains. Francine's agent, Tony, informs her that he's lined her up with some easy studio work back in New York.

Meanwhile, the show must go on, and Jimmy hires Bernice Bennett (Mary Kay Place) to stand in for the absent Francine. As Jimmy and Bernice sing "Blue Moon," it is instantly apparent that they cannot compete with Francine. As they continue to sing, we are presented with a montage in which the orchestra's three-week engagement turns into a limited engagement and is finally cancelled altogether. By the time the band finishes this song, the full house has cleared out and there are now only four couples remaining on the dance floor.

Back in New York, Francine is singing the Kander and Ebb original "There Goes the Ball Game" in a recording studio. Scorsese utilizes another sweeping wipe here, transitioning us back to Jimmy, who is now having an affair with Bernice and leaves the band. As the orchestra drives away, they drive toward an obvious matte painting. Jimmy soon returns to New York to be with Francine. As Jimmy sits at the piano and tinkers with a new tune—the film's title song, "New York, New York"—he and Francine discuss his three-day disappearance after leaving the band. As Jimmy explains that he needed time to himself, it becomes more and more apparent that he is not as committed to the relationship as Francine is.

Jimmy meets up with Cecil Powell (Clarence Clemons, of E Street Band fame) and some musicians who are playing at the Harlem Club, telling them that things didn't work out with Frankie Hart's band because they were "bad musicians." We then see Jimmy performing with these guys at the all-black Harlem Club, where his soulful playing is met with great acclaim. Jimmy shows up late to pick Francine up from the recording studio, driving an automobile that she's never seen before. The two of them then get into a heated argument in the parked car, and Jimmy ends up in a screaming match with a driver who wants his parking spot. The argument between Jimmy and Francine escalates, and Jimmy makes it clear that he's unwilling to pay more attention to his pregnant wife than to his music.

In the next scene, Jimmy and Francine discuss going to see Paul Wilson (Barry Primus) and the band perform at the Up Club. The following night the two of them go to the Up Club, where they meet with Artie Kirks (Lenny Gaines) of Decca Records. Artie attempts to talk business with Jimmy, but Jimmy refuses to listen. He declares that he doesn't want to spend any more time in this club and demands to Francine that they leave. Francine says she will stay, and Jimmy storms off to the bar, where he then proceeds to get drunk. In between sets, Jimmy admits to Paul that he's better leading the band than Jimmy himself ever was. Paul thanks him for the compliment and tells Jimmy that everyone thinks he's a great guy—"even your wife." Jimmy takes this as an insult, but says nothing. Moments later, once the band is back onstage, Jimmy's simmering anger comes to a boil and he attacks Paul. Jimmy is thrown out of the club.

We see Jimmy and Francine outside New York City Hospital the next day. Jimmy gives her several bouquets of flowers and apologizes. That night, Francine brings Artie and Tony to the Harlem Club to tell Jimmy that they want to sign her to a recording deal at Decca Records. Jimmy is in the bathroom doing cocaine but comes out to have the conversation. Once again jealous of his wife's successes, Jimmy is visibly unhappy but says nothing. He soon excuses himself and climbs onstage, playing with Cecil and the band. Seeing Francine leave the club, Jimmy goes after her. Thinking she's left in a cab, he jumps into his car. Francine is hiding in the backseat and attempts to surprise him, but Jimmy becomes enraged. He tells her that she should never have kept the baby and that she looks disgusting. Francine breaks down and starts hitting Jimmy. The argument intensifies and Jimmy flies into a rage, trying to hit Francine and punching the car windows. This stressful argument ultimately causes Francine to go into labor.

The following day, Jimmy arrives at the hospital to see Francine. We do not know where he's been, but we learn that he was not present for the birth of the child. Francine tells him that she named the baby Jimmy, which irritates him. He says she has taken away his right to help select a name for the child, and he also thinks she has named the child this to make him feel bad. He then says he does not want to see the child. He tells her that things are not going to work, kisses her, and says goodbye. Outside Francine's room, a nurse offers to take Jimmy to see the baby, but he declines the invitation.

The next scene takes place several years later. Little Jimmy, who is now five or six years old, is sleeping on a couch inside the music studio. Francine is recording a new song, the Kander and Ebb original "But the World Goes 'Round." The lyrics of the song clearly apply to Francine's relationship with Jimmy, but in the song she tells us that she's moving on with her life. (The lyrics include such lines as "sometimes your dreams get broke into pieces, but that doesn't matter at all" and "sometimes a friend starts treating you bad, but the world goes 'round.") We then see that Francine has landed the lead role in the musical *Happy Endings*, which is being performed at the New York Music Hall. We see Francine performing an elaborate musical number—a short film within the film—titled "Happy Endings." The inclusion of this number is meant to be ironic as the film's story line will offer no such happy ending.

We see Jimmy sitting in a theater, watching the closing of the film version of Francine's successful musical. A newsreel then plays, telling us (and Jimmy) about Francine's successful career.

We next hear a radio deejay known as Midnight Bird (Casey Kasem) playing his new theme song "New York, New York Theme," performed by the Jimmy Doyle Sextet. A close-up of the *Down Beat Magazine* top ten list shows us that the song is number one in the nation. (A closer inspection of the top ten also reveals the presence of not only such icons as Charlie Parker and Ella Fitzgerald, but also Georgie Auld, the musician who actually plays the sax in this film. The song attributed to him is titled "Man with a Horn.") We learn that Jimmy has opened his own nightclub, Jimmy Doyle's Major Chord. Inside the club, Jimmy plays a song and then makes way for Cecil and his band.

Jimmy attends Francine's show at the Starlight Terrace, where she sings "New York, New York." After the show, Jimmy comes by Francine's dressing room, briefly giving us the false hope of a happy ending. Jimmy tells her that he's proud of her "in a way." He excuses himself and talks briefly with Jimmy Jr. He then leaves but telephones Francine, telling her that he wants to talk with her. She agrees, and he tells her that he's waiting outside the stage door. At first both Francine and Jimmy are excited, but then each of them change their minds; Francine decides not to meet him, and Jimmy opts to leave. The camera then holds on the empty, rainy New York street, and the closing credits roll.

Notes

1. Keyser, Les, *Martin Scorsese* (New York: Twayne Publishers, 1992), 85.

2. Goodman, Mark, "Tripping with Martin Scorsese," *Penthouse*, May 1977, 69.

3. Goodman, "Tripping with Martin Scorsese," 78.

4. Kelly, Mary Pat, *Martin Scorsese: A Journey* (New York: Thunder's Mouth Press, 1991), 102.

5. Carson, Greg, *Liza on "New York, New York,"* documentary (Metro-Goldwyn-Mayer, 2005).

6. Hodenfield, Chris, "Martin Scorsese's Back-Lot Sonata," *Rolling Stone*, June 16, 1977, 42.

7. Mardik Martin, interview by the author, October 10, 2008.

8. Thompson, David, and Christie, Ian, eds., *Scorsese on Scorsese* (Boston: Faber and Faber, 1989), 72.

9. Carson, Greg, *The "New York, New York" Stories*, documentary (Metro-Goldwyn-Mayer, 2005).

10. Kroll, Jack, "De Niro: A Star for the 70s," *Newsweek*, May 16, 1977, 82.

11. Agan, Patrick, *Robert De Niro: The Man, the Myth, and the Movies* (London: Robert Hale, 1989), 75.

12. Kroll, "De Niro," 83.

13. McKay, Keith, *Robert De Niro: The Hero behind the Masks* (New York: Ultra Communications, 1986), 68.

14. Hodenfield, "Martin Scorsese's Back Lot Sonata," 42.

15. Hodenfield, "Martin Scorsese's Back Lot Sonata," 42.

16. McKay, *Robert De Niro*, 72.

17. Baxter, John, *De Niro: A Biography* (New York: HarperCollins, 2002), 162.

18. McKay, *Robert De Niro*, 71.

19. Parker, John, *De Niro* (London: Victor Gollancz, 1995), 122.

20. Hickenlooper, George, *Reel Conversations: Candid Interviews with Film's Foremost Directors and Critics* (New York: Citadel Press, 1991), 27.

21. Biskind, Peter, *Easy Riders, Raging Bulls* (New York: Simon & Schuster, 1998), 325.

22. McKay, *Robert De Niro*, 68.

23. Dougan, Andy, *Untouchable: A Biography of Robert De Niro* (New York: Thunder's Mouth Press, 1996), 100.

24. Kelly, *Martin Scorsese*, 107.

25. Woods, Paul A., ed., *Scorsese: A Journey through the American Psyche* (London: Plexus Publishing, 2005), 96.

26. Carson, *The "New York, New York" Stories*.

27. McKay, *Robert De Niro*, 75.

28. Thompson and Christie, *Scorsese on Scorsese*, 72.

29. *Variety* review is quoted in Dougan, Andy, *Martin Scorsese: Close Up* (New York: Thunder's Mouth Press, 1998), 119.

30. Maltin, Leonard, *Leonard Maltin's TV Movies, 1981–1982* (New York: Signet, 1980), 212.

31. Kelly, *Martin Scorsese*, 111.

32. Thompson and Christie, *Scorsese on Scorsese*, 72.

33. Agan, *Robert De Niro*, 77.

CHAPTER FOUR

Raging Bull (1980)

In the fall of 1978 everything clicked together and I kind of woke up and said, "This is the picture that has to be made, and I'll make it that way. There are reasons why it has to be made." I understood then what Jake was, but only after having gone through a similar experience myself.

—Martin Scorsese

The Backstory

The year was 1973, and Robert De Niro was in Italy to film Bernardo Bertolucci's *1900*. Just before filming began, De Niro received a book, *Raging Bull*, in the mail from one of its authors, Peter Savage. The book was the autobiography of boxer Jake La Motta (cowritten with Joseph Carter and Savage). Out of curiosity, De Niro opened the book and started reading, immediately seeing potential for a film adaptation—and a plum role for himself. "There was something about it—a strong thrust, a portrait of a direct man without complications," De Niro explains. "Something at the center of it was very good for me. I felt I could evolve into the character."[1]

Although most critics assess the book as a whitewash of La Motta's troubled past, it still failed to present a likeable man. Born in the Bronx in 1922, La Motta learned to box in jail while serving time for robbery. La Motta, nicknamed "the Bronx Bull," was never once knocked out in his 106 fights. After a suspension for throwing a fight, La Motta later won the middleweight championship. He held the title for two years. The boxer was ultimately forced to retire after losing a long battle with his weight. He physically abused his wives and was famous for his violent tantrums. La Motta was later imprisoned for pimping underage girls in his nightclub. After all this, the former fighter reemerged as a sad caricature of the man he had once been, working as an unfunny stand-up comic and strip club emcee.

Some film critics would later ask why anyone would want to make a film about Jake La Motta, and in the beginning this was a common reaction; no one except De Niro could envision a good film being made from La Motta's book.

Hoping Martin Scorsese would be able to see the potential he saw in the project, De Niro called him on the set of *Alice Doesn't Live Here Anymore* and told him about it. De Niro admitted to Scorsese that the book was poorly written but told him that he thought it would make a terrific film. He also expressed interest in playing La Motta and told Scorsese right then and there his idea about transforming his body first into that of a boxer and later into that of a man fifty or sixty pounds heavier.

But Scorsese had no interest in the project, saying that he hated boxing. According to Scorsese, the only boxing that made sense to him occurred in the 1926 Buster Keaton film *Battling Butler*, in which Keaton simply entered the ring and hit his opponent over the head with a chair.

De Niro was relentless, and he eventually convinced Scorsese that *Raging Bull* could be adapted into a film. Despite this, Scorsese still wasn't moved. In the years to come, De Niro and Scorsese would collaborate on *Taxi Driver* and *New York, New York*, but De Niro refused to let his pet project die. The two continued to have conversations about *Raging Bull* even while making those films, and De Niro is said to have practiced shadowboxing in his dressing room during the filming of *New York, New York*.

Scorsese still wasn't all that interested in making *Raging Bull*, but he agreed to meet with La Motta's friend and cowriter Peter Savage. Nothing much resulted from this meeting, although Scorsese ultimately wound up casting Savage in bit roles in both *Taxi Driver* and *New York, New York*. But De Niro continued to talk about the possibilities of *Raging Bull*. At some point Scorsese relented and asked his old friend and collaborator Mardik Martin to write the screenplay.

Martin worked on *Raging Bull* for about two years. He interviewed "about 30 people" for the project, and spent nine days talking with Jake's second wife, Vickie La Motta.[2] His first draft was 210 pages, but Martin says Scorsese still didn't read it. To appease Scorsese, Martin began integrating elements of the director's own history into the screenplay (such as a story regarding his grandfather's fig tree in Staten Island). Martin ultimately wrote three drafts of *Raging Bull*—each one straying further from De Niro's original vision of the film.

"In 1977," Scorsese recalls, "De Niro read the script and said, 'What's going on? This is not the picture we agreed upon.' And I said, 'Well, look, I don't know what else it ought to be.'"[3]

Both De Niro and Scorsese were dissatisfied with Martin's script. De Niro loathed the additions that had nothing to do with La Motta's real-life story, and Scorsese thought there was too much boxing in the screenplay and not enough of La Motta's life outside the ring. And both De Niro and Scorsese were unhappy that each element of the story was presented from several different people's viewpoints. "We started writing the script for *Raging Bull* during *New York, New York*," Scorsese explains, "and I just want to say—for the record—that I never gave [Martin] any direction. I was running around writing the script for *New York, New York*—what we would shoot the next morning—and everyone was working on it. But when Mardik came in with *Raging Bull* it was like *Rashomon*. He got 25 different versions of the story because all the characters were still alive."[4]

Scorsese was still on the fence regarding *Raging Bull*. One person who pushed him to make the film was novelist Norman Mailer, who had written about La Motta in his novel *The American Dream*. "He encouraged me a lot," Scorsese recalls. "'He's a fantastic guy,' Mailer told me. 'I never used any real people in my novels except Jake. He's been very underestimated, both as a man and as a boxer.'"[5]

De Niro and Scorsese decided it was time to hire another screenwriter. De Niro paid a visit to the set of *Hardcore*, which Paul Schrader was directing. He then explained the situation to Schrader and asked him to come onboard the project. Schrader was now a director himself and had no interest in writing screenplays for other directors. Nevertheless, he agreed to meet with De Niro and Scorsese. The three men sat down to dinner at Musso and Frank's Grill in mid-1978, and Schrader agreed to do some rewriting on *Raging Bull*.

However, once Schrader started reading Mardik Martin's drafts of the script, he knew the project would require more than mere rewriting. He then went out and started conducting his own research for *Raging Bull*. He worked on the screenplay for six weeks. Once Schrader learned the dynamics of the relationship between Jake La Motta and his brother Joey, the whole story clicked for him. "My main contribution to it was the character of Joey La Motta," Schrader says.

> Jake didn't like his brother much, so he wasn't in the first draft and there was no drama there. I did some research, met Joe, and he struck me as much more interesting. You had these two young boxer brothers, the Fighting La Mottas, and one was sort of shy while the other one had a lot of social tools, so Joey quit fighting and managed his brother. The only thing Jake was good at was taking a beating, and meanwhile, Joey was off managing and getting all the girls. So injecting that sibling relationship into the script made it a financeable film.[6]

Schrader then combined two of the characters, dramatically improving the screenplay. "[Schrader] said the next big change would be that you combine the Peter Savage character with the Joey La Motta character," Scorsese explains. "These are characters; they're based on real people, but these aren't the real people. It's a creation that comes out of everybody. But it was dramatically efficient to combine the two characters together and make it the brother, make it bound by blood."[7]

Schrader added another scene that he felt was integral to the film's story. In the scene, La Motta attempts to masturbate in his jail cell. However, he cannot complete the act because images of the violence he inflicted upon women keep popping into his head. Scorsese recalls, "'Jake has to masturbate in his cell,' [Schrader] told me at dinner. I found the idea interesting. In the novel, there was a complete obsession with the female sex. It was a new approach to the subject, basing it on sexuality."[8]

Schrader, De Niro, Scorsese, and producer Irwin Winkler met to discuss this latest draft of the screenplay. Scorsese loved the sibling aspect of the script, but both De Niro and Scorsese still had misgivings about elements of Schrader's draft. De Niro was unhappy about a scene in which Jake pours ice over his erect penis, as well as the masturbation scene. "I don't know where Paul got [the masturbation scene]," De Niro says, "but that had nothing to do with anything I remember about Jake, or what Marty and I felt about what we were trying to do."[9] Scorsese was unhappy with Schrader's attempts to humanize La Motta and make him more audience friendly. Eventually Schrader became upset and threw the screenplay across the room at Scorsese, telling him that if he wanted someone to take dictation he should have hired a secretary instead of a screenwriter. Scorsese smiled and finished the meeting politely, but the collaboration with Schrader on *Raging Bull* was finished.

"I still hadn't found my connection to the material," Scorsese recalls. "I was also in a very destructive state and I wasn't satisfied with the work I was doing on *New York, New York* and a couple of other things. I felt I was losing something from the passion I felt on *Taxi Driver*, and I certainly was losing connection with the passion that produced *Mean Streets*. And that was my concern—could I ever feel strongly about something again? And I went back and forth, back and forth."[10]

Scorsese ultimately found his connection to the material in an unexpected place. On Labor Day 1978, Scorsese suffered a near-death experience at the Telluride Film Festival, which he'd attended with De Niro, Martin, and girlfriend Isabella Rossellini. While there, Scorsese started bleeding from every orifice of his body—possibly due to an interaction between prescription medications and bad cocaine. At the hospital Scorsese was told that he had no platelets and was experiencing severe internal bleeding. Doctors told Scorsese that if he didn't change his lifestyle he would most likely die.

The Band's front man, Robbie Robertson, with whom Scorsese had lived and partied while making *The Last Waltz*, came to Scorsese's hospital room. Robertson was worried about Scorsese's health. He told him to slow down and asked him if he really felt like he needed to make *Raging Bull*. "Can you go on with your life without doing this?" Robertson asked.[11] Scorsese began to analyze his life, questioning himself about many things, *Raging Bull* among them.

Then a second visitor came to Scorsese's hospital room. It was De Niro, who advised him to change his ways, asking him if he wanted to live to see his daughter grow up and get married. De Niro then changed the subject to *Raging Bull*. "You know," De Niro said, "we can make this picture. We can really do a great job. Are we doing it or not?"[12] And now, for the first time, Scorsese realized that he *had* to make the film. He now recognized the self-destructive aspects of Jake La Motta within himself and saw *Raging Bull* as a rehabilitation of sorts. So he said yes, he would make the film.

Soon Winkler had set up the project at United Artists (UA) by telling them if they wanted a sequel to the hit film *Rocky*, which he had produced, they would have to agree to make *Raging Bull*, as well. However, Schrader's jail cell scene was a problem for them as they could see no way to shoot it without showing the physical act of Jake's masturbation. If they did this, the film would most certainly be slapped with an X rating, ensuring that it would find relatively few exhibitors willing to show it.

So Winkler arranged a meeting between Scorsese and UA produc-tion heads Steven Bach and David Field. De Niro was also present at the meeting—wearing blue jeans with bare feet. Bach and Field expressed concerns regarding Schrader's script. Their problems with *Raging Bull*, it seemed, went well beyond such wording as "Close-up on Jake La Motta's erection"; their primary concern with the project was the character of La Motta himself. Field asked if there was any screenwriter who could make something more of La Motta than what he was in Schrader's script. When Scorsese asked Field what exactly he thought La Motta was in the script, he answered flatly, "A cockroach." This irked De Niro, who said quietly, "He is not a cockroach." And then he repeated it: "He is *not* a cockroach."[13]

Scorsese then convinced Bach and Field to underwrite a trip to the West Indies island of St. Martin so he and De Niro could rework the screenplay. "Bob De Niro and I took the script to an island that Bob wanted to go to and we worked for about three weeks, he and I alone," Scorsese recalls. "And in that period we wrote the whole script and, in a sense, rehearsed the whole picture, rewrote all of the dialogue, everything."[14]

"Marty and I liked parts of Schrader's script but not others," De Niro explains. "We still had to make it our own. So we revised the script and went over every scene."[15]

After their stay on St. Martin, De Niro and Scorsese returned with a completely different screenplay. This draft was approved by UA. Scenes and characters had been removed, others had been reduced, and some characters and situations were combined. Neither De Niro nor Scorsese took any credit for their writing. The finalized script bore De Niro's initials, but no evidence of Scorsese's contributions. Final credit for the screenplay was given to Mardik Martin and Paul Schrader.

De Niro prepared for his role by spending a lot of time with Jake La Motta. The two sparred for more than 1,000 rounds, and De Niro ultimately became skilled enough that he broke the former champ's ribs and nose, and knocked out a few teeth. Under La Motta's tutelage, De Niro became a good enough fighter that La Motta told reporters that he had the skills to become a professional boxer. For his research, De Niro also followed La Motta around with a tape recorder for more than a year. "He asked me all kinds of questions about my wives, my girlfriends—the kinds of questions a psychiatrist would ask," La Motta says. "He would ask me about when I was a kid, and he would always be watching my expressions and my reactions to things. He became obsessed with learning to act like me, talk like me, think like me, fight like me. When he does something, he goes all out."[16] De Niro even went so far as to participate in three authentic boxing matches. Billed as the second coming of Jake La Motta, De Niro won two of the three bouts.

During this period De Niro practically lived with La Motta and his third wife, Deborah. "As a teacher, he was very good," De Niro recalls of La Motta. "He was patient. He wanted it to be right. He'd tell me when it was off. We had a good relationship. He had a remarkably high tolerance. He never got angry."[17] However, the same could not be said of Deborah La Motta, who would later cite De Niro's constant presence in their lives as one of the reasons for ending her marriage.

One day while they were hanging out at Scorsese's suite at the Sherry Netherland, La Motta did something odd that helped to define his character for De Niro. For no apparent reason, La Motta stood up and started banging his head into the wall. "De Niro saw this movement and suddenly got the whole character from him, the whole movie," Scorsese recalls. "We knew we wanted to make a movie that would reach a man at the point of making that gesture with the line, 'I'm not an animal.'"[18]

In researching the role, De Niro also spent time with Jake La Motta's second wife, Vickie La Motta. De Niro, all business, was surprised when Vickie La Motta tried to get him to have sex with her. "I wanted to," she would later say. "In fact, I thought: How could I not? An affair seemed the most normal thing to do. But Bob wanted things to be businesslike. I should have just attacked him or something. But I got shy. If I were just attracted to him sexually and didn't like him, I would have known just how to make it happen. But I was intimidated and did everything wrong."[19]

One day at his apartment, Scorsese screened some 8mm footage of De Niro boxing for director Michael Powell. While watching De Niro sparring with La Motta, Scorsese mentioned that something about the footage was wrong, but he couldn't put his finger on what exactly that was. Powell then observed that the color of the red boxing gloves seemed too bright. Scorsese agreed. Remembering the black-and-white newsreel boxing footage he'd seen a child, Scorsese then came to the conclusion that he would need to shoot the film in black and white if he wanted it to feel authentic to the time in which its story takes place. In addition to this, Scorsese was concerned about the preservation of old films, which tended to fade over time. Why should he shoot *Raging Bull* in color only to see those colors badly faded only a few years later? Besides, Scorsese would later say, shooting in black and white would give the film a different look from the other boxing films of the time, which all tended to be brightly colored.

Scorsese also decided that the cast should be rounded out with unknown actors, so casting director Cis Corman began scouring the boxing world for fighters, trainers, and ring announcers to cast in the film. She then cast a number of amateur and professional boxers to appear as La Motta's opponents.

While casting for the role of Joey La Motta, De Niro saw a promising unknown named Joe Pesci in a 1975 film titled *Death Collector*. Having made only the one film, Pesci had retired from acting and was now

operating a restaurant in the Bronx. It was there that Scorsese located Pesci. De Niro and Scorsese then had dinner with him. They both had concerns that he might be too old for the role, but ultimately wound up casting Pesci as Joey La Motta. "We felt that Joe was so interesting for the part, and so terrific," De Niro says. "He was just too special to not use him."[20]

Casting the role of Vickie La Motta proved to be a headache for Corman, who couldn't find anyone they all felt was right for the role. At one point Jake La Motta's daughter Stephanie was considered for the role, but De Niro nixed this idea as he felt it would be strange to be married in the film to someone he considered his daughter. Then Pesci suggested an eighteen-year-old named Cathy Moriarty, who was a dead ringer for Vickie La Motta. Moriarty had no acting experience, but she left quite an impression on Scorsese, De Niro, and Corman. "As soon as she walked into my office, I knew we had our Vickie," Corman says. "Cathy possessed a sophistication that many young women in the Forties had. She was older than her years."[21] Moriarty read for Scorsese and De Niro almost daily for three months. "It was like taking private acting lessons," Moriarty recalls. "They never once said I had the part or anything, and I knew they were seeing other actresses too. But I was just happy to be learning about acting from two of the best people in the business. I just kept on going, reading with Bobby and taking Marty's instructions."[22] Eventually Cathy Moriarty was cast as Vickie La Motta.

For the role of Salvy, Scorsese cast another unknown who had appeared in the film *Death Collector*. This actor was Frank Vincent, who ultimately became a staple in Scorsese's films. "I had been in the music business for a long time, so I didn't really know the word 'star-struck,'" Vincent explains.

> I knew who both De Niro and Scorsese were, but it didn't really seem like such a big deal at the time. I had just seen Bob in *The Deer Hunter*, so at the audition I said, "I loved you in *The Deer Hunter*," and he said, "Well, I loved you in *Death Collector*." So it didn't really seem like such a big deal. Now after I left there, I talked to some people I knew, and they said, "You really auditioned with Scorsese?" It was such a big monumental thing, and at the time it didn't really impress me the way it should have.[23]

Principal photography began in April 1979. Scorsese filmed the fight sequences first. Although these sequences comprised less than fifteen minutes of the finished film, they took three months to film. Footage of the ring and crowd, as well as the boxers climbing into the ring, was filmed at the Olympic in Los Angeles. The fights themselves were shot on soundstages. It was very important to Scorsese that these scenes allow viewers to see the fights from the boxer's perspective. To accomplish this, he used one camera, which was in the ring with the fighters. There were relatively few shots of the crowd, as Scorsese did not want *Raging Bull* to look like *Rocky*. (This proved to be a wise decision, considering the filmmakers were never able to assemble a large enough audience of extras to properly surround the ring. The small audience they had was constantly being moved to different sides of the ring for different shots.) Scorsese also used elaborate choreography in the scenes to ensure that they looked realistic and that no one got hurt. "We treated the fights like a dance," cinematographer Michael Chapman recalls. "Shooting them was somewhat like shooting the performers in *The Last Waltz*, in which we had everything extensively choreographed ahead of time."[24]

Adding to the realism of these scenes was the transformation that De Niro had undergone, having built up his 145-pound body to a lean, muscular 160 pounds. During this period, De Niro stayed in character around the clock. He was no longer Robert De Niro—he was Jake La Motta. "De Niro was always in character, and he was very, very intense," first assistant director Allan Wertheim explains. "If you spoke to him, you had to address him as either Jake or Champ. That was what he would respond to best."[25] Cathy Moriarty recalls De Niro being so dedicated to his role as La Motta that one day while she was giving him a ride home, De Niro jumped out of the car to run down the highway, as if training for a fight. "You have to realize that Bob wore a prosthetic during that shoot," Frank Vincent explains. "He had a fake nose and all that make-up on. As an actor, those things sort of keep you in the character."[26]

On the set, De Niro and Scorsese frequently excused themselves to discuss character motivations just as they had on their previous collaborations. "Whenever Bobby and Marty wanted to talk about something, there was no doubt that shooting would stop," Wertheim recalls. "They would kind of go off on their own and confer in the distance, and we just had to wait for them to return."[27] However, the dynamics of these sessions were changing, and De Niro was becoming less reluctant to talk to the director around others. "A lot of times I used to like to talk to him in private, in front of no one," De Niro says. "We've worked so much with each other now, we trust each other. Not that we didn't trust each other before, but I think now if there's another person around, we can still talk."[28] Scorsese agrees that the level of trust between him and De Niro increased dramatically on *Raging Bull*. "At times he would say, 'Let me try something' and I would trust him and say 'Go ahead,'" Scorsese explains. "I knew that inevitably—especially if we were in a situation where we had to improvise something or were in a situation and we had to roll with it and something happened by accident—I knew that he was the one person who would find the truth in the situation."[29]

During filming, De Niro would introduce new dialogue or new actions to catch other actors off guard and stimulate more realistic responses.

One day he actually slapped Cathy Moriarty, who had been promised that all of the film's violence would be simulated. "I didn't know what to do, I was so shocked," Moriarty says. "But that was the way Vickie would have reacted."[30] De Niro coaxed a similar startled response from Pesci in a scene in which La Motta asks his brother if he slept with his wife. Instead of asking this, De Niro asked Pesci if he had sex with his own mother, thus eliciting a genuine expression of shock.

Once all the scenes featuring the young Jake La Motta were filmed and in the can, the production was halted for four months. During this time, De Niro transformed his body once again, gaining an astonishing sixty pounds in order to accurately portray the older La Motta. To do this, De Niro spent the hiatus in Italy and France, eating everything he could get his hands on. After binge eating for only a week, De Niro had already put on seven pounds. "It was very easy," De Niro says. "I just had to get up at six-thirty in the morning and eat breakfast at seven in order to digest my food to eat lunch at 12 or one in order to digest my food to eat a nice dinner at seven at night. So it was three square meals a day, that's all. You know, pancakes, beer, milk."[31] Once De Niro had gained the weight, he found himself uncomfortable, unable to even tie his own shoes. His thighs rubbed together, creating rashes, and he began to snore when he slept. The doctors monitoring his weight were alarmed by the high blood pressure he was now experiencing.

Nevertheless, De Niro was happy. He believed that putting on the weight helped him tap into his character in ways that he would not have been able to otherwise. "The internal changes, how you feel and how it makes you behave—for me to play that character, it was the best thing I could have done," De Niro explains. "Just by having the weight on, it made me feel a certain way and behave in a certain way."[32]

During the hiatus, Scorsese and editor Thelma Schoonmaker began cutting the existing footage of *Raging Bull*. Scorsese also traveled to Japan, where he married his third wife, Isabella Rossellini.

Once filming resumed, Scorsese found it difficult to work around De Niro's dramatically increased weight. De Niro now had sore feet and thighs, breathed like an asthmatic, and tired much more quickly. As a result, Scorsese had to change the way he normally worked. "With the bulk he put on, he wasn't doing forty takes," Scorsese recalls, "it was three or four takes. The body dictated."[33]

Filming soon wrapped and *Raging Bull* officially went into postproduction. Schoonmaker and Scorsese then began editing all night in Scorsese's apartment. Wearing a kimono he'd purchased on his honeymoon, Scorsese would study Michael Powell's films frame by frame in search of inspiration. Sometimes Powell himself would come to the apartment during editing. Cutting the film was a relatively simple task compared to editing the sound, which took sixteen weeks. Scorsese obsessed over each sound in the film, asking others to listen for obscure sounds buried deep within the sound mix. He and sound editor Frank Warner would then rerecord these sounds repeatedly until he found one that satisfied him. Warner, who had worked previously on films such as *Taxi Driver* and *Close Encounters of the Third Kind*, conceived and created a bevy of original sounds for the film. Each punch and popping flashbulb in *Raging Bull* had its own unique sound. However, Warner became extremely protective of his creations and refused to reveal how he'd created them, even to Scorsese. Eventually Warner became so paranoid that he destroyed the tapes so his sounds could never be used again.

With an eye on the impending release date, Irwin Winkler repeatedly urged Scorsese not to edit *Raging Bull* a single frame at a time. Scorsese, however, was insistent on working in this manner. Winkler finally convinced Scorsese to screen the film for UA executives, even though he was still tinkering with the sound. The screening was held at the MGM screening room on Fifty-fifth Street and Sixth Avenue. The film played, and when the lights came up, the room was deathly silent. There was no customary applause, and no one spoke for a matter of minutes. Fearing that his career was over, Scorsese leaned his head against a wall in the back of the theater in defeat. Then UA chieftain Andy Albeck stood and approached Scorsese, telling him that he was "an artist." A relieved Scorsese began breathing again.

Winkler eventually had to order Scorsese to relinquish *Raging Bull*. It was midnight on the Sunday before the film was to be released, and Scorsese was upset about the sound in a scene in which a character orders a drink. Scorsese kept saying that he couldn't hear the words "Cutty Sark." Winkler could hear the words clearly, but Scorsese could not and wanted to keep working on the sound. Because the film had to get to the lab *that night*, Winkler told him he was finished tinkering with the sound. This infuriated Scorsese, who vowed to remove his name from the film. Eventually cooler heads prevailed and Scorsese left his name on *Raging Bull*.

Even if Scorsese had issues with the final mix of the film, Schoonmaker was convinced that it was flawless. "*Raging Bull* was seamless," she says. "It was perfect. We participated to a certain extent, but it felt as if we were being guided through it by this omniscient hand."[34]

Raging Bull opened on November 14, 1980, at the Sutton Theater in New York City. Coming in the wake of *Rocky*, audiences were divided by the film. Critics found it equally divisive; some proclaimed it the year's finest film, while others dismissed it altogether. (*Variety*'s headline announced that the film "may have wobbly legs.")

Andrew Sarris of the *Village Voice* praised the film for its brilliant performances. "After *Raging Bull*," Sarris wrote, "Scorsese must be placed right up there with Cukor, Bergman, and Kazan as a director capable of drawing inspired performances." Sarris went on to discuss the film's obvious contrast to *Rocky*: "The difference between *Raging Bull* and *Rocky* is the difference between undiluted vinegar and pure corn, between Off-Broadway absurdism and Capraesque sentimentality, between Dante's Inferno and Hollywood heaven."[35] *Newsweek*'s Jack Kroll also heaped praise on the film, saying, "*Raging Bull* is the best American movie of the year, Scorsese's best film, and at long last replaces Robert Wise's *The Set-Up* as the best film about prizefighting ever made." Kroll also lauded De Niro's turn as "his most stunning yet."[36]

Most reviews—positive and negative—gave De Niro kudos for his amazing physical transformation and bravura performance. "De Niro is always absorbing and credible, even when his character isn't," *Time* magazine critic Richard Corliss observed. "When the film is moving on automatic pilot, De Niro is still sailing on animal energy, carrying his able, unknown costars with him."[37] However, *New Yorker* reviewer Pauline Kael, who had previously been a staunch defender of De Niro's work, offered a different opinion of the actor's performance: "He put on so much weight that he seems to have sunk in the fat with hardly a trace of himself left," Kael wrote. "What De Niro does in this picture isn't acting, exactly. I'm not sure what it is. Though it may at some level be pleasurable. He has so little expressive spark that what I found myself thinking wasn't about La Motta or the movie but the metamorphosis of De Niro."[38]

Stanley Kauffmann of the *New Republic* called the film "electrifying and rich," but then added, "I have to hope that De Niro will make more films with other directors, though he and Scorsese clearly work well together, they stay within a relatively narrow spectrum, and the limits are demonstrably Scorsese's, not De Niro's."[39]

La Motta himself also praised De Niro's portrayal. "Bobby came from heaven," he would later say.[40] La Motta publicly supported the film, but was privately hurt by the way it depicted him.

Raging Bull didn't shatter any box office records, but it eventually earned back its budget (different sources cite the film's budget as being anywhere between $14 million to $18 million), breaking even.

When awards season came around in early 1981, *Raging Bull* featured prominently in most competitions. De Niro won a handful of Best Actor honors, Scorsese received a Directors Guild nomination, and Schoonmaker won an Eddie for Best Edited Feature Film. The film received seven Golden Globe nominations for Best Motion Picture, Best Director (Scorsese), Best Screenwriter (Schrader and Martin),

Best Actor (De Niro), Best Supporting Actor (Pesci), Best Supporting Actress (Moriarty), and New Star of the Year (Moriarty). However, only De Niro won. *Raging Bull* then received an impressive eight Academy Award nominations. These included Best Picture, Best Director (Scorsese), Best Screenwriter (Schrader and Martin), Best Actor (De Niro), Best Supporting Actor (Pesci), Best Supporting Actress (Moriarty), Best Cinematography (Chapman), Best Editing (Schoonmaker), and Best Sound (Donald O. Mitchell, Bill Nicholson, David J. Kimball, and Les Lazarowitz). The film won two Oscars—for De Niro's performance and Schoonmaker's editing.

Today critics are no longer divided over the film, and *Raging Bull* is widely considered the finest film produced in the 1980s. The American Film Institute (AFI) has named it the number one American sports film ever produced, and it ranked as the fourth greatest film in the history of American cinema on the AFI's 2007 "100 Years . . . 100 Movies" list.

The Film

The film's white opening credits are superimposed against grainy black-and-white footage of boxer Jake La Motta (Robert De Niro) shadow-boxing in an otherwise empty ring. This is significant as Jake will be his own worst enemy throughout the film. The film's title appears in bold red lettering. The sequence, set to Pietro Mascagni's "Intermezzo" (from the opera *Cavalleria Rusticana*), has a surreal, dreamlike feel.

A title card tells us that the first scene takes place in New York City in 1964. The film opens with a sign outside the Barbizon Plaza Theater announcing "An Evening with Jake La Motta." A middle-aged Jake La Motta stands alone in his dressing room, rehearsing for the show. He recites an original poem titled "That's Entertainment," which pokes fun at his years of fighting and the bum he's become. "I know I'm no Olivier," he says, "but if he fought Sugar Ray, he would say, that the thing ain't the ring, it's the play. So give me a stage, where this bull here can rage."

A superimposed title card informs us that it's now 1941. Jake is fighting Jimmy Reeves (Floyd Anderson) in Cleveland. Although he's still undefeated, Jake is behind in points. In his corner between the ninth and tenth rounds Jake is told that he needs to knock Reeves out to win the fight. His brother Joey La Motta (Joe Pesci) advises him to bite and kick Reeves if he needs to.

Once the bell rings, Jake takes a few punches. He moves in on his opponent, knocking him down. Flashbulbs explode and the crowd roars with approval. Soon Reeves is back on his feet, and Jake pummels him, sending him reeling back down to the mat. Reeves gets up again, and Jake is all over him, pounding him down to the mat for a third time. The referee counts to nine, but the bloodied, semi-conscious Reeves is saved by the bell. Jake begins strutting around the ring, raising his arms as the victor. The ring announcer then declares Reeves the victor by unanimous decision and it becomes apparent that the match was fixed by the Mafia. Jake has just lost his first decision. With this announcement, Jake raises his arms again, further inciting the angry crowd. Chairs are thrown through the air, a woman is trampled, and mayhem ensues.

A superimposed title card informs us that the next scene takes place in the Bronx in 1941. Joey and Salvy (Frank Vincent), a small-time Mafia foot soldier, are walking down the street, discussing the fight. Salvy informs Joey that this injustice would never have occurred had Jake allowed the Mafia to control his career. Joey explains that Jake wants to work alone, and that if Salvy doesn't like it, he should talk to him himself.

Inside Jake's apartment, he and his wife, Irma (Lori Anne Flax), get into an argument over a steak. As Jake mulls over the injustice of the fight with Jimmy Reeves, Irma cooks his steak. Jake continuously tells Irma not to overcook the steak, eventually raising his voice. This angers Irma, who throws the steak onto Jake's plate. Jake becomes enraged. He knocks the dinner table over and starts yelling and throwing things.

The camera cuts back to Joey, who is still talking with Salvy outside the apartment. With the faint sounds of screaming coming from within the apartment, Joey promises Salvy that he will talk to Jake about the Mafia's offers. Joey enters the apartment where Jake and Irma are still arguing. A neighbor knocks on the wall and calls Jake an animal, inciting Jake to threaten to eat the man's dog. Jake threatens to kill Irma, and Joey attempts to calm his brother. Joey reminds him that there are other fights on the horizon, but Jake laments that he will never fight heavyweight champion Joe Louis because he has small hands. Jake says he's better than Louis. Jake then asks Joey to punch him in the face. When Joey says no, Jake ridicules him and questions his sexuality. Finally Joey gives in and punches Jake in the face repeatedly. All the while, Jake is slapping him and urging him to hit him harder.

In Gleason's Boxing Club, Jake spars with Joey, beating up on him. Salvy and two other wiseguys, Patsy (Frank Adonis) and Guido (Joseph Bono), enter the establishment and watch Jake. Angry that his brother has been talking with Salvy, Jake beats Joey unmercifully. Salvy and the other wiseguys get up to leave, and Salvy advises Jake to be careful not to hurt himself. Jake reprimands Joey again for talking about his career with Salvy. Joey becomes so angry that he begins punching Jake, even going so far as to pull off his boxing gloves and hurl them at him.

In the next scene we see Jake and Joey at a public swimming pool. Salvy and the other wiseguys are also there. Jake zeroes in on an attractive fifteen-year-old named Vickie (Cathy Moriarty) and questions his brother about her. When Joey tells Jake that Vickie isn't the kind of girl one sleeps with and then forgets, Jake asks him if he had sex with her. Joey says that he went out on several dates with her, but never slept with her. Jake continues to watch Vickie, causing Joey to remind his brother that he's married.

Jake and Joey, both well dressed, groom themselves in front of a mirror inside Jake's apartment. As they leave (under the pretenses that they are going out for business), Irma insults them, calling them homosexuals. Once they are outside, Irma begins screaming at them from the window, insulting them further.

Jake and Joey attend the Annual Summer Dance sponsored by St. Clare's Church. They sit at a table in the back of the room with some friends. A Catholic priest stops by the table, and the guys ask him to bless their table. Jake spots Vickie sitting at a table with several other women. When Vickie gets up to leave with Salvy, Jake follows them outside, where he watches them leave together.

In the next scene, Joey introduces Jake and Vickie through the chain-link fence surrounding the public swimming pool. (It has been said that the fence is symbolic of the barriers that will be created between Jake and Vickie by Jake and his brother's relationship.) Joey introduces Jake as the next champ. When Vickie admires Jake's car, he invites her to go for a ride with him. She accepts.

In a camera angle shot through the front window of Jake's car, we then see the would-be lovers driving. Jake asks Vickie to move closer to him, and she does. Jake puts his arm around her. In the next scene, Jake and Vickie are playing miniature golf. Vickie putts the golf ball under a model of a church, but the ball is lost. Vickie asks what this means, to which Jake replies that it means the game is over.

Knowing no one will be there, Jake takes Vickie to his father's apartment. The two of them sit at the table, drinking glasses of water. Jake once again encourages Vickie to move closer to him, and she complies. Jake asks her to sit on his lap, and she does. Jake offers to show her the rest of the apartment. He gives her a tour that concludes with them in the bedroom. Vickie walks over to look at a photograph of Jake and Joey "foolin' around." As Jake moves in to kiss her, the photograph of he and his brother is still visible between them (once again symbolizing how the relationship between the brothers will come between the lovers). Jake pulls her toward the bed and out of the frame. The camera remains on the photograph of Jake and Joey for another five seconds.

The film cuts abruptly to a boxing match. A superimposed title card tells us that Jake is fighting Sugar Ray Robinson (Johnny Barnes) in Detroit in 1943. (Two years have passed since Jake's defeat to Jimmy Reeves and his first meeting with Vickie.) Jake and Robinson appear to be evenly matched, and the two take turns delivering a barrage of body blows. In the eighth round, Jake knocks Robinson through the ropes. This is the first knockdown of Robinson's career. The two boxers continue to pummel each other until the fight's conclusion, at which time Jake is declared the winner.

Next we see Jake and Vickie in the bedroom. Jake asks Vickie to kiss his "boo-boos." Vickie undresses Jake, reminding him, "You made me promise not to get you excited." The two move closer and closer toward making love, but Jake ultimately relents, telling her that he can't have sex as he's about to fight Sugar Ray Robinson again. He goes to the bathroom and pours ice cold water down the front of his pants to cool himself down. As he does, Vickie enters the bathroom and begins to kiss him passionately.

We then move to the rematch between Jake and Sugar Ray Robinson. The fight once again takes place at Olympia Stadium in Detroit in 1943. (The fights are just three weeks apart.) Round seven finds Robinson ahead in points, and the commentators state that Jake may need to knock him out if he wants to win. Jake delivers a powerful left, sending Robinson to the mat for the second knockdown of his career. Despite this, Robinson ultimately wins the fight by unanimous decision.

In the dressing room, a furious Joey smashes a chair against the wall. He declares that the only reason the judges awarded Robinson the fight is because he is going into the army the following week. Vickie comes to the door, but Jake refuses to see her. He asks Joey to drive her home so he can be alone for a while. Alone, Jake stares at his image in the mirror, contemplating his career. Jake sits alone, soaking his swollen hands in ice water—an image meant to remind us of Jake's pouring ice water down his pants. The implication here is clear—on some level Jake blames Vickie for his loss, seeing her as a distraction.

Here Scorsese presents us with a montage of color "home movies" of Jake, Vickie, and Joey (similar to the home movies of *Mean Streets*) intercut with images from six of Jake's fights. The montage covers the time between January 1944 and March 1947. During this period Jake fights Fritzie Zivic, Jose Basora, George Kochan, Jimmy Edgar, Bob Satterfield, and Tommy Bell. While the home movies are comprised of actual footage, the fights are mostly represented with black-and-white stills. The home movies depict Jake and Vickie's wedding, Joey's wedding, and Jake and Vickie horsing around a swimming pool.

A superimposed title card reads "Pelham Parkway Bronx, New York 1947." We see a slightly larger Jake, who now weighs 168 pounds, reprimanding Joey for scheduling him a fight against Tony Janiro (Kevin Mahon) when he's overweight. As Jake and Joey discuss Jake's prospects of a title fight, Jake yells at Vickie for not bringing him his coffee fast enough. When Vickie makes an offhand comment about Janiro being an up-and-comer who's good-looking, Jake becomes jealous. Joey goes back to talking about serious business, but the suspicious Jake raises concerns that his wife may be cheating on him. Jake tells Joey to keep an eye on his wife while he's away. Joey advises Jake to take his wife out for dinner to make nice with her.

That night at the Copacabana nightclub, a comedian introduces Jake as "the world's leading middleweight contender." Jake and Vickie are at the club with Joey, who's there with a woman who is not his wife. Vickie gets up to go to the restroom and is greeted by Salvy, who kisses her on the cheek. Jake once again becomes jealous and grills Vickie when she returns to the table. Joey goes to Salvy's table and talks with Tommy Como (Nicholas Colasanto), the neighborhood boss. Tommy then motions for Jake to come over to the table. Conversation is made about Janiro, and Salvy makes a remark about Janiro's attractiveness.

Later that night Jake enters the bedroom where Vickie is sleeping. He wakes her and asks her if she ever thinks of other men when they make love.

A superimposed title card announces the fight between Jake and Janiro. Jake unmercifully beats Janiro, violently smashing his nose into a bloody mess. A shot of the disapproving Vickie tells us that she is fully aware of Jake's reasons for beating Janiro so badly. As Jake is declared the winner, Tommy Como leans over to a friend and observes that Janiro isn't pretty anymore.

In another scene in the Copacabana, Joey is talking with another man about Jake's chances at a title shot, as well as the damage he did to Janiro. As he's talking, Joey sees Salvy's crew enter the nightclub—with Vickie in tow. Joey takes Vickie away from the table and reprimands her. She says she's tired of Jake's jealousy. She says that Jake won't have sex with her anymore. When Vickie returns to the table, Joey follows her and orders her to get her belongings and go. Salvy attempts to intervene and Joey becomes enraged, acting like Jake. Joey breaks a glass over Salvy's head and starts beating him. The fight then moves outside, where Joey beats Salvy further, even going so far as to smash his body in the door of a cab.

In the next scene, a sit-down is held at the Debonair Social Club with Tommy Como presiding. Tommy listens to both Joey's and Salvy's sides of the story and ultimately decides that the matter should be forgotten. Tommy orders Joey and Salvy to shake hands and asks them not to hold any grudges. Both men agree. Tommy asks Salvy to leave the table. Tommy then tells Joey that Jake is making him look bad in the neighborhood by not allowing him to manage his fights. Joey informs him that Jake respects him but wants to try to make it without help. Tommy explains that Jake won't get a title shot without his help, no matter whom he defeats. Tommy asks Joey to talk with Jake about this once again.

After the meeting with Tommy Como, Joey meets Jake in the pouring rain at the swimming pool. The location reminds Jake of his first meeting with Vickie, and he once again starts to question her fidelity. Joey advises Jake to either throw his wife out on the street or be miserable for the rest of his life. The subject then turns to the sit-down with Tommy Como, and Joey tells Jake that the Mafia wants him to throw his upcoming fight against Billy Fox (Ed Gregory).

Before the fight, promoter Jackie Curtie (Peter Savage, the coauthor of the book *Raging Bull* upon which the film is based) tells Jake that there are rumors floating around that he's going to throw the fight. Curtie informs him that Jake, who was formerly the favorite, is now a twelve-to-five underdog. To this Jake insists that he's going to defeat Fox, saying that he doesn't go down for anyone.

A superimposed title card informs us that Jake is fighting Billy Fox at New York's Madison Square Garden in 1947. Once the match begins, it is instantly apparent that Jake is throwing the fight. Although he is too proud to fake being knocked out, he allows the inadequate Fox to beat him. Jake does a poor job faking the loss, and the crowd turns on him. Fox ultimately wins by TKO (technical knockout). Jake then cries in the arms of his trainer, who advises him to stop fighting. "What did I do?" Jake asks himself aloud. We see a copy of the November 22, 1947, issue of the *New York Daily News*. The headline reads, "BOARD SUSPENDS LA MOTTA." (The two photographs on the front of the newspaper depict the real-life La Motta rather than De Niro.) Jake tells Joey that he took the fall for the Mafia and asks him what more they want from him. Jake reads in the newspaper that the purse from the fight has been held pending the district attorney's investigation. Joey reminds Jake that Tommy Como will remember what Jake has done for him and that he'll get his title shot.

A superimposed title card reads, "Two Years Later Detroit June 15, 1949." Jake and his opponent, Marcel Cerdan (Louis Raftis), are both staying at the Book-Cadillac Hotel. They are scheduled to fight at Briggs Stadium, an outdoor arena, but the fight has been delayed for twenty-four hours due to rain. In his room, Jake paces, obviously in a bad mood. Joey convinces Jake to order a steak from room service, telling him that he can chew it up and spit it out in order to maintain his weight. When Vickie says she only wants a piece of cake, Joey talks her into ordering a cheeseburger. Jake becomes jealous regarding Joey's influence over his wife. Tommy then stops by the hotel room to check in on Jake. When Tommy goes to leave, Vickie kisses him on the cheek. As Jake watches, we see a close-up of a second kiss—this time on the lips. Tommy compliments Vickie on her beauty. Once Tommy is gone, Jake becomes angry with Vickie and slaps her. When Joey defends Vickie, Jake threatens to deal with him later.

In the next scene, Jake is warming up by punching a padded Joey in the midsection. Still angry at Joey for defending Vickie—and, in his mind, possibly sleeping with her—Jake beats his brother harder than necessary. They then make their way to the ring.

A title card superimposed over an image of the two fighters touching boxing gloves introduces the fight between Jake and French middleweight champion Marcel Cerdan. Scenes from the fight are shown over the span of a minute and ten seconds, and the angry Jake pummels his opponent. At the start of the tenth round, the fight is declared a TKO, and Jake wins the title belt.

A superimposed title card tells us that we are back at Jake's home on Pelham Parkway in New York. The year is 1950. Jake's weight has ballooned, and he is eating a submarine sandwich and drinking a beer. Vickie enters the house after a shopping trip. She innocently kisses both Jake and Joey, and Jake once again becomes jealous. He then begins questioning Joey about the incident at the Copacabana with Salvy two years before. Jake insists that Joey admit that Salvy slept with Vickie. The two of them argue, and Jake then becomes adamant that Joey had sex with Vickie. Insulted that Jake has asked him this, Joey refuses to answer. Jake, of course, mistakes this for guilt. Joey leaves.

Now left alone with Vickie, Jake asks her where she's been. She answers that she went to the movies to see *Father of the Bride* with her sister. Jake then asks her about the night at the Copacabana and asks her why she had sex with his brother Joey. Jake slaps Vickie repeatedly, and she runs and locks herself in the bathroom. Relentless, Jake breaks down the door and starts slapping her around again. Fed up with all of this, Vickie gives Jake a mock confession in an attempt to incite him further; she tells him that she had sex with Salvy, Tommy, and Joey. Jake slaps her around some more and walks out. Enraged, Jake storms out of the house and makes his way down the street to Joey's house. Joey and his family are eating dinner. Jake forces his way into the house and savagely beats Joey in front of his wife and children. Vickie and Lenore (Theresa Saldana) attempt to pull Jake off Joey. Jake becomes angry and punches his wife in the face, knocking her unconscious.

We see Jake sitting in his empty house, staring at a blank television screen. Vickie returns to gather her belongings, and Jake begs her for forgiveness. She embraces him, and all is presumably forgiven.

The film then cuts to Jake being punched in the jaw. A superimposed title card tells us that Jake is fighting Laurent Dauthuille (Johnny Turner) in Detroit in 1950. Dauthuille is beating Jake badly until the final seconds of the fifteenth round, at which time Jake knocks his opponent out. After the fight, Vickie convinces Jake to call Joey and apologize. Jake agrees but finds himself unable to speak when Joey answers.

We see Jake once again fighting Sugar Ray Robinson. Robinson is beating Jake into a bloody pulp. This is reminiscent of the beating Jake gave Tony Janiro. A slow-motion punch sprays the crowd with Jake's blood, and the referee stops the fight in the thirteenth round, making Robinson the new champion. Defeated but still proud, Jake taunts Robinson, proclaiming, "Hey, Ray, I never went down, man! You never got me down, Ray! You hear me? You never got me down!" As Robinson is announced the winner, we see a shot of Jake's blood dripping from the ropes.

A title card informs us that we are now in Miami, and six years have passed since Jake's bloody defeat at the hands of Sugar Ray Robinson. A much heavier Jake is sitting beside his swimming pool at his new house, talking with a reporter. He tells the reporter that he's retired. "It's over for me," he says. He says that he is now content to spend his time with his wife and family. He also tells the reporter that he's opening his own nightclub, which he appropriately dubs "Jake La Motta's." We then see Jake at the club, where he is emceeing and playing (very poorly) comedian. Interestingly, he tells a joke about two men sharing the same woman—a reflection of his lifelong anxieties regarding

Vickie. Later Jake allows two underage girls to drink alcohol after they kiss him to prove that they are old enough.

Vickie arrives outside the club in the wee hours of the morning to inform Jake that she's leaving him. She tells him that she has a lawyer and that she will get custody of the children. She then drives away.

Jake is awakened in the next scene by police officers. He is arrested on a morals charge for pimping girls out of his club. One of the girls that Jake allegedly set up with male customers—one of the girls he kissed at the bar—was only fourteen years old. After being released on bail, Jake goes to Vickie to pick up his championship belt. Jake tells Vickie that his lawyer has informed him that he can get the case dropped in exchange for a $10,000 bribe. Jake removes the jewels from the belt and takes them to a jewelry store, where he is informed that he could have gotten far more money for the intact belt itself. When he cannot raise the $10,000, Jake is detained in the county jail.

A superimposed title card tells us that Jake is now in the Dade County Stockade and that the year is 1957. Deputies struggle with Jake to get him inside his cell. Once inside the cell, Jake reflects on his life. He then begins to pound his head and his fists into the cement wall. Jake breaks down, wailing about his shortcomings and the predicament he's now in.

A title card introduces "New York City 1958." Jake is performing as a stand-up comic at the Carnevale Lounge in the Hotel Markwell. We soon learn that Jake's "career" has sunk so low that he now introduces strippers. While escorting one of the strippers, known as "Emma 48s," to her cab, Jake spots his brother Joey across the street at a coffee shop. Jake follows him, begging for forgiveness, but Joey refuses to acknowledge him. Finally Jake catches him getting into his car. He hugs Joey repeatedly, apologizing all the while, but Joey seems unaffected. He promises to call Jake and then climbs into his car.

We next see Jake rehearsing his new nightclub act at the Barbizon Plaza Theater. It is now 1964, and six years have passed since Jake's chance meeting with his brother Joey. Jake's new act consists of dramatic readings of works by such writers as Paddy Chayefsky, William Shakespeare, and Budd Schulberg. Jake stares into the mirror and flatly recites the "I coulda been a contender" monologue from *On the Waterfront*. A stagehand (Martin Scorsese) interrupts Jake's rather wooden rehearsal to tell him that he is on in five minutes. Jake looks into the mirror and says, "Go get 'em, champ." He then begins shadowboxing, chanting, "I'm the boss, I'm the boss, I'm the boss."

The final title card quotes John 9:24–25, which concludes with the line, "Once I was blind and now I can see." The film then closes with a dedication to Scorsese's late New York University film teacher Haig P. Manoogian.

Notes

1. McKay, Keith, *Robert De Niro: The Hero behind the Masks* (New York: Ultra Communications, 1986), 91.

2. Martin, Mardik, interview by the author, October 10, 2008.

3. Kelly, Mary Pat, *Martin Scorsese: A Journey* (New York: Thunder's Mouth Press, 1991), 123.

4. Dougan, Andy, *Martin Scorsese: Close Up* (New York: Thunder's Mouth Press, 1998), 63.

5. Henry, Michael, "*Raging Bull*," *Positif*, April 1981, 87.

6. Jackson, Kevin, *Schrader on Schrader* (Boston: Faber and Faber, 1990), 131.

7. Bouzereau, Laurent, "*Raging Bull*": *Before the Fight*, documentary (Metro-Goldwyn-Mayer, 2004).

8. Henry, "*Raging Bull*," 87.

9. Evans, Mike, *The Making of "Raging Bull"* (London: Unanimous Ltd., 2006), 46.

10. Bouzereau, "*Raging Bull*."

11. Dougan, *Martin Scorsese*, 63.

12. Biskind, Peter, *Easy Riders, Raging Bulls* (New York: Simon & Schuster, 1998), 387.

13. Biskind, *Easy Riders, Raging Bulls*, 390.

14. Hickenlooper, George, *Reel Conversations: Candid Interviews with Film's Foremost Directors and Critics* (New York: Citadel Press, 1991), 28.

15. Dougan, Andy, *Untouchable: A Biography of Robert De Niro* (New York: Thunder's Mouth Press, 1996), 121.

16. Yakir, Dan, "Two Sticklers and a Slugger," *After Dark*, November 1980, 29.

17. McKay, *Martin Scorsese*, 93.

18. Biskind, *Easy Riders, Raging Bulls*, 385.

19. Agan, Patrick, *Robert De Niro: The Man, the Myth, and the Movies* (London: Robert Hale, 1989), 93.

20. Bouzereau, *"Raging Bull."*

21. Wiener, Thomas, *"Raging Bull's* Secret Punch," *American Film*, November 1980, 35.

22. Parker, John, *De Niro* (London: Victor Gollancz, 1995), 158.

23. Vincent, Frank, interview by the author, September 30, 2009.

24. Wiener, Thomas, "Martin Scorsese Fights Back," *American Film*, November 1980, 34.

25. Wertheim, Allan, interview by the author, March 20, 2009.

26. Vincent, interview.

27. Wertheim, interview.

28. "Dialogue on Film: Robert De Niro," *American Film*, March 1981, 47.

29. Wiener, "Martin Scorsese Fights Back," 36.

30. Wiener, *"Raging Bull's* Secret Punch," 20.

31. "Dialogue on Film," 40.

32. Dougan, *Untouchable*, 133.

33. Kelly, *Martin Scorsese*, 143.

34. Kelly, *Martin Scorsese*, 150.

35. Andrew Sarris is quoted in Brode, Douglas, *The Films of Robert De Niro* (Secaucus, NJ: Citadel Press, 1996), 132.

36. Jack Kroll is quoted in Brode, *The Films of Robert De Niro*, 132.

37. Richard Corliss is quoted in Brode, *The Films of Robert De Niro*, 132.

38. Pauline Kael is quoted in Brode, *The Films of Robert De Niro*, 132.

39. Stanley Kauffmann is quoted in Brode, *The Films of Robert De Niro*, 132.

40. Agan, *Robert De Niro*, 98.

CHAPTER FIVE

The King of Comedy (1982)

It's so grim. For me it's about how my fantasies and De Niro's fantasies have come about. We were like the guy in that movie. We wanted to get into show business. We were fascinated by celebrities. Now we're part of it. It's very strange.

—Martin Scorsese

The Backstory

In 1970, *Newsweek* film critic Paul Zimmerman caught an episode of *The David Susskind Show* about autograph collectors. He then read a feature in *Esquire* about a man who obsessed over television talk shows. Seeing a link between the rabid autograph hounds and people who were obsessed with celebrity in general, Zimmerman began to see these fans as being "like assassins."[1] This synchronicity would serve as the genesis of *The King of Comedy*. Based on these ideas, Zimmerman hammered out a screenplay titled *Harry, the King of Comedy*. Director Milos Forman soon expressed interest, and screenwriter Buck Henry was brought in to polish the material. There was continued talk of Forman directing the project for some three years, but the project was ultimately aborted. Zimmerman then dusted off his original script and started showing it around Hollywood.

One of the people he showed it to was Robert De Niro, who was vocal about his desire to develop his own projects for himself to star in. De Niro read the screenplay and liked what he saw. He told Zimmerman that he really liked the screenplay but had a number of projects in mind to make first. "Bobby understood the bravery of Rupert Pupkin, his chutzpah, the simplicity of his motives," Zimmerman would later say. "Bobby said he liked the single-minded sense of purpose. People speak of Bobby as an instinctive actor but he also understands these characters on an intellectual level. I think Bobby understood Rupert because he's an obsessive person himself."[2]

De Niro showed the screenplay to Scorsese, hoping to convince him to direct it. During this same period, De Niro was also trying to persuade Scorsese to adapt boxer Jake La Motta's autobiography *Raging Bull* into a film. Scorsese, however, had little interest in either project (although he ultimately wound up making both). Scorsese was already writing a screenplay about stand-up comedy with another film critic, *Time*'s Jay Cocks. Scorsese also didn't care for Zimmerman's script. He thought it trite and saw it as being something of a one-line joke. Based on these things, Scorsese passed on the project, telling De Niro that he was the wrong man for the job.

Zimmerman and De Niro continued to hone the screenplay, tightening it further with each draft. Meanwhile, De Niro was shopping it around Tinseltown but finding little interest. After five years of searching for financing, De Niro convinced a would-be producer named Arnon Milchan to fund the film. Milchan committed to a budget of approximately $14 million. De Niro then began searching for a director. He soon convinced Michael Cimino, whom he'd worked with on *The Deer Hunter*, to helm the film. However, Cimino soon became entangled in the debacle that was *Heaven's Gate*, and he lost interest in De Niro's project.

De Niro went on to make *Raging Bull* with Scorsese. Having made three films in fairly quick succession, Scorsese was not in good health. Nevertheless, he went on an international tour to promote film preservation. As a result, Scorsese soon found himself in the hospital once again, this time suffering from exhaustion and pneumonia. And once again, De Niro showed up at Scorsese's bedside in an effort to convince him to make a film. This time it was *The King of Comedy*. De Niro made the project sound as though it would be a breeze, and, as Scorsese says, he was sick and "susceptible to an easy film."[3] And with the John Hinckley assassination attempt on Reagan still fresh in his mind, Scorsese now saw Zimmerman's examination of dangerously obsessive fans in a different way. His and De Niro's newfound fame also made it easier to relate to the material. So he agreed to make the film and collaborate with De Niro for a fifth time.

To prepare for his role as Rupert Pupkin, an autograph collector and would-be comic, De Niro spent time with real-life autograph hounds. He watched them at work, questioned them about their lifestyle, and even visited their homes to see where they lived. He also began frequenting comedy clubs so he could watch amateur comedians perform. He then imitated their rhythm and timing. Between this research and the chance discovery of what became Rupert's wardrobe in the film, De Niro locked in on the character. "I had certain ideas about him," De Niro explains, "and that's why it was fun—because with Marty I can say, 'Let's try this or that.' Like the suit Pupkin wore—we just went into a Broadway store, and it was right on the mannequin, the whole outfit. It was just, wrap it up and take it home, you know?"[4]

Zimmerman had originally written the screenplay with talk show host Dick Cavett in mind, but Scorsese wasn't interested in Cavett. When he envisioned the character Jerry Langford, he saw real-life talk show king Johnny Carson. Scorsese then approached Carson, but Carson wasn't interested. He had made a living doing things in one take, so he had little patience for having to perform the same material six or seven times—let alone the twenty or thirty takes that Scorsese and De Niro frequently employed. When the talk show host balked, Scorsese promised that he would get everything he needed in only two or three takes. Carson, however, remained unmoved.

Orson Welles was considered for the role, but Scorsese felt he wasn't "show business" enough. Scorsese then thought of Frank Sinatra, which caused him to think of other Rat Pack members. When Scorsese thought of Dean Martin, his mind then went to Martin's old comedy partner, Jerry Lewis. Scorsese then contacted Lewis, who was working in Lake Tahoe. Scorsese and Lewis had two meetings about the project, and Scorsese felt Lewis was right for the role. However, De Niro still had to be convinced.

"What we went through before we decided we were gonna do it!" Lewis says. "Bobby and I had five meetings, five separate meetings in six months."[5] This lengthy process perplexed Lewis, who had himself already directed twelve films by this time. "Bobby has to know the people he's gonna work with," Lewis explains. "What he needs from them, I can't tell you—whether he has to know that they're genuine, whether he has to know that they're just goddamn good actors, that they'll commit—I'm not too sure, but he has to know some stuff."[6] During those meetings, De Niro interrogated Lewis about his thoughts on the script, his outlook on celebrity, his relationship with his parents, and his views on filmmaking. Finally Lewis passed De Niro's test and was cast as Jerry Langford.

"Jerry Lewis seemed to be the best candidate for the part, because he wasn't just a talk show host," Scorsese says. "He is a comic, a director, an actor. He incorporates all the different aspects of show business. By 'show business' I mean Hollywood and Las Vegas, and that was important. He was also really open to a lot of ideas and was a valuable contributor. And he helped with the 'intangibles' like body moves. He knew when you had to be a certain way. He knows lenses—I purposely did long takes on him so I could study him."[7]

After the contracts were signed and Lewis was officially part of the cast, De Niro telephoned Lewis and warned him that they could not be friends. Now fully in character as Rupert Pupkin, De Niro informed him that "I really want to kill you in this picture."[8] Lewis later made the mistake of asking De Niro to lunch, to which De Niro replied, "I wanna blow your head off, so how can we have dinner?"[9] Of this incident, Lewis would later remark, "De Niro obviously has never heard Noel Coward's advice to actors—that their job was to say the lines and not bump into the furniture. He just could not forget the part at the end of the day's work."[10]

Lewis played a significant role in the development of his character. He met with Scorsese, De Niro, and Zimmerman to discuss his insights into celebrity. Having been internationally famous for some four decades, Lewis was the only one of them who really knew anything about being a celebrity. By this time, De Niro was a household name, but he was so chameleon-like that hardly anyone ever recognized him when he went out. "They don't know celebrity," Lewis says. "They only know anonymity."[11] Lewis regaled them with stories of celebrity, many of which were integrated into the film. For instance, a scene in which an ungrateful fan tells Langford he "should get cancer" was based on a real-life encounter that Lewis had with a fan. In addition to helping define his character, Lewis also wore his own clothes in the film, and his character's Pekinese dog was his own.

The next role that needed to be cast was Masha, Rupert's pugnacious cohort. De Niro wanted Meryl Streep, with whom he'd worked on *The Deer Hunter*. "I asked Meryl to come in and meet Marty and talk about it because I thought she'd be terrific," De Niro recalls. "She's very, very funny. She's a great comedienne. She came in, but I don't think she wanted to do it, obviously, for whatever reason, I never really knew. But I knew that she *could* do it."[12] The role then went to an edgy young comedienne named Sandra Bernhard, who'd previously appeared in bit parts in films like *The Hand* and *Cheech and Chong's Nice Dreams*. "From the moment I auditioned for the part, I was obsessed with getting it," Bernhard explains. "I'd never felt that way about a role before; I felt comfortable with the character right away."[13]

Other roles in the film were filled by friends and past collaborators. Rupert's romantic interest was played by De Niro's estranged wife, Diahnne Abbott, who had also appeared in *Taxi Driver* and *New York, New York*. Scorsese's mother, Catherine Scorsese, lent her voice to Rupert's unseen mother. Mardik Martin, who had cowritten *Mean Streets* and *Raging Bull*, appeared as a man in the bar. Liza Minnelli shot a scene for the film that ultimately wound up on the cutting room floor. Minnelli did, however, appear in the film by way of a cardboard cutout in Rupert's room. Other roles in the film were filled by *Tonight Show* producer Fred De Cordova and De Niro and Scorsese's agent Harry Ufland.

Because the film focused largely on the world of television, Scorsese decided to film *The King of Comedy* as one would film a television show. His plan was to use largely empty sets, flat lighting, and old-fashioned box-like framing. Michael Chapman, Scorsese's go-to director of photography, declined to work on the film as he didn't like this concept. Instead, Scorsese hired Fred Schuler to be his cameraman. Prior to this, Schuler had worked as camera operator on both *Taxi Driver* and *The Last Waltz*.

Scorsese and De Niro both liked Zimmerman's screenplay, but they wanted to personalize the material just as they had on *Raging Bull*. So the two of them took the script and a novelization Zimmerman had penned to an undisclosed location on Long Island, secluded themselves, and rewrote the script. Protective parent Zimmerman was worried about this revision of his material, but he soon found that Scorsese and De Niro had dramatically improved *The King of Comedy* without changing much of the original scenarios and character motivations. "The script Marty and Bobby returned to me was all mine—with maybe one new scene," Zimmerman would later say.[14] The tone of the new script had changed, though; instead of being an outright comedy, this draft was much darker.

While in preproduction on *The King of Comedy*, the always busy Scorsese began planning a possible twenty-hour television miniseries about the history of early Christianity and its ties to paganism. This, however, came to an end when the Directors Guild of America threatened to go on strike. If the strike happened, any film without a significant amount of footage already in the can would be shut down. As a result, producer Arnon Milchan ordered Scorsese to start shooting on June 1, 1981—a full month earlier than planned. Scorsese told Milchan that they weren't ready to begin filming, but Milchan would not back down. Scorsese says he then looked at De Niro and asked, "Can you do it?" De Niro responded with a simple "Yes."[15] So Scorsese agreed to go to work on the film, even though he was still suffering from physical exhaustion and the aftereffects of pneumonia.

"*The King of Comedy* was an uphill battle for me," Scorsese admits. "It was more Bob's project than mine and I wasn't a big help at the time. The motives for making a film are very important to me. They have to be good motives. Mine weren't very clear when I started out on this picture."[16] Because of this, Scorsese found himself in constant search of motivation. "It was a very interesting movie, but I had to keep reinventing reasons for doing it and caring about it," Scorsese explains. "That can be dangerous. Imagine making a picture and not caring about it. What's it going to look like?"[17]

Scorsese's lack of motivation coupled with his sickness resulted in him sometimes not showing up on the set until well into the afternoon. Since Lewis arrived on the set each day at nine in the morning, he wasn't terribly thrilled. Making matters worse, Lewis spent the first few days of filming watching Scorsese shoot scenes that did not involve him. Then, at the end of the day, after Lewis had endured take after take of De Niro making minimal modifications in each, Scorsese would decide not to film Lewis' scenes. Finally, after Lewis had had enough, he approached the director. He told him that he was a professional and would sit and wait if that was what was needed—after all, he was being well paid for his time—but that he would appreciate being told in advance when he wasn't going to be needed.

As a result of Scorsese's ongoing sickness, the day's shooting was eventually restricted to an intense three-hour period from four to seven in the evening. "*King of Comedy* was maybe three hours a day shooting," Scorsese says. "But I was tired, had just had pneumonia and had to start the picture before I was ready because of an imminent directors' strike. Now I shoot 10 hours. By the end of that film, I realized I wouldn't be able to sustain a career that way any longer."[18]

All of these methods were foreign to Lewis, who, as a director, had run a very tight ship. "If they had hired me as part of the filmmaking team," Lewis says, "I'd have killed them both, because it was against everything I was taught." Always the consummate professional, Lewis said nothing. "When I am a passenger on the other captain's ship, I'm just a passenger. And it means if I see this ship going down because this fucker's pulling the cork out, he ain't gonna hear anything from me."[19]

Lewis was also shocked to see Scorsese and De Niro spending so much time refining a single scene. One day Lewis was appalled to see Scorsese and De Niro shoot an astounding 29 takes for a scene with no dialogue. When Lewis realized that the following day's shooting covered four pages of dialogue, he turned to a crew member and told him if Scorsese didn't use 138 takes for that scene, he'd purchase him a new car. Lewis, however, eventually came to see the method within this madness. "In order to work with Bobby you have to make a deal with the devil," he explains.

> Bobby is no fool. He knows his craft. And that his craft needs time, it needs his gut to go for it. Marty would tell him from now until next Tuesday that take five was super. But De Niro knows fucking well that

if he goes into take 12 and 14 and 15 he'll find an "if" and an "and." If he does take 20, he'll pick up a quick turn, and on take 28 he's got lips tightening, which he never had through the first 27 takes. I watched him feign poor retention just to work a scene. I watched him literally look like he couldn't remember the dialogue. He knew the fucking dialogue. It was masterful. There's nothing he did that didn't stagger me.[20]

Utilizing the same technique he had used to coax an authentic reaction out of Joe Pesci in *Raging Bull*, De Niro strayed from the script to make Lewis genuinely angry for a scene in which Rupert Pupkin shows up uninvited at Jerry Langford's country house. With Lewis completely unaware that the cameras were rolling, De Niro stood just out of the frame and began hurling anti-Semitic remarks at him. Caught off guard by these remarks, which included insults such as Hitler should have been allowed to live so he could finish what he started, Lewis went completely ballistic. He began screaming at De Niro, inadvertently delivering a terrific performance. He later realized he'd been duped but remained angry. De Niro came to Lewis' dressing room and apologized, but Lewis swore to him that he would never work with him again.

After the film was released, Lewis ultimately saw what a brilliant performance he'd given with the help of De Niro. As a result, he for-

gave the younger actor. "Working with Bobby De Niro, for me, had to be the one of a kind chance any actor would remember for the rest of his life," Lewis says, "It has to be the same kind of feeling actors had for the first time they worked with the likes of Marlon Brando, Rod Steiger, Paul Newman, James Cagney, and so on. He is the ultimate professional. De Niro has the tremendous capacity for helping the other actors totally forget that there are cameras, crew, or anything around. He gets you so involved with what you are doing that you find yourself doing things you didn't know you could do."[21]

Bernhard also managed to make Lewis feel uncomfortable. While filming a scene in which her character has him tied up, she began to improvise more and more. Lewis had no idea what she was going to throw at him next. Bernhard had never felt that Lewis really liked her, so she took advantage of Lewis being taped up and went all out, delivering a powerfully frightening performance. "Being intimidated by a young woman isn't really Jerry's forte," Bernhard explains. "I don't think it would've worked if it had been this nice, sweet off-screen relationship." Scorsese also attests to Lewis' discomfort during this scene. "The sexual threat to Jerry was very important, but he used to crack up laughing," Scorsese says. "Then it became difficult to deal with, and his comments and jokes became edgier."[22]

Shooting lasted twenty weeks and exceeded its $14 million budget by $5 million. By the end, Scorsese sometimes became so exhausted that he had to lie down during filming. The shoot was unbearable for Scorsese.

The editing of the film was also a nightmare for the director. "I got myself into such a state of anxiety that I just completely crashed," Scorsese recalls. "I'd come downstairs from the editing room, and I'd see a message from somebody about some problem, and I'd say, 'I can't work today. It's impossible.' My friends said, 'Marty, the negative is sitting there. The studio is going crazy. You've got to finish the film.'"[23] During this period, the *New York Daily News* reported that distributor Twentieth Century Fox was so enthused with *The King of Comedy* that they were taking it off their summer schedule in order to unveil it during awards season. The truth, however, was that Scorsese was still editing and the studio was demanding reshoots. A press release on the subject even went so far as to declare that the studio thought it might become one of the five greatest films ever made.

Once the film was completed, test screenings were held in several major U.S. cities. Twentieth Century Fox executive David Field recalls, "We loved Rupert Pupkin, but the preview audience hated him, saw him as this sick terrorist. In Kansas City, we got such bad numbers, it became funny."[24]

The film was released on February 18, 1983. Marketed as a mainstream comedy, it failed to find an audience. The $19 million film earned less than $2 million at the box office. After a month in release, the studio decided to pull the film from theaters.

"I think maybe the reason [The King of Comedy] wasn't well received was that it gave off an aura of something people didn't want to look at or know," De Niro has said.[25] Scorsese rightfully felt the film was misunderstood. "People in America were confused by The King of Comedy and saw Bob as some sort of mannequin," he says. "But I felt it was De Niro's best performance ever. The King of Comedy was right on the edge for us; we couldn't go any further at that time."[26]

Most criticism of the film was tepid. The New Yorker's David Denby called The King of Comedy a "clever, sometimes brilliant movie, but ice-cold and not really likeable . . . it produces, at best, a nervous giggle—too bitter, too angry to make anyone laugh."[27] Variety's review read, "The King of Comedy is a royal disappointment, although another off-center teaming of director Martin Scorsese and actor Robert De Niro will work up excitement in certain limited quarters. But it's an enthusiasm that's not likely to be shared by the majority."[28] Pauline Kael of the New Yorker trashed the film: "Putting a grossly insensitive, coldhearted deadhead at the center of a movie is a perverse thing to want to do, and Martin Scorsese's The King of Comedy isn't an ordinary kind of bad movie. It's so—deliberately—quiet and empty that it doesn't provide even the dumb, mind-rotting diversion that can half-amuse audiences at ordinary bad movies."[29]

De Niro once again received praise for his work in the film. Vincent Canby of the New Yorker called the turn "one of the best, most complex and flamboyant performances of his career."[30] Newsweek's Jack Kroll agreed, calling the performance "another indelible portrait to his growing gallery."[31] Vogue critic Molly Haskell also agreed: "If there was any doubt that Robert De Niro is the greatest and most unsettling actor in movies today . . . then The King of Comedy should dispel it."[32]

The King of Comedy was selected as the opening film for the 1983 Cannes Film Festival, where it vied for—and lost—the festival's top prize. The British Critics' Circle voted it the year's top film. In addition, *The King of Comedy* received five British Academy Award nominations, winning only one award for its screenplay. It received no Oscar nominations.

In 1989, an *American Film* poll of critics listed *The King of Comedy* as one of the decade's ten best films. As was the case with *Raging Bull*, which topped the list, the same critics who had trashed the picture at its release had now warmed to the film. As author David Ehrenstein suggests in his book *The Scorsese Picture*, critics who "initially found the works disturbing" may have later found that "they couldn't get them out of their minds."[33]

The Film

The King of Comedy begins with a brief credit sequence consisting of white lettering against a black background. Only the names of producer Arnon Milchan, Martin Scorsese, and Robert De Niro appear. The film then begins with the opening title sequence of a *Tonight Show*–like late night talk show, *The Jerry Langford Show*. Announcer Ed Herlihy rattles off the names of tonight's guests: Tony Randall, Richard Dreyfuss, Rodney Dangerfield, and Dr. Joyce Brothers. Herlihy then announces the show's host, Jerry Langford (Jerry Lewis), who steps out from behind the curtains. Once the applause stops, Langford introduces the band and engages in Johnny Carson–like banter.

The film cuts to a lot behind the television studio where hundreds of autograph hunters are waiting for Jerry to leave the building. One of these is Rupert Pupkin (Robert De Niro). With help from bodyguards, Jerry makes his way through the crowd and gets inside his limousine. He is then accosted by an obsessed female fan named Masha (Sandra Bernhard), who was hiding in the limo. After a momentary struggle, Jerry breaks free and climbs out of the limo. We then see a freeze-frame shot of Masha's hands against the inside of the window. According to Martin Scorsese, this shot is symbolic of the barriers—physical and otherwise—that stand between stars and their fans. The song "Come Rain or Come Shine" by Ray Charles begins to play over the soundtrack. This shot of Masha's hands appears on the screen for a full thirteen seconds before the film's title is superimposed against it. The rest of the credits are then superimposed against the freeze-frame shot, as well.

Once the credit sequence has concluded, the film begins where it left off. Jerry is momentarily trapped outside the limo and is being mobbed by legions of adoring fans. Seeing an opportunity to get Jerry's attention, Rupert tries to separate the fans from Jerry. After Masha has been removed from the limo, Jerry climbs back inside. An overanxious Rupert follows him into the limo. Rupert asks Jerry for a moment of his time, but Jerry is obviously uncomfortable and doesn't want to talk to him. Rupert then shows Jerry a gash in his hand that he incurred while he was trying to keep the mobbing fans away from him. Jerry relents and instructs his driver to drive. Rupert informs Jerry that he's a stand-up comic and has idolized him for some time. Rupert believes that meeting Jerry may be his big break into comedy. Jerry tries to explain that an untested comic can't just walk onto a national television program, but Rupert is convinced that he's ready for an appearance on *The Jerry Langford Show*. Finally Jerry tells Rupert to call his secretary, and he'll listen to his act. Rupert tells him that this scene has played out in his head many times prior to this. "Did it always turn out this way?" Jerry asks. "Yeah, it did," Rupert responds. Jerry makes a backhanded joke about Rupert needing to get over his shyness, but it goes over Rupert's head. Once they arrive at Jerry's apartment building, Rupert continues pestering him with bad jokes and an invitation to dinner. Jerry finally breaks free of Rupert and enters the apartment building. Rupert stares down at the monogrammed handkerchief Jerry gave him for this bleeding hand.

The next scene is a dream sequence—the product of Rupert's delusions of self-importance. In the scene, the tables have turned, and it is now Jerry who needs Rupert. The two of them are having dinner together—this time at the behest of Jerry. Jerry alludes to the fact that he needs a break from the show, and he hesitantly asks Rupert to take over as host for six weeks. This is a matter that they have discussed before, and the aloof Rupert—now in the position of power—doesn't want to do it. "I'll give you anything, but don't ask me to do six weeks," Rupert pleads. "I can't take over the show for six weeks. I can't even take over

my own life for six weeks!" In alternating cuts between the fantasy dinner and reality, we see that Rupert is actually in his basement talking
aloud to himself. In the real world, Rupert's mother (Catherine Scorsese) yells at him for making noise so late at night. In his fantasy world,
autograph seekers ask Rupert for his signature but pay no mind to Jerry.
Finally Rupert agrees to fill in on Jerry's show for the six weeks.

Back in the real world, we see Jerry entering his apartment, where
his existence is apparently a lonely one. He watches Samuel Fuller's
Pickup on South Street on a small television as he eats dinner alone. The
telephone rings and Jerry answers it. It's Masha, the crazed woman who
attacked him in the limo. He asks her how she got his phone number,
but Masha doesn't answer. An irritated Jerry hangs up on her, leaving
the phone off the hook.

Rupert enters a seedy little bar and gives a single red rose to Rita
(Diahnne Abbott), the bartender. We learn that Rupert went to high
school with Rita but was too shy to tell her that he liked her. Rupert
now asks Rita out, and the film cuts to the two of them having dinner
together. Rupert asks who her favorite actor or actress is, to which Rita
answers "Marilyn Monroe." Rupert then produces his autograph album
and shows her Monroe's autograph. While showing Rita signatures in

the album, Rupert tells her that Woody Allen is a close personal friend of his. He then shows her a page bearing his own signature. He tears it out of the album and gives it to her as a gift, telling her that soon everyone will want one of their own. He tells her that he is going to be appearing on *The Jerry Langford Show* and that he's the new king of comedy. He spins a fantasy tale that ends with both Rupert and Rita in Hollywood and tells her that he wants her to be the queen to his king. Rita is at first uncomfortable with Rupert's delusions but begins to believe his stories when he suggests that they spend a weekend at Jerry's summer home.

We next see Rupert sitting in his basement between life-sized cardboard cutouts of Liza Minnelli and Jerry. Pretending that he's actually on Jerry's show, Rupert makes talk show chitchat with the cardboard Liza and Jerry. The one-sided conversation is interrupted, however, when Rupert's mother yells down to inform him that the bus has arrived early.

Rupert attempts to call Jerry's office twice but is told to leave a message both times. He leaves a message for Jerry to call him at his office number, which actually belongs to a Times Square pay phone. Because most of the other pay phones are broken, a long line forms behind Rupert. Even as fights erupt over the pay phones, Rupert maintains his position. We then see him still waiting as the city grows dim around him, but Jerry never calls. Rupert then goes to Jerry's office building and attempts to get in to see Jerry. After sitting in the waiting room for a long period of time, Rupert is eventually seen by Cathy Long (Shelley Hack), the assistant to the executive producer. She tries to brush him off, but Rupert fails to take the hint. She finally agrees to listen to a tape of Rupert's comedy act, and he tells her he will bring it to her soon.

Outside the building, Rupert is approached by Masha. The two are apparently old friends. She asks if Jerry said anything about her, to which Rupert says no. He tells her that he and Jerry have a "real relationship," and not some "fantasy world" make-believe connection. With each far-fetched tale that Rupert spins, it becomes more apparent that he actually believes the things he is saying. Equally delusional is Masha, who says that right now she and Jerry are just having "communication problems." She then asks Rupert to deliver a handwritten note to him. Using the same approach that both Jerry and Cathy Long have used with him, Rupert agrees to this request so Masha will leave him alone.

In his basement, Rupert records a tape of his comic material. He titles it "The Best of Rupert Pupkin." While recording his stand-up material, Rupert stands in front of a wall-sized photograph of an audience laughing. As he tells his unfunny jokes, there is a laugh track accompanying him. As Rupert records his tape, his mother frequently yells at him to talk and play his music at a lower volume as she's trying to sleep.

The next day, Rupert gives the tape to Cathy Long. Rupert then imagines he's having a conversation with Jerry, who's praising his talent. Jerry prods for pointers, asking Rupert how he does what he does. Jerry says that the material is top-notch and that he envies Rupert's talent. Rupert now imagines Jerry inviting him and his "special young lady" to stay at his country estate for the weekend.

In the next scene, we see Jerry walking down a busy New York street. People yell out and catcall to him as he walks. A woman on a pay phone asks Jerry for his autograph. He obliges, signing her magazine. She then asks him to talk on the phone to her nephew. When he politely says no, she exclaims that she hopes he gets cancer. As he walks, Jerry catches a glimpse of Masha following him. He becomes nervous and speeds up, but she remains just behind him. Finally he breaks into a sprint, and Masha gives chase all the way to the studio where he works. Once Jerry is inside the building, the dejected Masha spots Rupert entering and smiles.

Inside, Rupert asks to see Jerry but is told that Cathy Long will be speaking to him once again. He informs Cathy that he would prefer to see Jerry. As he sits in the waiting room, Rupert once again imagines himself as a guest on Jerry's show. Rupert is introduced to a mystery guest, who is revealed to be George Kapp, his high school principal. Kapp informs Rupert that he's now a justice of the peace. After Rita is introduced, she and Rupert are married on national television in a scene staged similar to the 1969 *Tonight Show* wedding between Tiny Tim and Miss Vickie. During the proceedings, Kapp publicly apologizes—and even begs for forgiveness—for "all the things we did to you." The fantasy sequence is broken up, however, when Cathy Long greets

Rupert in the waiting room. She tells him that the tape shows him to have a lot of potential but that she doesn't feel he's ready to appear on the show yet. She encourages him to work in front of a live crowd and says that once he starts working, he should call her back. Rupert becomes somewhat hostile, asking her, "Are you speaking for Jerry?" She says that she is speaking for Jerry and that Jerry has complete faith in her judgment. Rupert tells her that he does not have faith in her judgment. After the conversation has concluded, Rupert sits down in the waiting room to wait for Jerry himself. The receptionist asks Rupert to leave, but he does not. A security guard soon emerges and escorts Rupert out of the building.

Rupert runs into Masha outside. Masha informs him that Jerry is inside the building and calls Rupert naïve for believing it when he was told otherwise. Masha instructs Rupert to go back inside and assert himself. This gets Rupert pumped up, and he angrily storms back inside. When the receptionist tells him that Jerry isn't in, Rupert threatens to have her fired. He then marches through the building in search of Jerry. This time Rupert is carried out by several security guards and warned that if he ever shows his face there again, he will be arrested. Masha sees this and mocks Rupert, who informs her that he'll be staying at Jerry's home for the weekend.

In the next scene, Rupert and Rita arrive at Jerry's country home to stay for the weekend. Rita has no clue that Rupert has not been invited. Jerry's manservant Jonno (Kim Chan) informs them that Jerry is not in, but Rupert hands him his suitcases and enters the house anyway. As Rupert shows Rita around the house, a concerned Jonno telephones Jerry and informs him that the couple is "ruining the house" and that he's "getting a heart attack already." Rita plays one of Jerry's records—"Ain't Nobody's Business" by Otis Spann—and she and Rupert dance together. Rita goes upstairs and Rupert follows.

Jerry arrives. Momentarily speechless, he is introduced to Rita by Rupert. As Rupert tries to make casual conversation, Jerry stands angrily with his arms crossed. "You know I could have the both of you arrested?" Jerry asks. Rupert, still delusional, laughs this off. Jerry calls him a moron, but Rupert laughs this off, as well. Jerry becomes angrier by the second and finally informs Rupert that he initially told him to call his secretary because he wanted to get rid of him. When Rupert says that he made a mistake, Jerry angrily barks, "So did Hitler!" Finally Rupert takes the hint and leaves.

The following day, Rupert and Masha wait outside Jerry's apartment building with a fake gun. The two of them follow Jerry on his way to work, arguing as they do. They pull up beside Jerry, and Rupert jumps out to take him at gunpoint but drops the gun on the pavement. He then picks up the gun and forces Jerry into the backseat of Masha's car. The two kidnappers take their hostage back to Masha's house, where Rupert informs Jerry that he's to call his producer, Bert Thomas. Masha holds the fake gun to Jerry's head. Jerry calls Bert Thomas' (Fred De Cordova) office, but when he tells Thomas' secretary who he is, she thinks it's a gag and hangs up. Jerry finally gets Thomas on the phone and reads from cue cards. Rupert has the cards turned around and in the wrong order, so Jerry has a brief difficulty reading them. The message he reads is, "I have a gun at my head. If a man who identifies himself as 'The King' is not allowed to be the first guest on tonight's show, you'll never see me alive again." Thomas agrees to meet this demand.

Rupert asks Jerry why he didn't listen to the tape when he asked him to. Jerry says if that's the reason he has kidnapped him, the two of them should go back to his office and listen to the tape. Rupert tells him no. "Friendship is a two-way street," the delusional Rupert informs him. Rupert and Masha prove themselves to be not only inept kidnappers, but also extremely unprofessional ones; the two of them constantly argue as Jerry watches. Rupert turns his attention back to Jerry, asking him again why he never listened to his tape. Jerry tells him that he's a very busy man, trying to stay afloat of all his responsibilities. Jerry attempts to talk his way out of the predicament, promising that if Rupert and Masha let him go he will not press charges. Rupert declines the offer and tapes Jerry to a chair.

In a meeting with the television producers and the head of the network, the FBI advises them to allow Rupert to perform at the show's taping but not air the episode. FBI Inspector Gerrity (Thomas M. Tolan) says he fears that the kidnappers could be terrorists, wishing to deliver some sort of code on national television that would result in the deaths of many people.

After Rupert has left for the taping, the sexually aggressive Masha lights dozens of candles and removes the tape from Jerry's mouth. "I feel completely impulsive tonight," she warns. "Anything could happen." She then begins to tell an uncomfortable Jerry how frequently she thinks about him. "I love you," she says. "I've never told my parents that I love them." Jerry remains silent as Masha attempts to seduce him.

At the television studio, there is a disruption when guest and author Clarence McCabe (Bill Minkin) isn't on the security list to be admitted. McCabe explains that he has written a book titled *The Vanishing Siberian Tiger*, and he is supposed to be the third guest on the night's show. As this is happening, Rupert manages to evade security, walks right into the building, and approaches Cathy Long, informing her that he's "The King."

Back at Masha's place, Masha wants to have sex with Jerry on top of the dinner table. She pushes the candles and plates off onto the floor and begins serenading him with "Come Rain or Come Shine": "You're gonna love me, like nobody's loved me." As she sings, Masha caresses Jerry—still taped to the chair—suggestively. She sits on his lap.

Meanwhile, Inspector Gerrity questions Rupert about Jerry Langford's whereabouts, but Rupert refuses to talk. He insists on seeing someone involved with the show. When Gerrity says that Rupert cannot see anyone from the show until he produces Jerry, Rupert smugly tells them he's dead. Rupert is then allowed to talk with Bert Thomas, who questions him about his monologue. Even as Gerrity informs Rupert of his Miranda rights, the delusional Rupert remains happy and carefree.

Back at the house, Masha tells Jerry, "Let's do something crazy tonight—just get insane!" She then shows Jerry just how insane she is when she starts screaming ecstatically. She then proceeds to peel off her clothes.

The Jerry Langford Show begins taping with Tony Randall filling in as guest host. The night's guests include Shelley Winters, Gore Vidal, and Tony Bennett. Instead of an opening monologue, Randall informs the crowd that they're about to get a glimpse of the future. "It isn't often that you can call someone a sure thing in the entertainment business," Randall says, reading dialogue written by Rupert. "After all, the verdict is always in your hands, isn't it? But I think tonight after you've met my first guest, you'll agree with me that he's destined for greatness—in one way or another." He then introduces the "newest King of Comedy," Rupert Pupkin.

Masha is about to kiss Jerry, but Jerry convinces her to take the tape off.

Meanwhile, Rupert has just finished his set and is being interrogated by the FBI agents. Rupert informs them that they won't get Jerry back until after he's had a chance to see the night's episode aired on national television from the bar where Rita works.

Back at Masha's house, Jerry is now free from his bonds. He picks up the gun but realizes at once that it's fake. He slaps Masha and flees. Masha gives chase in only her underwear and bra, but to no avail.

At the bar, Rupert switches the television to *The Jerry Langford Show* so he can show Rita his appearance. We now see Rupert's act for the first time. It's not particularly funny, but the crowd laughs anyway. Scorsese then cuts to Jerry, who is walking across the darkened city to safety. He stops in front of an appliance shop and disgustedly watches Rupert performing on his show. The film then cuts back to Rupert in the bar. Rita is momentarily proud of Rupert but is then appalled when he is handcuffed in front of her by FBI agents. As the FBI agents escort Rupert to their car, Inspector Gerrity tells him that his jokes were terrible. "If you wrote that material, I got one piece of advice for you," Gerrity says. "Throw yourself on your knees in front of the judge and beg for mercy."

A brief montage shows several news programs discussing Rupert's stunt. One of them says that Rupert's set was viewed by a record 87 million American households. We then see photographs of Rupert gracing the covers of *Time, Newsweek, People, Rolling Stone,* and *Life.* Now heralded as "the kidnapping king of comedy," Rupert is sentenced to six years in prison in Allenwood, Pennsylvania. One news report given on the anniversary of Rupert's stunt informs audiences that Rupert still considers Jerry Langford a close personal friend and mentor. We are also told that Rupert has sold his memoirs, *King for a Night,* for more than $1 million. After serving two years and nine months, Rupert is freed from prison. At the film's conclusion, we find that Rupert is resuming his career in show business. We see him onstage for an unspecified television show—possibly his own—where he is greeted with wild enthusiasm. Perhaps it is for all the wrong reasons, but Rupert has finally become the star he always dreamed he would be.

Notes

1. McKay, Keith, *Robert De Niro: The Hero behind the Masks* (New York: Ultra Communications, 1986), 113.

2. Dougan, Andy, *Untouchable: A Biography of Robert De Niro* (New York: Thunder's Mouth Press, 1996), 146.

3. Keyser, Les, *Martin Scorsese* (New York: Twayne Publishers, 1992), 126.

4. Paris, Barry, "Maximum Expression," *American Film*, October 1989, 36.

5. Levy, Shawn, *King of Comedy: The Life and Art of Jerry Lewis* (New York: St. Martin's Griffin, 1996), 419.

6. Levy, *King of Comedy*, 419.

7. Cameron-Wilson, James, *The Cinema of Robert De Niro* (London: Zomba Books, 1986), 102.

8. Levy, *King of Comedy*, 420.

9. Brode, Douglas, *The Films of Robert De Niro* (Secaucus, NJ: Citadel Press, 1996), 149.

10. Baxter, John, *De Niro: A Biography* (New York: HarperCollins, 2002), 225.

11. Levy, *King of Comedy*, 420.

12. Paris, "Maximum Expression," 36.

13. Cameron-Wilson, *The Cinema of Robert De Niro*, 105.

14. Keyser, *Martin Scorsese*, 127.

15. Dougan, Andy, *Martin Scorsese: Close Up* (New York: Thunder's Mouth Press, 1998), 72.

16. Kelly, Mary Pat, *Martin Scorsese: A Journey* (New York: Thunder's Mouth Press, 1991), 153.

17. Dougan, *Untouchable*, 149.

18. Randall, Stephen, and the editors of *Playboy* magazine, eds., *The Playboy Interviews: The Directors* (Milwaukie, OR: M Press, 2006), 352.

19. Levy, *King of Comedy*, 422.

20. Levy, *King of Comedy*, 422.

21. Cameron-Wilson, *The Cinema of Robert De Niro*, 103.

22. Thompson, David, and Christie, Ian, eds., *Scorsese on Scorsese* (Boston: Faber and Faber, 1989), 91.

23. Biskind, Peter, "Slouching toward Hollywood," *Premiere*, November 1991, 70.

24. Kelly, *Martin Scorsese*, 159.

25. Brode, *The Films of Robert De Niro*, 149.

26. Dougan, *Martin Scorsese*, 73.

27. David Denby is quoted in Brode, *The Films of Robert De Niro*, 150.

28. The *Variety* review is quoted in Dougan, *Martin Scorsese*, 124.

29. Pauline Kael is quoted in Brode, *The Films of Robert De Niro*, 150.

30. Vincent Canby is quoted in Brode, *The Films of Robert De Niro*, 150.

31. Jack Kroll is quoted in Brode, *The Films of Robert De Niro*, 150.

32. Molly Haskell is quoted in Brode, *The Films of Robert De Niro*, 150.

33. Ehrenstein, David, *The Scorsese Picture: The Art and Life of Martin Scorsese* (New York: Birch Lane Press, 1992), 112.

CHAPTER SIX

GoodFellas (1990)

I knew it would make a fascinating film if we could keep the same sense of a way of life that Nick had in the book . . . and still have an audience care about these characters as human beings: to be as close to the truth as possible in a fiiction film, without whitewashing the characters or creating a phony sympathy for them.

—Martin Scorsese

The Backstory

Martin Scorsese was filming *The Color of Money* in Chicago in 1985 when he read a review of crime journalist Nicholas Pileggi's book *Wiseguy: Life in a Mafia Family* in the *New York Times*. Pileggi's tome chronicled the rise and fall of real-life Mafia foot soldier Henry Hill. The book had not yet landed in bookstores, but Scorsese made a few calls and managed to obtain galley proofs of the work from Simon & Schuster. Once he began reading the book, the director knew instantly that it held great potential for a film; through the details recounted in the book, Scorsese found himself transported back to the people and places he'd known growing up in Little Italy. The film Scorsese envisioned would be like a 16mm documentary that followed the lives of a Mafia crew for some thirty years. "I was interested in the minutiae of how to live as a wise guy," Scorsese explains. "I wanted to get into the frame of mind of a guy who works that way every day."[1]

Fascinated by this idea, Scorsese immediately telephoned Pileggi at his office at *New York* magazine. Pileggi, however, was out. When he returned to find a note instructing him to call Martin Scorsese, he thought it was a practical joke being played on him by *New York* reviewer David Denby, and he tossed the note into the wastebasket. Undeterred, Scorsese persisted, eventually reaching the writer at home. "My name is Martin Scorsese," he informed him. "I'm a film director. I've been looking for this book for years."[2] To this, Pileggi informed him that he had been waiting for this call all his life and that Scorsese was the man he'd long envisioned helming a film adaptation. However, there was currently a bidding war over the material. Despite this, Pileggi told Scorsese that they had a deal. Once Scorsese learned that his old friend Irwin Winkler, who had previously produced both *New York, New York* and *Raging Bull*, was one of the parties who had been bidding on *Wiseguy*, he reteamed with the producer. Winkler then sold *Wiseguy* to Warner Bros. with Scorsese attached as director.

Although he'd worked as a ghostwriter on *Raging Bull* and *The King of Comedy*, Scorsese had not worked as a screenwriter in an official capacity since *Mean Streets*. Despite this, Scorsese planned to work closely with Pileggi in adapting the screenplay. Pileggi knew very little about screenwriting or film structure, but Scorsese taught him as they went. Scorsese screened *Jules et Jim* for the writer to show him the narration technique he intended to employ for the film. The two then made a list of episodes they wanted to appear in the film. Scorsese's idea was that only the highs and lows of the characters' lives over the three decades would be shown. This was achieved by cutting transitional scenes altogether, allowing them to cherry-pick the most interesting episodes from the book. Pileggi would first write a scene and then give it to Scorsese, who would then rewrite it by hand. Scorsese also jotted down the titles of songs he wanted to incorporate into scenes in the margins. From 1986 to 1987, Scorsese and Pileggi produced eleven drafts of the screenplay. Early drafts followed the story in chronological order. Then Scorsese came up with the idea to present the murder of Billy Batts at the beginning of the film to hook audiences.

Scorsese then went to work on several other projects, including an Armani commercial, a Michael Jackson video ("Bad"), *The Last Temp-*

tation of Christ, and a segment for Woody Allen's anthology film *New York Stories* ("Life Lessons"). During this time, Scorsese began to question whether or not he should return to the gangster genre. As a favor, Scorsese's hero Michael Powell took a look at the screenplay. Because of his failing eyesight, Powell was read the screenplay by his wife, editor Thelma Schoonmaker. Seeing a unique approach to the genre, Powell convinced Scorsese that he had to make the film. "It is a stunning script," Powell wrote in a letter, "and will make a wonderful film."[3]

After four years and eleven drafts, Scorsese was finally ready to fully commit himself to the project. The first thing he wanted to do was change the title of the project since there was already a television series called *Wiseguy* and a film titled *Wise Guys*. Scorsese then changed the title to *GoodFellas*. Despite the commercial success of *The Color of Money*, Warner Bros. didn't want to bank on Scorsese alone. They insisted that a big-name actor be brought onboard before they would agree to make the picture. Scorsese showed the screenplay to Robert De Niro and asked him who he thought he should cast in the role of Jimmy "the Gent" Conway (based on Jimmy Burke). De Niro then suggested that he himself take the role. This pleased both Scorsese and Warner Bros., and the studio agreed to finance the film for $26 million.

Henry Hill, the film's main character, was the next to be cast. It was once again De Niro who suggested the perfect actor for the role. "Hey, why don't we use the kid from *Something Wild?*" De Niro suggested.[4] The actor he was recommending from the 1986 Jonathan Demme film was Ray Liotta, who, as it turned out, had already read Pileggi's book. Liotta was then brought in to audition and had to wait another eight months before being given the part. Once he landed the role, he was ecstatic to be working with two of his filmmaking heroes. "I wanted to get into film," Liotta explains, "and was very influenced by De Niro and Scorsese. . . . And now, here I am with both of them. They're great. I like their commitment and passion."[5]

For the role of Karen Hill, Henry's wife, Scorsese thought of actress Lorraine Bracco. The actress was married to his friend and collaborator Harvey Keitel, and she had auditioned for him previously for a part in his dark comedy *After Hours*. Scorsese didn't make Bracco audition for the role. Instead, he held a meeting at his apartment with both Bracco and Liotta to ascertain if they had chemistry. The three of them spent several hours discussing the characters Henry and Karen Hill. At the end of the conversation, Scorsese offered the role to Bracco. However, there was a dispute regarding the amount of money Bracco would receive for appearing in the film. Bracco didn't feel the amount was enough, but her husband convinced her to take the role anyway. "You should never miss an opportunity to play a great role and work with a great director over money," Keitel advised.[6] Inspired by her husband's devotion to the craft, Bracco accepted the role.

Liotta and Bracco soon discovered that they worked well together as Henry and Karen Hill. "Just right from the beginning, I trusted her, she trusted me," Liotta says. "And we were kind of the new kids on the block."[7] At the beginning of the shoot, Scorsese would refer to the two of them as "the kids," which amused them. "By the end of the film, we weren't kids anymore," Bracco laments. "We literally lived through the sad decline of the Hills—Henry's descent into drugs, and Karen's descent into being a partner in her husband's crimes."[8]

When Frank Vincent first spoke to Scorsese about the film, he envisioned himself as mob boss Paul Cicero. Scorsese, however, saw him as a character named Billy Batts. Scorsese urged him to accept the role, and Vincent did. "You don't argue with Marty and say, 'No, I don't wanna play this,'" Vincent says.[9]

For the role of Paul Cicero (based on Paul Vario), Scorsese cast actor Paul Sorvino. Sorvino wanted very badly to appear in a Martin Scorsese film, but he wasn't sure he could relate to the character well enough to do a decent job playing him. Sorvino said nothing but wondered for some time how he would ever be able to give a convincing performance. As a middle-aged Italian man, Sorvino looked the part. However, he wasn't convinced he could appear as menacing as the role required. After several months of searching within himself for the character, Sorvino decided he couldn't do it. He began to worry that he would ruin the film, and he started searching for a way to get out of making it. Then one night Sorvino walked past a mirror and did a double take. When he'd looked into the mirror, he'd seen a very different, very intimidating expression on his face. The expression had lasted only the briefest of moments, but there was something about it that literally frightened him. He then realized that he was capable of playing Paul Cicero, as he had just seen his face in the mirror.

Casting the character of the volatile Tommy DeVito (based on Tommy DiSimone) was rather easy for Scorsese. Although the real-life

Tommy was much taller, Scorsese envisioned Joe Pesci in the role even as he'd first read Pileggi's book. While making the film, Scorsese offered Pesci a singular mandate: "I don't want to see you act. I want to see you behave."[10] Rather than study his character's every motivation the way De Niro did, Pesci instead created his own imagined version of the man. "What I do is think of someone I know very well who is the same type," Pesci says, "and play him. I do *my* Tommy DiSimone. I do Joe Pesci as if I were this killer, this crazy, funny, wisecracking person."[11]

Pesci says he doesn't know why Scorsese frequently pairs him up with De Niro as brotherly characters, but he believes it has to do with their having a kindred spirit. "I guess it's because the first time we worked together, he had this feeling that we got along that way onscreen and offscreen," Pesci says. "There's this connection. It's very easy for us to work together, no matter if he plays the bad guy or I play the nicer guy, or vice-versa. . . . Maybe input that I give Marty is a lot of the same input that Bob gives. We like Marty's ideas the same way. We take direction from him, and we really get enthusiastic."[12]

De Niro learned about his character by studying Pileggi's files of information that did not appear in the book. He also spoke to the real-life Henry Hill about Jimmy Burke's reactions and mannerisms; he asked Hill everything from how Jimmy Burke held a shot glass to how he poured a bottle of ketchup. Hill recalls that De Niro would sometimes call him "four or five" times a day. In the end, this attention to detail helped De Niro give a fully realized portrayal of Jimmy Burke. "Robert De Niro plays Burke as well as Burke could play himself," Hill would later remark.[13]

Liotta also did his fair share of homework to learn about his character. He not only met with the real Henry Hill, but also studied cassette tapes given to him by Pileggi that featured Hill telling his story, chomping on potato chips as he did. Those close to the actor urged him to take a break from studying to go outside sometimes, but Liotta was afraid of botching the performance and persisted in his studies.

Bracco did not have access to the same wealth of materials that De Niro and Liotta had, so she, like Pesci, had to create her own version of her character. "Marty trusted me, and because of that trust, I was free to create Karen Hill," Bracco says. "I had to create my character from the inside, psychologically, because I was unable to meet the real Karen Hill, and there weren't any live models around. People weren't coming up to me and saying, 'Meet my mob wife.' So, while I was basically in

the dark, I was lucky to have Marty and Nick Pileggi as my ever-present guides on this journey."[14]

Location filming began on May 1, 1989, in Astoria, Queens. The earliest scenes to be shot were those of Henry Hill's childhood. Other locations used included Kennedy Airport and the Copacabana nightclub.

It had been nearly a decade since their previous collaboration, and Scorsese and De Niro's working relationship changed once again on *GoodFellas*. They were still extremely comfortable with one another, but after working with many other people during their time apart, they were now able to communicate without talking as much about each scene. "We had evolved a different kind of relationship," Scorsese says. "He'd just say 'What do you need?' and I'd say, 'I need this or that,' and he'd say, 'Okay, let's try that.' We used to laugh sometimes in the trailer afterwards, saying 'Do you remember years ago? We used to talk so much. What were we talking about?'"[15]

"[Scorsese] knows so well what actors need, and how to help them," Pileggi observes.[16] Liotta agrees with this assessment. "He knows what he wants to do," Liotta says, "but you really feel like you're creating and he's letting you go to do what you've come up with."[17]

On *GoodFellas*, Scorsese once again utilized a lot of improvisation. Using what he'd learned while working on *New York, New York*, he let the actors improvise heavily during rehearsals. He then integrated elements of that improvisation into the final script. One such discovery was Sorvino's slapping Liotta during a conversation about mobsters selling drugs like common criminals. There was no slap in the script, but Sorvino felt the need to smack Liotta in the scene. Scorsese liked this, and he decided to keep the slap as he felt it was a genuine reaction on the part of Sorvino's character. "He lets you improvise a lot," explains actor Frank DiLeo. "He encourages you to do what you feel is right. He says, 'React like you yourself would react in real life.'"[18] While filming a scene in which Sorvino's character is being arrested, DiLeo improvised several lines. Scorsese immediately stopped the scene. "What do you think you're doing?" the director asked. "Where did those lines come from? They're not in the script!" Believing that Scorsese was genuinely upset with him, DiLeo feared that he might be fired. Then Scorsese said, "That was brilliant! Do it again."[19] And the lines stayed in the film.

A key scene—perhaps the film's most famous—also grew out of these improvisational sessions. "Probably the most memorable improvisation I've ever seen was the Joe Pesci–Ray Liotta improvisation at the nightclub," Irwin Winkler says.[20] This is a tension-filled scene in which joking between Pesci's and Liotta's characters suddenly becomes serious. Pesci's murderous character snaps and begins asking, "How am I funny?" The scene starts out as a humorous one, but the tone suddenly shifts and the audience quickly comes to the realization that this is a deadly serious matter that could result in the death of the film's protagonist. This scene did not appear in Scorsese and Pileggi's screenplay, but was suggested by Pesci, based on a similar incident he had once witnessed. A master of improvisation, Pesci spun out of control into a frightening madman, delivering what is perhaps his finest performance to date. It is also interesting to note that Scorsese filmed this entire sequence in a medium shot rather than a close-up. This allows the audience to see the expressions of the other men at the table gradually shift from ones of happiness to something much more grim. Once the scene is concluded, laughter fills the soundtrack. This laughter was not only that of the actors, but also that of Scorsese and the crew.

Scorsese believes this to be one of the film's most important scenes because it shows the true dangers of being associated with the Mafia. "The scene that Joe Pesci asked to be put in, and improvised with

Ray—'You think I'm funny?'—is really the most authentic, I think, in the picture," Scorsese explains. "Because it shows that if you're willing to go this way, this is what you have to be. This is what's going to happen to you. . . . You could be killed any second. You could be killed. They don't care who's around."[21]

Another iconic sequence evolved as the result of Scorsese being told that he could not film the entrance to the Copacabana nightclub. Scorsese then chose to utilize a single unbroken steadicam shot that tracks through a side entrance, through the kitchen, and into the dining area. This scene required a hundred or so extras to be simultaneously perfect throughout the duration of the shot, and moving actors and props—namely, a table that is being whisked out for Henry and Karen—to be expertly choreographed, and their execution of duties to be performed seamlessly. This was a very complex scene to shoot, yet Scorsese managed to film it in a single day.

According to Scorsese, filming this scene in this manner became very important because it speaks to Henry's place in the world. "Henry's whole life is ahead of him," Scorsese says. "He's the young American ready to take over the world, and he's met a girl he likes. Because he works with these guys and he's smart and something of an outsider, and so can make a lot of money for them, he gets his reward. His reward is not having to wait in line at the bakery or worry about getting a parking ticket—and getting into the Copa that way. . . . So it had to be done in one sweeping shot, because it's his seduction of her, and it's also the lifestyle seducing him."[22]

During the filming of a scene in which Liotta's character knocks a gun from Bracco's hand, the gun was flung wildly off camera, striking cinematographer Michael Ballhaus in the forehead. As blood began pouring down Ballhaus' face, Scorsese exclaimed, "Not again!"[23] This was the second time in as many collaborations with Scorsese that Ballhaus had been injured by friendly fire. While working on their previous collaboration, The Last Temptation of Christ, actor Willem Dafoe had thrown a bag filled with coins—striking Ballhaus in the exact same spot on his forehead. Luckily, Ballhaus' injuries weren't serious. He was patched up and then went back to work.

Much of the film's power was created in the editing room by Scorsese and editor Thelma Schoonmaker. By intercutting whirling cameras, zooming close-ups, and using freeze frames heavily influenced by

Francois Truffaut's *The 400 Blows*, they crafted an extraordinary film that moves at a breakneck pace. Skillful editing was especially important in crafting the scenes depicting Henry Hill's final day as a gangster. In these scenes, a series of quick cuts set to the frenetic sounds of the Rolling Stones' "Monkey Man" expressed Hill's mind-set at the time and helped to create an ever-building tension that kept audiences on the edge of their seats. After Scorsese learned that test audiences were agitated by these scenes—just as he had intended—he recut the scene again, making it even more frantic.

GoodFellas was released on September 21, 1990. The film grossed $49 million in the United States alone, and eventually made another $20 million on video. Reviews were largely glowing, and many critics predicted that it would be the finest film of the new decade, much like *Taxi Driver* and *Raging Bull* had arguably been the finest of their respective decades.

Barry McIlheney of *Empire* assessed the film as such: "Violent in the extreme—this is a movie where heads literally get kicked in—and simply relentless in its grip over more than two hours, *GoodFellas* falls short only in its limited emotional range, never quite achieving the full sweep of Coppola or Leone over the same terrain. In its own narrow, near-claustrophobic perspective, however, driven along by a classic soundtrack and with no shortage of master directorial brush strokes,

it is hard to imagine a bigger picture than this."[24] Roger Ebert of the *Chicago Sun-Times* wrote, "Most films, even great ones, evaporate like mist once you've returned to the real world; they leave memories behind, but their reality fades fairly quickly. Not this film, which show's America's finest filmmaker at the peak of his form. No finer film has ever been made about organized crime—not even *The Godfather*."[25] Pauline Kael of the *New Yorker* criticized De Niro's performance as pedestrian but praised the film itself, calling it "a triumphant piece of filmmaking—journalism and sociology presented with the brio of drama." She then added, "What you respond to is Scorsese's bravura: the filmmaking process becomes the subject of the movie."[26]

The film received two of its finest compliments from the real-life Hills. "In *Goodfellas*, Martin Scorsese captures everything—good and bad—with almost total accuracy," Henry Hill says. "Had I had the opportunity to direct the movie myself—if I knew anything about directing—I don't think I could have done a better job. All the details are just right. The Brooklyn neighborhood in the movie looks and feels just like my own did."[27] Karen Hill agrees. "I saw *GoodFellas* three times," she says. "Before I saw it the first time, my anxiety and fear were very high. But as it turned out, I was able to relive 25 years of my life on the screen. . . . I thought the movie was fast and furious. And correct."[28]

GoodFellas also fared well at awards time. The film received seven British Academy Award nominations, winning five awards, including Best Film, Best Director (Scorsese), and Best Screenplay (Scorsese and Pileggi). Thelma Schoonmaker was nominated for an Eddie from the American Cinema Editors, and Michael Ballhaus received a nomination for Best Cinematography from the British Society of Cinematographers. The film also received nominations from the Directors Guild, the Writers Guild, and virtually every other awards group. Scorsese received the prestigious Silver Lion Award for Best Director at the Venice Film Festival. *GoodFellas* received six Academy Award nominations in the categories of Best Picture, Best Director (Scorsese), Best Screenplay (Scorsese and Pileggi), Best Supporting Actor (Pesci), Best Supporting Actress (Bracco), and Best Film Editing (Schoonmaker). These six nominations led to a single Oscar for Pesci.

In 2007, the American Film Institute ranked *GoodFellas* as the ninety-second greatest film in the history of American cinema.

The Film

The film opens with credits that zip from the right side of the screen like speeding cars. The film then begins in the middle of its narrative. A title card tells us that it is "New York, 1970." We see a car speeding down the highway in the middle of the night. It is being driven by Henry Hill (Ray Liotta). Jimmy Conway (Robert De Niro) is asleep in the passenger's side, and Tommy DeVito (Joe Pesci) is riding in the backseat. We—and the characters—hear a thumping sound coming from the trunk of the automobile. Henry pulls the car off the road, and the three men step out to investigate the sounds. As *Martin Scorsese: A Biography* author Vincent LoBrutto observes, the three men are "lit in hellfire red by the taillight."[29] They open the trunk, exposing the bloodied Billy Batts (Frank Vincent), whom they'd believed to be dead. Tommy pulls out a huge butcher's knife and stabs Batts seven times. Jimmy then shoots four slugs into the already motionless body. Henry closes the trunk door.

A zoom shot pushes in on Henry's face, which is then held in a six-second freeze frame. The main title sequence begins as Tony Bennett sings "Rags to Riches." The credits are white on black, save for the film's title—*GoodFellas*—which is presented in blood red.

A title card tells us that it's now "East New York, Brooklyn, 1955." The adult Henry serves as narrator during scenes featuring a younger incarnation (Christopher Serrone). As we see the young man peering out of his window at the gangsters gathering at the Pitkin Ave. Cab Company (a scene inspired by Norman's peephole voyeurism in *Psycho*), the adult Henry explains his lifelong dream of being one of the gang—literally. Henry explains that the gangsters were treated like royalty. A few of the wiseguys begin to roughhouse, but the mere sight of neighborhood Mafia boss Paul Cicero (Paul Sorvino) stops them cold.

The young Henry soon goes to work at the cab stand. The older Henry explains that his parents were excited about this at first. His father (Beau Starr) was happy that his son had a job, and his mother (Elaine Kagan) was pleased that the Ciceros were from the same part of Sicily that she was. As the Cleftones' "Can't We Be Sweethearts" plays over the soundtrack, we see young Henry skipping school to work at the cab stand, where he is treated like part of the family. Henry feels like an adult and is quite pleased with his new life.

Henry says that his parents soon changed their minds about his working at the cab stand. They saw it as a part-time job, while Henry saw it as a full-time one. One night Henry's ever-angry father confronts him about a letter stating that he hasn't been to school in months. Flying into a rage, his father beats him with a strap. A freeze-frame shot of his father beating him remains on the screen for a full fifteen seconds as narrator Henry tells us that the true source of his father's rage was his hanging out at the cab stand. Despite the beating, Henry continues to work there. When young Henry tells the gangsters about his father's reaction to the letter from school, they accost the mailman who delivered the letter—sticking his head into a hot pizza oven. This is depicted in a ten-second freeze-frame shot. The wiseguys demand that all letters from Henry's school be delivered to the cab stand ultimately results in the Hills receiving no mail at all.

We are introduced to Paul Cicero. The older Henry explains that "Paulie" only speaks with a few people, and he is extremely powerful. He explains that payments to Paulie are tribute—like those paid in Sicily—and are for protection from criminals who would rip them off.

Henry is assigned the task of lighting fire to the automobiles at a rival cab company. As we watch the younger Henry light cars on fire, Henry the narrator explains that people treated him differently because of his ties to the wiseguys. Shop owners would give him things without wait, and neighborhood children carried his mother's groceries all the way home from the supermarket one day. This, he states proudly, was done out of respect. Henry tells us that he made more money at thirteen than most of the adults in the neighborhood. When the automobiles finally explode, a running Henry is caught in a stylish sixteen-second freeze frame.

We see Henry arrive on his mother's doorstep one day dressed lavishly in a beige double-breasted suit, silk shirt, tie, and black lizard shoes. To this his mother gasps, "My God! You look like a gangster!" Since this is the desired effect, Henry beams proudly. As the sounds of Giuseppe di Stefano's "Firenze Sogna" fills the soundtrack, the film cuts to a bloodied man running down the sidewalk. Henry grabs aprons from the pizzeria and wraps the bleeding hand of the shot man. This moment is a turning point for Henry as it is the first time he has ever seen someone who has been shot. Henry knows that Paulie doesn't want anyone dying in his building as this would bring unwanted heat from the police, but he feels the need to help the man anyway. Tuddy

Cicero (Frank DiLeo) calls Henry a jerk for wasting aprons on the bleeding man, saying that he needs to toughen him up.

"Speedo" by the Cadillacs fills the soundtrack, and the film cuts to nighttime at the cab stand. Henry delivers food and beverages to the wiseguys, who are playing cards and socializing. Here Henry meets Jimmy Conway for the first time. He is immediately taken with Jimmy, who works the room, handing out big money tips to the doormen, dealers, and the bartender. Jimmy slips a $20 bill into Henry's pocket. Jimmy's face is captured in an eight-second freeze frame as Henry the narrator explains that Jimmy's favorite thing in the world to do is steal. We then see Jimmy at work hijacking a truck. Henry explains that most of the loads are practically given to Jimmy by the drivers in exchange for a piece of the action.

Henry is introduced to Tommy DeVito (Joseph D'Onofrio), who is the same age as he is. Henry then goes to work for Jimmy, selling untaxed cigarette cartons out of a car trunk. Henry is then arrested by two city detectives and brought to trial. As Henry leaves the courtroom to the sounds of Giuseppe di Stefano's "Parlami d'Amore Mariu," he is greeted by Paulie and the rest of the wiseguys. This event is essentially Henry's bar mitzvah in the world of the wiseguys—a rite of passage that indicates he's reached maturity. Jimmy tells Henry that he is proud of him for not squealing to the police, and he gives him a "graduation present"—a $100 bill. The screen then freezes for six seconds on Henry, surrounded by the wiseguys.

The story jumps forward eight years. As Billy Ward and His Dominoes sing "Stardust," a title card informs us that the setting and time are "Idlewild Airport, 1963." We see the now adult Henry and Tommy trying to steal a portion of the $30 billion in cargo that went through the airport annually. Again the truckers themselves assist in their own robberies by tipping off the wiseguys to all the best shipments. The music and the scene change. As Mina sings "This World We Live In," we are introduced to a bevy of gangsters inside Sonny Bunz's (Tony Darrow) Bamboo Lounge. A stylish dolly shot takes us through the nightclub, and we are introduced to the following individuals: Anthony Stabile (Frank Adonis), Frankie Carbone (Frank Sivero), Fat Andy (Louis Eppolito), Frankie the Wop (Tony Lip), Freddy No Nose (Mikey Black), Pete the Killer (Peter Cicale), Nicky Eyes (John Manca), Mikey Franzese (Joseph Bono), and Jimmy Two Times (Anthony Powers), who we learn has been given this moniker because he repeats everything he says. Soon an employee of the airport named Frenchy (Mike Starr) arrives, tipping off Jimmy and Henry to a major shipment of untraceable cash moving through the airport over the weekend. Jimmy and Henry make plans to steal the money.

We next see Tommy, Henry, and a group of wiseguys sitting around a table in the nightclub. Tommy is sharing a humorous story, and the wiseguys are laughing. Henry makes an offhand comment to Tommy that he's funny, and suddenly the tone of the scene changes, turning dark. For the first time we see Tommy's hair-trigger temper as he becomes angered by this remark, taking it as an insult. "How am I funny?" he asks, becoming angrier by the second. "Funny like I'm a clown? I amuse you? I make you laugh?" Finally Henry breaks the tension by using humor to calm his friend. Immediately after this tension is relieved, Tommy is insulted by Sonny Bunz, who asks him to pay his tab. Tommy then breaks a bottle over Sonny's head. Afraid for his life, Sonny then goes to Paulie for help. Paulie shrugs off the complaints about Tommy's behavior but ultimately becomes a silent partner in Sonny's business in exchange for protection. Sonny, unaware of the complexities of the deal he has just made, appears happy with the arrangement. Narrator Henry explains that Sonny is now obligated to pay Paulie each week as Paulie runs up tabs on the bar's credit and has his guys loot the supplies and sell them at a lower price. Once Sonny can no longer afford to keep the business open, the wiseguys torch the place so that Paulie can make more money from the nightclub's insurance.

As the nightclub burns, Tommy asks Henry to go on a double date with him. Tommy is trying to sleep with a "Jew broad" named Diane (Katherine Wallach) from the Five Towns who won't date an Italian man unless she's accompanied by her friend Karen (Lorraine Bracco). Henry wants no part of this, but reluctantly agrees to go on the double date to help his friend. The role of narrator now switches to Karen, who explains that Henry treated her rudely during their date. Diane and Tommy insist that Karen and Henry meet them again on the following Friday, but Henry stands her up. Instead of acting sullen and dejected, Karen chooses to track Henry down and confront him. She finds him congregating at the cab stand with his friends and accuses him of lying.

It is during this confrontation that Henry realizes that he truly likes the fiery Karen.

When Henry goes to Karen's house to pick her up for their next date, she makes him hide a crucifix pendant from her mother (Suzanne Shepherd), who believes he's half-Jewish. "Just the good half," Henry tells her mother. As the Crystals sing "Then He Kissed Me," Henry leads Karen into the Copacabana club. The camera follows them in a legendary three-minute uninterrupted tracking shot through the club. As Henry tips everyone in sight, a prime front row table is set up just for the couple. Karen is dazzled by the confidence with which Henry carries himself, as well as the preferential treatment he receives at the club. Comedian Henny Youngman takes the stage and begins cracking jokes. Youngman's joking continues on an overlapping soundtrack as we see Tommy and Henry taking part in the Air France cargo heist. The Chantels sing "Look in My Eyes" as narrator Henry explains that they stole $420,000 without using a gun. He then explains that they gave Paulie a $60,000 share of the take as tribute.

Karen takes Henry to a beach club, where she introduces him to her neighbor Bruce (Mark Evan Jacobs). During another date at the Copacabana, singer Bobby Vinton (Robbie Vinton) sends a bottle of champagne to Henry's table. Karen doesn't question how all of this good fortune could come to a twenty-one-year-old man who claims to be in construction.

A tacky television commercial for Morrie's Wig Shop airs on a television inside Morrie Kessler's Wig and Beauty Salon. Morrie (Chuck Low) complains about having to pay high interest rates on a loan from Jimmy. Hearing this, Jimmy becomes angry and starts to strangle Morrie with a telephone cord. Jimmy is angry that Morrie has enough money to pay for his television commercials but can't seem to come up with the money he owes him. Karen calls during this altercation to inform Henry that Bruce has attempted to rape her. Henry's retribution is swift as he drives to Bruce's house, gets out of his car, and pistol whips him violently. Henry then marches back to Karen's house and hands her the bloody gun, asking her to hide it for him. In a voice-over, Karen explains that most women she knew would have ended a relationship once their boyfriend handed them a gun to hide. This is not the case with Karen, however, as she is turned on by the violence and perceived danger.

As the Harptones' "Life Is but a Dream" plays over the soundtrack, Henry and Karen are married in a traditional Jewish wedding ceremony at the home of Karen's parents. This simple ceremony is followed by a lavish catered wedding reception at the Chateau Bleu. In a dizzying scene, Karen is introduced to the members of Henry's other "family." A line of well-wishers presents Karen with envelopes filled with $100 bills as wedding gifts. The joy of the wedding day is soon contrasted with a scene in which Henry is confronted by his new mother-in-law, with whom they now live, for staying out all night without calling his wife.

Karen attends a party hosted by Jimmy's wife, Mickey (Julie Garfield). Here for the first time Karen begins to understand the differences between life as a gangster's wife and the life of normal married women. Karen observes that the wiseguys' wives all have bad skin, look beat-up, and dress in gaudy, cheap-looking ensembles. The other wives at the party talk about how bad their children are, and they share stories of beating them with broom handles. Karen soon assimilates into this world with ease and begins making excuses for the crimes and lifestyle of Henry and his friends. When Karen asks her husband about the chances of his going to prison, he shrugs this off, saying that the only people who go to prison are people who want to go to prison. As ridiculous as this explanation is, Karen accepts it. Karen as narrator explains that she and Henry did everything with the other wiseguy families and that no outsiders were allowed. Here Scorsese employs a montage of photographs depicting birthday parties, christenings, and births featuring Henry, Tommy, Jimmy, and the wives.

As author Maria T. Miliora explains in *The Scorsese Psyche on Screen*, the religious themes that frequently present themselves in Scorsese's work are once again on display here. "Thematically, this film shows that gangsterism creates its own church, so to speak," Miloria writes. "Its members adhere to a common belief system, spend much of their time together, and feel that they are special—better than other people—because of their membership in this elite society. This group of insiders, moreover, feels contempt for and is suspicious about those outside their group."[30]

As the Crystals perform "He's Sure the Boy I Love" over the soundtrack, a title card tells us that it's now "June 11, 1970, Queens,

New York." Inside the Suite Lounge, a celebration is being held for mobster Billy Batts (Frank Vincent), who has just returned from a six-year stint in prison. During the party, Batts offends Tommy by asking him to shine his shoes. Henry diffuses the situation, and Tommy leaves. As Donovan's "Atlantis" plays, the party disperses at the end of the night. Tommy returns, and he, Henry, and Jimmy brutally stomp and beat Batts until he is unconscious. Believing Batts is dead, they wrap him in tablecloths and transport him somewhere upstate to bury him. Before embarking on this road trip, they stop at Tommy's mother's (Catherine Scorsese) house to borrow a shovel and a knife. Tommy's mother wakes up and serves them a full pasta dinner in the middle of the night. Tommy explains the blood on his shirt by saying that he hit a deer with the car. He then tells her that he needs to borrow a butcher's knife to cut the deer's hoof from the grill of the automobile.

Once the three men are back on the road, the opening scene in which Batts is violently stabbed and shot is repeated. They bury the body in the middle of the woods, and Henry as narrator explains the trouble they are now in. While murder has reluctantly become an accepted part of Mafia life, Tommy violated a sacred law by murdering Batts, a "made" man from another crew who is deemed untouchable. Henry explains that this breach of acceptable Mafia conduct could get all three men killed if anyone found out.

Narrator Henry explains that in the gangsters' world, Friday nights at the Copacabana are reserved for the men's mistresses. Henry is now cheating on Karen with a woman named Janice Rossi (Gina Mastrogiacomo). Meanwhile, the search is on for Billy Batts. Paulie questions Henry about Batts, but Henry maintains that he knows nothing. As the Shangri-Las perform "Remember (Walkin' in the Sand)" over the soundtrack, Jimmy explains to Henry that Batts' burial location has now become a problem as the land has been sold to a condominium developer. As a result, the three men must return to the woods to unearth Batts' decaying remains.

Henry rents his mistress, Janice, an apartment around the corner from the Suite Lounge. This arrangement enables Henry to spend the night with her "a couple nights a week." As a result of her affair with Henry, Janice begins screwing up at her job as a bridal shop employee, and Henry has to "straighten out" her boss. We see Henry, Jimmy, and Tommy beating her boss, telling him that she "can do whatever she wants."

During a card game in the basement of the Suite, the wiseguys are being served drinks by Spider (Michael Imperioli). Pretending that he's Humphrey Bogart in *The Oklahoma Kid*, Tommy shoots at Spider's feet, telling him to dance. In doing so, Tommy accidentally shoots Spider in the foot. Later, Karen becomes angry with Henry because he hasn't been home in two weeks. She accuses Henry of cheating on her. She throws his car keys out the window in an attempt to stop him from going out, but it's to no avail. In a second card game in the basement of the Suite, Spider disrespects Tommy in the face of belligerent insults. The hair-triggered Tommy becomes angry and shoots and kills Spider. An angry Karen learns where her husband's mistress is staying and goes to her apartment building, accompanied by her small children. Karen calls the superintendent via the apartment building's intercom and informs him that there is "a whore living in 2-R." Karen then threatens Janice, telling her to find a man of her own. In the next scene, Karen straddles her sleeping husband and shoves a .38 in his face. Upon waking up, Henry lulls her into a false sense of security and then knocks the gun away. Henry becomes enraged and turns the gun on her. He screams at her, and then leaves to move in with Janice. Paulie and Jimmy soon arrive at the apartment, advising Henry to return to his family so she won't go to the Feds and testify against him.

A superimposed title card announces that it's now "Tampa, Florida, Two Days Later." Henry and Jimmy are arrested for beating a bookie and threatening to feed him to hungry lions. As a result, the two men are convicted and sent to prison in Lewisburg for ten years. Bobby Darin's "Beyond the Sea" plays over the soundtrack, and we see that the mobsters—including Paulie, who's serving a year for contempt—are given special privileges. The guards treat the wiseguys with respect, and they live in luxurious conditions, drinking Scotch and wine over large steak and pasta dinners.

Henry soon resorts to selling drugs in prison—an activity that Paulie does not condone. Karen smuggles in contraband such as salami, booze, and drugs but becomes angry when she sees Janice's name in the visitors register. She complains to Henry that she is cut off and that no one will help her. Because of this, Henry must traffic more drugs to support his family. Henry is ultimately released after serving four years.

Tony Bennett croons "The Boulevard of Broken Dreams" as the Hills' previous life resumes once again at a dinner party hosted by

Paulie. Paulie then takes Henry aside and sternly advises him against the continued trafficking of drugs. Paulie's warnings fall on deaf ears, however, and Henry continues to deal drugs. Henry begins cutting the cocaine at the home of a second mistress, Sandy (Debi Mazar). This operation soon becomes so big that Henry needs help, so he includes Jimmy and Tommy. The rewards of this new venture are apparent when Karen shows off her lavishly (and tastelessly) decorated home to Morrie and his wife Belle (Margo Winkler).

Jimmy begins masterminding a new airport cargo heist that has been suggested by Morrie. The heist is pulled without a hitch, and the $5 million score ends up being the largest in history. A rogue's gallery of wiseguys are in on the score: Frenchy, Joe Buddha (Clem Caserta), Frankie Carbone, Johnny Roast Beef (John Williams), and driver Stacks Edwards (Samuel L. Jackson).

Meanwhile, Henry's drug trafficking operation has grown so large that he even has the family baby-sitter, Lois Byrd (Welker White), working for him as a courier smuggling cocaine from Pittsburgh. Henry cuts and prepares the cocaine at Sandy's house while Sandy, now a full-fledged junkie, gets high.

As the Ronettes sing "Frosty the Snow Man," Jimmy and the wiseguys celebrate at a Christmas party at Robert's Lounge. Jimmy has instructed everyone to act normal so as not to bring any unwanted attention their way, but Johnny Roast Beef shows up with a new Cadillac convertible and Frankie Carbone shows off his wife's brand new high-priced mink coat. Making matters worse, Morrie is continuously bothering Jimmy about his share of the heist money. When it is learned that Stacks Edwards failed to properly dispose of the getaway truck, Tommy is dispatched to murder him. The scene in which Tommy murders Stacks is then replayed in slow motion from a different angle, highlighting Tommy's dispassionate attitude toward the murder.

Jimmy and Tommy inform Henry that Tommy is about to undergo the ceremony to become a made man. He will then be a full-fledged untouchable member of the Mafia. Since Jimmy and Henry aren't full-blooded Italians, they cannot become made men. But by having Tommy—one of their own—made, their interests will be looked after, effectively making them "made" by proxy.

Morrie continues to complain about not receiving his share of the heist money, eventually leading to his being murdered by Tommy with an ice pick. As the piano bridge of Derek and the Dominoes' "Layla" plays over the soundtrack, Jimmy's accomplices in the heist begin to turn up dead. In a memorable montage, Johnny Roast Beef and his wife are discovered dead in their car by small children, the corpses of Frenchy and Joe Buddha are shown in a garbage truck, and Frankie Carbone's body is found hanging from a meat hook inside a refrigerated trailer.

On the day of Tommy's ceremony to make him a made man, Henry tells us that Jimmy is overjoyed. A well-dressed Tommy is led into a dark room to undergo the ceremony. Seeing no one inside the room, Tommy begins to realize that something is amiss just as he is shot in the head in retaliation for the Billy Batts murder. "It was real greaseball shit," Henry says. "They even shot Tommy in the face so his mother couldn't give him an open coffin at the funeral."

A black-and-white title card informs us that it's now "Sunday, May 11th, 1980, 6:55 A.M." As Harry Nilsson's "Jump into the Fire" plays, we see a very different Henry snorting cocaine. The strung-out Henry looks horrible; his eyes are red, he is jittery, and he is paranoid. He attempts to deliver gun silencers to Jimmy, but Jimmy tells him they are the wrong size and refuses to take them. The songs on the soundtrack shift from "Memo from Turner" by the Rolling Stones to "Magic Bus" by the Who as Henry encounters a variety of obstacles such as a traffic jam and a worrisome doctor who thinks he's sick. Throughout this intense sequence, the paranoid Henry looks over his shoulder, convinced that helicopters are following him. At home, Henry assists with the preparation of dinner while instructing baby-sitter-turned-smuggler Lois before a drug pick-up. The songs continue to change rapidly, from "Monkey Man" by the Rolling Stones to George Harrison's "What Is Life," as the sequence becomes more and more frantic with Henry stashing guns, making phone calls, hiding out, arguing with his mistress, and making drug transactions. Henry is obsessed that his telephone is tapped and is convinced that a helicopter is shadowing his every movement throughout the day. Moving cameras and rapid cutting effectively induce feelings of agitation in the viewer during these scenes.

Henry soon finds the gun of a narcotics agent to his head. "For a second, I thought I was dead," Henry the narrator explains. "But when I heard all the noise I knew they were cops. Only cops talk that way. If they had been wiseguys, I wouldn't have heard a thing. I would've been dead." As narcotics officers bang on the front door of the house, Karen flushes $60,000 worth of heroin down the toilet. She then attempts to hide a pistol in her panties.

A black-and-white title card reads, "The Aftermath." Henry is interrogated by FBI agents, and he learns that his paranoia was well founded; his phone was tapped and helicopters were in fact following him. Sandy, Lois, and Henry's connections in Pittsburgh are also arrested. Henry as narrator explains that his primary concern is to straighten things out with Paulie, who will be worried that he might "rat them out." When Karen's mother puts her house on the line, Henry is released on bail. Henry seeks to square things not only with Paulie, but also with Jimmy, who, as his partner, must also fear reprisal.

When Henry goes to see Paulie, he is given the kiss-off; Paulie hands him a wad of cash ($3,200) and tells Henry he must now turn his back on him. Karen visits Jimmy at his pinball machine warehouse, and he gives her some money to help them out. In a tense scene, it is insinuated that Jimmy tries to have her whacked (although we are never told if this is a legitimate threat or simply Karen's paranoid delusions). By this time, Henry's paranoia has increased, as well. "If you're part of a crew, nobody ever tells you that they're going to kill you," Henry tells us. "It doesn't happen that way. There weren't any arguments or curses like in the movies. So your murderers come with smiles. They come as your friends, the people who have cared for you all your life, and they always seem to come at a time when you're at your weakest and most in need of their help." Henry meets Jimmy one last time, just to be sure of his intentions. The two meet in a crowded diner where Jimmy cannot have him killed. Henry finds his old friend agitated and distracted. Here Scorsese brilliantly employs a zoom shot—the same technique used by Alfred Hitchcock in Vertigo—to convey Henry's sense of the world closing in around him. Remembering that Jimmy previously had all of his Lufthansa heist partners murdered to keep from being imprisoned, Henry feels distrust for his old friend and partner. Jimmy asks Henry to travel to Florida to perform a hit, and the screen freezes on Jimmy's face for seven seconds. "That's when I knew I would never have come back from Florida alive," Henry tells us. A second freeze frame is then employed, holding on Henry's knowing face for five seconds. A second zoom shot is also used here to conclude the scene, this time pulling slowly away from the table. This signifies Henry's departure from the wiseguy world he has been part of for three decades.

Henry and Karen talk to FBI agent Edward McDonald (himself) about entering the witness protection program. Henry insists that he be relocated somewhere warm, and he and Karen are told that they can never see their families again. This conversation is crosscut with scenes of Paulie and Jimmy being arrested. The FBI agent again reminds Henry and Karen that they will be killed by their former associates if they don't play by the FBI's rules. In the courtroom, Henry fingers Paulie, Jimmy, and the rest of his cohorts.

At the end of the film, Henry shows no remorse for betraying his former friends but bemoans his lengthy prison sentence in suburbia. As punk rocker Sid Vicious sings his version of "My Way" over the soundtrack, Henry imagines Tommy at his door in a medium close-up. Reminiscent of Edwin S. Porter's classic *The Great Train Robbery*, Tommy fires a gun at the screen six times at point-blank range.

The film ends with a black-and-white postscript informing us that Henry remains in the witness protection program, where he has run afoul of the law once more for narcotics. The postscript also informs us that Henry and Karen finally separated in 1989 after twenty-five years of marriage. Paulie died in prison in 1988 at the age of seventy-three, and Jimmy is serving twenty years to life in a federal prison and will not be eligible for parole until he's seventy-eight.

Notes

1. Altobello, Stephen, *Getting Made: The Making of "GoodFellas,"* documentary (Warner Bros., 2004).

2. Denby, David, "Time on the Cross," *New York*, August 29, 1988, 50.

3. Thompson, David, and Christie, Ian, eds., *Scorsese on Scorsese* (Boston: Faber and Faber, 1989), 153.

4. Bishop, Kathy, "Ray Liotta," *Rolling Stone*, November 1, 1990, 62.

5. Kelly, Mary Pat, *Martin Scorsese: A Journey* (New York: Thunder's Mouth Press, 1991), 269.

6. Bracco, Lorraine, *On the Couch* (New York: Berkley Books, 2006), 113.

7. Altobello, *Getting Made*.

8. Bracco, *On the Couch*, 114.

9. Altobello, *Getting Made*.

10. Keyser, Les, *Martin Scorsese* (New York: Twayne Publishers, 1992), 202.

11. Kelly, *Martin Scorsese*, 263.

12. Emery, Robert J., *The Directors: Martin Scorsese*, documentary (AFI, 2000).

13. Woods, Paul A., ed., *Scorsese: A Journey through the American Psyche* (London: Plexus Publishing, 2005), 190.

14. Bracco, *On the Couch*, 114.

15. Dougan, Andy, *Martin Scorsese: Close Up* (New York: Thunder's Mouth Press, 1998), 93.

16. Altobello, *Getting Made*.

17. Altobello, *Getting Made*.

18. DiLeo, Frank, interview by the author, October 1, 2009.

19. DiLeo, interview.

20. Altobello, *Getting Made*.

21. Schickel, Richard, *Scorsese on Scorsese*, documentary (TCM, 2004).

22. Dougan, *Martin Scorsese*, 94.

23. Bracco, *On the Couch*, 118.

24. Barry McIlheney is quoted in Brode, Douglas, *The Films of Robert De Niro* (Secaucus, NJ: Citadel Press, 1996), 217.

25. Ebert, Roger, *Scorsese by Ebert* (Chicago: University of Chicago Press, 2008), 120.

26. Pauline Kael is quoted in Brode, *The Films of Robert De Niro*, 217.

27. Woods, *Scorsese*, 190.

28. Sangster, Jim, *Scorsese* (London: Virgin Books, 2002), 200.

29. LoBrutto, Vincent, *Martin Scorsese: A Biography* (Westport, CT: Praeger Publishers, 2008), 300.

30. Miliora, Maria T., *The Scorsese Psyche on Screen* (Jefferson, NC: McFarland, 2004), 106.

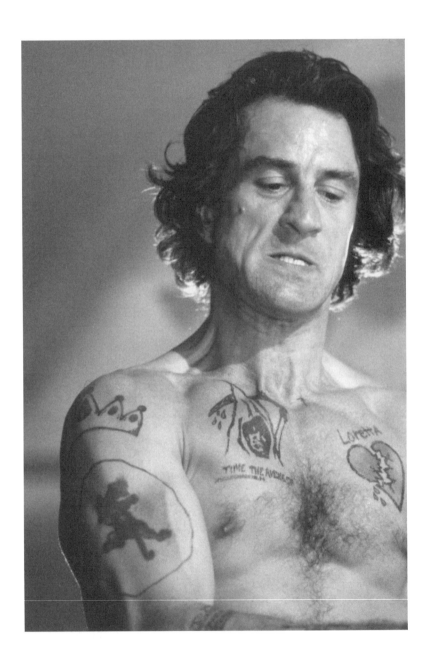

CHAPTER SEVEN

Cape Fear (1991)

Max was never gonna stop. He's just not gonna stop. He's gonna go and go and keep coming and keep coming after them. And that's frightening. It just takes one person to do that in your life, and your entire life is undone. That was what was interesting to us.

—Martin Scorsese

The Backstory

In the late 1980s, filmmaker Steven Spielberg was circling a remake of the 1962 J. Lee Thompson thriller *Cape Fear*. For a time, he'd considered producing a Stephen Frears–helmed version of the film based on a screenplay by mystery novelist Donald Westlake. Once this incarnation of *Cape Fear* unraveled and both Frears and Westlake had left the project, Spielberg approached a young screenwriter named Wesley Strick about taking a pass at the material. Spielberg, who'd been impressed by Strick's writing on Frank Marshall's *Arachnophobia*, sent the writer a copy of the original film. Strick saw the film as a failed attempt at imitating Alfred Hitchcock and hated it. Spielberg then met with Strick, who provided him with a laundry list of reasons why he felt *Cape Fear* didn't work. Apparently seeing Strick's abhorrence of the original film as the catalyst for a very different remake, Spielberg decided he was the perfect writer for the job.

Producer Spielberg then began the search for a director. After considering many filmmakers, Spielberg turned his gaze toward Martin Scorsese, who had just bowed out of directing *Schindler's List*. (Scorsese and Spielberg would ultimately, in essence, trade projects.) Scorsese, however, had little interest in making the picture. By this time, Scorsese's frequent collaborator Robert De Niro had become attached to the project to play the villain Max Cady. "Bob De Niro and Spielberg asked me to read the script while I was finishing up *GoodFellas*," Scorsese explains. "And by the end of editing the film, I had read *Cape Fear* three times. And three times I hated it. I mean really hated it."[1] While Scorsese had been a fan of the original film, he found Strick's screenplay, which had been written to fit Spielberg's directorial sensibilities, too black and white. Happy familial scenes, such as one featuring the Bowdens sitting around a piano singing together, were unthinkable for Scorsese. "I thought the family was too clichéd, too happy," Scorsese recalls. "And then along comes the boogeyman to scare them. They were like Martians to me. I was rooting for Max to get them."[2] In an effort to convince Scorsese to direct the film, Spielberg staged a read-through of the screenplay for him in New York. In this read-through, De Niro read the role of Max Cady, Kevin Kline read the part of Sam Bowden, and Kline's wife, Phoebe Cates, read as Bowden's daughter.

As he had done previously with *Raging Bull* and *The King of Comedy*, De Niro began to pressure Scorsese, telling him that together they could make something unique. To some extent this appealed to Scorsese. "If he's excited by a project, or if he's excited by a character, I should say, and if I can understand that character . . . if I can see in the character something of what he sees, or if I can see my own way, and my way blends with his, it promises to be something kind of special," Scorsese observes.[3]

Finally, after Spielberg gave him the green light to rewrite the screenplay as he saw fit (as long as it retained a happy ending), Scorsese agreed to make the film. By once again incorporating elements of his religious beliefs into the screenplay—Scorsese saw Cady as a sort of punishment for Sam Bowden's infidelity—he saw how he could make something personal out of a big-budget mainstream genre film such as this. (Budgeted at $34 million, *Cape Fear* would be Scorsese's largest film to date.) Scorsese also saw his involvement with the project as a sort of apology to Universal for the backlash they'd endured with his controversial 1988 film *The Last Temptation of Christ*.

Both Scorsese and De Niro agreed that they wanted their version of *Cape Fear* to be a conscious homage to Hitchcock. De Niro explains, "We spent a lot less time reconsidering the *Cape Fear* film from 1962 than we did watching many of the old Hitchcock classics, which were truly our inspiration here."[4] Blatant nods to Hitchcock include a scene in which fireworks fill the nighttime sky (like in *To Catch a Thief*) and a parade scene in which the rest of the crowd's attention is turned toward the festivities while Bowden's attention remains fixed on Cady (similar to the tennis scene in *Strangers on a Train*). As a further nod, Scorsese kept the original film's score by frequent Hitchcock collaborator Bernard Herrmann, having it reworked by Elmer Bernstein. Scorsese also hired production designer Harry Bumstead, who had worked with Hitchcock on films such as *Vertigo* and *Topaz*.

Scorsese and De Niro then met with Wesley Strick to discuss the long list of changes they wanted made in his forthcoming drafts. In what Strick calls a four-hour "marathon meeting," the three men pored over each and every page of the script. Most of the changes they wanted involved elements that had been written specifically for Spielberg. Strick explains that he had "consciously styled it a bit for Steven Spielberg's sensibilities. There were a lot more 'movie movie' moments, and some cute touches of Americana. It was a bit antiseptic."[5] Strick recalls, "Marty continually would say, 'Steven does that beautifully. I don't do that. I work on a much smaller canvas.'"[6] In Scorsese's version of *Cape Fear*, the lawyer Sam Bowden would be a philanderer with questionable professional ethics and poor parenting skills rather than the clear-cut good guy he had been in the original film. And Scorsese's Cady—still very much an evil character—would be legitimately wronged by Bowden, thus giving him a very real motive for vengeance. Scorsese and Strick also created a palpable sexual tension between Bowden's wife and Cady, as well as an underlying sexual threat to Bowden's daughter that was obviously absent in the original film. It was important to Scorsese that the three family members be interesting characters rather than stereotypes. Scorsese also liked the idea that his family would have inner conflicts and tensions that were present before Cady's arrival, giving the villain something to work with and the ability to attack them from within the familial unit.

Scorsese envisioned his version of *Cape Fear* to have the atmosphere of a traditional horror film. To help him accomplish this, he hired Oscar-winning cinematographer Freddie Francis, who was also an accomplished horror film director. "The main thing was Freddie's understanding of the concept of the Gothic atmosphere," Scorsese explains. "He knows the atmosphere that I want for this picture. He knows the lighting—whatever it takes to get that incredible Gothic thriller look. He understands the obligatory scene of a young maiden with a candle walking down a long hall towards a door. 'Don't go in that door!' you yell, and she goes in! *Every time* she goes in! So I say to him, 'This has to look like The Hall,' and he understands that."[7] Francis also brought some ideas of his own to the table regarding the atmosphere of the film. "One of the ideas I had for the film," Francis would later say, "was how normal people living in a normal house change, so that the atmosphere of the house changes with them—it degrades as the story goes along. The thing starts off bright and sunny and then slowly gets more downbeat, reaching the lowest depths when we get into the tank for the final sequence. From the beginning, the house was a very light and airy place, but always recognized was the fact that it was hemmed in, as if the trees at any time could close in on the house like a lot of Triffids."[8]

Scorsese then focused on casting. Robert Redford was his first consideration for the role of Sam Bowden, as Redford seemed to possess many of the traits the character had possessed in the original film. However, Scorsese's desire to make a much darker *Cape Fear* caused him to reconsider. As he was considering other options, Scorsese had a chance encounter with actor Nick Nolte at a Museum of Modern Art screening of *GoodFellas*. Nolte, who had been overweight and bearded when Scorsese had directed him in *New York Stories*, was now trim and clean shaven. This transformation so impressed Scorsese that he cast Nolte in the role of Sam Bowden. Scorsese then cast Jessica Lange, whom he'd previously auditioned for the role of Vickie La Motta in *Raging Bull*, as Bowden's wife. Lange wasn't familiar with the original film, but the material didn't matter to her. She just wanted to work with Scorsese and De Niro. "That was, for me, more important than the part or the story," Lange recalls.[9] De Niro then conducted the initial interviews for the role of Bowden's daughter Danielle alone in Beverly Hills. De Niro thought seventeen-year-old Juliette Lewis—the very first actress he met with—was perfect for the role. Believing that it was impossible that they had found their Danielle so quickly, Scorsese and De Niro held subsequent auditions for the role. Lewis was forced to audition four more times, but she was ultimately awarded the role. It was then decided that three of the primary actors from the 1962 film—Gregory Peck, Robert Mitchum, and Martin Balsam—would be cast in supporting roles as a respectful nod to J. Lee Thompson's original version.

During this period De Niro was already hard at work, once again transforming his body for the role. To achieve the grossly muscular physique he envisioned for the character Max Cady, De Niro began a strict workout regimen with trainer Dan Harvey. De Niro would lift weights each day for three hours before arriving on the set. To allow the actor time to bulk up as much as possible, Scorsese scheduled scenes depicting a shirtless De Niro late in the production. In an effort to find the essence of his character, De Niro spent hours listening to tapes of imprisoned rapists and killers from the South. De Niro and dialogue coach Sam Chwat also listened to the tapes in an effort to find Max Cady's accent and rhythm of speech. De Niro also spoke extensively with psychologists and behavioral experts. Through his research, De Niro found new things to incorporate into the screenplay. When he learned of a rapist having bitten the cheek of his victim, he convinced Scorsese and Strick to add this detail. And when De Niro learned of religious fanatics speaking "Glossolalia"—what is known as "speaking in tongues"—he became convinced that Cady should do this as he drowns at the end of the film.

The screenplay had initially described Cady as having a few tattoos, but in spending time with the convicted rapists and killers, De Niro decided that the character's body should be covered with them. Scorsese agreed. Artist Ilona Herman was then hired to create the designs based on input from De Niro and Scorsese. Most of these designs would be religious in nature. Make-up company Temptu Inc. was then enlisted to apply temporary tattoos to De Niro's body that would not be affected by water or fire. Because De Niro's body size changed so dramatically as a result of his workout regimen, the tattoos ultimately expanded, causing headaches for the make-up artists.

De Niro worked closely with Wesley Strick to define his character. This led to the incorporation of many biblical quotations. "Every scene of Bob's, he would call me and say, 'Can Max say something else here about vengeance, from the Bible?'" Strick recalls. "So I would dutifully go and look up vengeance in my concordance, and go through the 29 quotes about vengeance, and find the best one."[10]

Cape Fear offered a number of firsts for director Martin Scorsese. One such first was allowing his screenwriter on the set. This decision proved invaluable as Strick was on hand to incorporate suggestions made by the actors, such as the introduction of a new scene written at the behest of Jessica Lange, who believed that her character and Cady should meet at least once before the film's climax. Strick also added dialogue regarding Cady's copious tattoos, which the writer had not known about prior to seeing De Niro on set. Other firsts for the director included the use of optical effects and Cinemascope, which he'd previously avoided because he felt that 70mm did not lend itself well to the pan-and-scan transfer to television.

Location filming was done in Fort Lauderdale, Florida. Harry Bumstead had searched high and low for the Bowden house, ultimately finding the location just one month before shooting. The house was extremely rundown, but Bumstead could see the potential in the place. He then added shutters to its exterior and a wooden banister to the interior staircase in place of its original iron one. The fact that the house had a two-story living room also worked as an advantage in that it was very similar to a set (although it didn't offer the maneuvering room of an actual set). The house was surrounded by tropical plant life, but it didn't have the mossy look of North Carolina, so a greensman was hired to hang moss from the trees. As perfect as the house appeared to be, Scorsese soon discovered one significant prob-

lem with the location—the house was situated directly beneath the
flight pattern of a nearby airport. Because of this, crew members had
to be stationed at the airport to communicate take-offs around which
shooting had to be coordinated.

Now on their seventh collaboration, Scorsese and De Niro had
developed their shorthand to the point where they didn't even need
to speak to one another to communicate what they wanted do for a
scene. The discussions they did have were largely held prior to shooting
rather than in lengthy conferences in the far corners of the set. "There's
total trust between [De Niro] and Marty," Freddie Francis would later
observe. "If Marty says it's fine, then Bob just walks away. I think they
both realize how important they are to each other. In some ways, it's
very strange being on the set with the two of them because they're so
close. Obviously, they've discussed their ideas beforehand, so there's
very little discussion or rehearsing on set. There's just a few words between Marty and Bob, and then off we go."[11]

Actress Illeana Douglas, who had already worked with both Scorsese
and De Niro on *GoodFellas* and *Guilty by Suspicion*, was impressed by
the way the two worked together. "There was a real sense of collaboration between [Scorsese and De Niro]," Douglas recalls.

I think they just trust each other implicitly. There's almost a sort of psychic communication between the two of them. They don't say a lot of words, but they're both on the same page. They can just give each other a look, and then they immediately know and understand what the other one wants to do. One of the great things, which is missing on a lot of movies, is the sense that when the two of them are working together it's very special. It's very quiet on the set, and there's a sense of enthusiasm. And that's something I've rarely felt working on other films.[12]

A scene in which Cady interacts with the teenage Danielle was originally scripted much closer to the story line of the original film. The scene, which takes place at the girl's high school, originally ended with Cady chasing her until she is left hanging from a second story window. However, both Scorsese and De Niro believed the scene would be far more frightening if Cady attempted to seduce the young girl. "The idea was to make it more insidious, to try and seduce her in a way, get ahold of her and seduce her," De Niro explains. "That's a much more severe, to say the least, way of getting revenge on the father."[13] Scorsese envisioned something much darker than mere seduction; he believed the film could only be effective if Danielle lost all trust in her father during this scene due to Cady's manipulation. Strick then rewrote the scene based on improvisational sessions between De Niro and Lewis. Several drafts of the scene were ultimately written before Scorsese felt that Strick had succeeded in capturing "the complete undoing"[14] of Danielle.

Still convinced that both the scene and Lewis' reactions could be pushed even further, De Niro persuaded Scorsese to allow him to surprise the young actress during filming by suggestively sticking his thumb into her mouth. When it came time to film the scene, the unsuspecting Lewis, who has since admitted to having a crush on De Niro, giggled nervously and gave a realistic performance. She would later recall, "They didn't tell me they were going to do that. Marty and Bob—they're sick, they're sick together."[15] Although Scorsese shot several takes of De Niro pushing his thumb into Lewis' mouth, he ultimately decided to use the first one as her reaction felt the most genuine. The final result was a scene that was far more disturbing than the events that had transpired in the original film.

One question that had to be answered during the writing process was how exactly Cady would follow the family when they escape to Cape Fear. Strick's initial idea was that Cady would be hiding in the trunk of their automobile, but he then thought better of it. Strick and Scorsese didn't feel that Cady's hiding in the trunk was shocking enough. Drawing inspiration from a scene in *Alien* in which the creature is attached to the face of a human being, Strick sought to make Cady's attachment to the family a much more personal and intimate one. It was then that he conceived the idea that the villain hide beneath the automobile itself. Strick had no idea if this feat could actually be accomplished in real life, but he liked the idea of it. It would ultimately be De Niro who would question how realistic this act was; constantly searching for truth within his roles, De Niro refused to stow away beneath the automobile unless Scorsese and Strick could prove to him that this act was indeed possible. A brave stuntman agreed to participate in this experiment and allow himself to be strapped to the undercarriage of the Bowden family's Jeep Cherokee. The automobile was then driven around in circles as Scorsese and company watched nervously. In the end, the stuntman survived the drive and Robert De Niro was adequately convinced that Max Cady could in fact stow away beneath the Cherokee.

The filmmakers originally planned to film scenes involving the Bowdens' houseboat on an actual river, but production designer Bumstead vetoed this idea. Bumstead observed that the inlet where they wanted to film was filled with water for part of the day and virtually empty the rest. He convinced Scorsese that filming this way would take much more time than the director could afford to spend. Scorsese and company then had a seven-foot-deep 90-by-100-foot tank of water built on a soundstage in Fort Lauderdale. By doing this, Scorsese and company could control their environment in a way that they could never have done had they filmed on an actual river. A ramp was also built so the boat could be put in and taken out of the water. Elaborate matte paintings would then be used for exterior shots of the boat sailing down the river. Violent rains were then provided by crew members spraying water hoses onto the exterior of the boat.

For a scene in which a debilitated Nick Nolte observes Cady violating his wife, Scorsese had envisioned a shot of the actor's eyes peering in through the rain-covered window. But when it was time to film the shot, Scorsese found that something was missing. He wasn't sure what it was about the shot, but he didn't find it to be as effective as he had envisioned. At this point, cinematographer Freddie Francis suggested that Scorsese film just a single eye peering in through the window. This was a simple solution, but Scorsese discovered that Francis' instincts were correct. The single eye peering in from the darkness proved to be much more effective and, to Scorsese's liking, a more Hitchcockian device.

Another problematic scene in this portion of the film was the one in which Danielle lights Cady's face on fire. Scorsese initially attempted to film this sequence with a stunt double but was ultimately unhappy with the scene as it required a number of cutaways. Scorsese believed the scene would be far more effective if he could find a way to allow the camera to linger on the burning face of De Niro. A stuntman wearing a flame-retardant suit was instructed to imitate De Niro's actions against a green screen. The stuntman was then set on fire, and the flames were digitally grafted to footage of De Niro's face. The fire in these close-ups actually consists of dozens of shots of flames rather than a single one. Because of the flickering nature of fire, the naked eye cannot detect the numerous shots integrated together.

Cape Fear opened on November 13, 1991, quickly becoming Scorsese's biggest commercial hit. The film earned more than $79 million in the United States. Reviews were largely positive, but many focused on what some considered excessive violence. Most reviews—even the most positive—commented that this most commercial of fare seemed to obscure many of the aesthetics that made Scorsese the filmmaking force that he is. Roger Ebert of the *Chicago Sun-Times* raved that "*Cape Fear* is impressive moviemaking, showing Scorsese as a master of a traditional Hollywood genre who is able to mold it to his own themes and obsessions."[16] *Rolling Stone* critic Peter Travers observed, "Though Scorsese doesn't always transcend the pulp in *Cape Fear*, watching him try allows us to share the exhilaration he experiences behind the camera."[17] David Ansen of *Newsweek* wrote, "It gives you a pumped-up, thrill-happy ride (assuming you have the stomach for violent pulp), but it doesn't linger in the mind as Scorsese's richest movies do."[18]

While some critics were less than pleased by the over-the-top nature of De Niro's character, most were taken with his performance. *Variety's* Todd McCarthy wrote, "Quite distinct from Mitchum's more laconic villain, De Niro's Cady is a memorable nasty right up there with Travis Bickle and Jake La Motta. Cacklingly crazy at times, quietly purposeful and logical at others, Cady is a sickie utterly determined in his righteous cause, and De Niro plays him with tremendous relish and is extremely funny in several scenes."[19] David Ansen went on to say in the aforementioned review that "it is De Niro—his body covered with tattoos and the tackiest wardrobe in the New South—who dominates the film with his lip-smacking, blackly comic, and terrifying portrayal of psychopathic self-righteousness."[20]

Cape Fear was ultimately recognized by a number of industry awards ceremonies, from the Oscars to the MTV Movie Awards. The film received two Academy Award nominations for Best Actor (De Niro) and Best Supporting Actress (Lewis), but it ultimately lost in both categories. Cinematographer Freddie Francis and editor Thelma Schoonmaker were both nominated by the British Academy of Film and Television Arts, and again both nominees lost. Other nominations included a run at the prestigious Golden Bear at the Berlin International Film Festival, and Golden Globe nods for both De Niro and Lewis.

The Film

Utilizing unused footage from John Frankenheimer's film *Seconds*, Saul and Elaine Bass styled an opening credit sequence that features a number of objects reflected in a pool of water. These seemingly random objects include a swooping vulture, a fearful eye, a grimacing mouth, a man's face, a human body, and finally a single drop of blood, which colors the water red just as the credit "Directed by Martin Scorsese" appears. (Author Vincent LoBrutto theorizes in his book *Martin Scorsese: A Biography* that "Scorsese's biblical reference to the blood of Jesus speaks here to the impending violence and his Old Testament approach to the 1962 narrative."[21]) We then see a negative image of human eyes, which turn blue. The camera pulls back and we see that these eyes belong to fifteen-year-old Danielle Bowden (Juliette Lewis), who begins the film with an opening narrative.

The film then shifts to Max Cady's (Robert De Niro) cell at Statesborough Prison, where the heavily tattooed inmate is doing push-ups. The walls of his cell are covered with drawings and photographs depicting religious figures and famous military leaders. The cell is also lined with books such as *100 Days to an Impressive Vocabulary*, *Trial Handbook for Georgia Law*, and Dante's *The Inferno*. Cady finishes his exercises, straightens his hair, and is then led out of the cell for release. As Cady walks away from the prison with nothing but the clothes on his back, a symbolic storm approaches in the sky behind him.

Next we see the seemingly idyllic home of Sam and Leigh Bowden (Nick Nolte and Jessica Lange) in New Essex, North Carolina. When Sam, Leigh, and daughter Danielle go to the movies (to see *Problem Child*), a man sitting in front of them proves to be a nuisance by laughing harder than is appropriate and puffing a big cigar. The man is, of course, Max Cady. Frustrated, the Bowdens then go to an ice cream parlor where they discuss the "annoying loser" from the movie theater. When Sam attempts to pay for his family's ice cream, he is told that it has already been paid for by Cady, who is sitting outside in a red Mustang convertible. Sam leads his wife and daughter to a table, but when he turns back toward Cady, the man has vanished.

In the next scene, we see Sam playing racquetball with his secretary, Lori (Illeana Douglas). Sam touches her several times, and it is clear through his flirtatious actions and their dialogue that they are on the verge of an affair. After Lori drives away, Sam climbs into his car, where he is confronted by Cady. "Could it be that you don't remember me?" Cady asks. Cady then introduces himself and reminds Sam just who he is. Fourteen years earlier, Sam defended Cady in his trial for a vicious sexual assault; Sam lost the trial and Cady went to prison. Sam nervously attempts to kid around with Cady, who declares that he will learn about loss at the end of the conversation.

With fireworks filling the sky outside (reminiscent of *To Catch a Thief*), the Bowdens discuss Danielle's recent experimentation with marijuana before they go to bed. Sam and Leigh then engage in joyless sex, and Scorsese presents us with another negative image—this time a close-up of their interlocked hands and wedding rings. The color fades to yellow as a bored-looking Leigh opens her eyes as though she's thinking of something or someone else. The color then fades to red as she sits in front of the mirror and reapplies her makeup. Leigh peers outside through the shutters, seeing Cady sitting on the fence staring back at her. The frightened Leigh then wakes Sam, but Cady is gone when Sam goes looking for him. Sam then tells Leigh that he knows who the man was. Leigh questions her husband about Cady's motives for harassing him, but Sam is evasive and pretends not to know what Cady wants. The following morning the problems in Sam and Leigh's marriage make themselves known when Leigh comments that owning a gun might be a bad idea because the married couple would use it on each other.

In a discussion with his partner Tom Broadbent (Fred Thompson), Sam explains that he has filed for a restraining order against Cady. He then finally comes clean about why Cady might seek to harm him or his family: fourteen years before, Sam had sabotaged his client Cady's trial by burying evidence that might have freed him. Sam then explains that there's no way the illiterate Cady could have read the report. In the next scene, Cady stops Sam in the street. During this second conversation Cady reveals that he taught himself how to read while in prison and then acted as his own attorney, applying seven times for an appeal. Sam attempts to pay Cady off to leave him alone, but Cady has no interest in his money. Cady explains that he was raped in prison and that there can be no monetary compensation for what he's endured.

Sam goes back to work after his conversation with Cady, but his work is interrupted when Leigh telephones with an emergency—the Bowden's family dog, Benjamin, which was apparently locked inside the house, has been poisoned to death. Sam then goes to the police, where Lieutenant Elgart (Robert Mitchum) explains that he has many ways of "leaning on an undesirable," including a full-body cavity search. As Sam and Elgart watch Cady being searched from behind a one-way mirror, the two men are astounded by the number of tattoos on his body (most of which are comprised of Bible passages). Once he is informed that Sam has no proof that Cady killed the dog, Elgart says he cannot make a case against Cady stick.

The next scene finds the Bowdens attending the local Independence Day parade. The family's fun is soon interrupted, however, when Sam spots Cady staring at Leigh through mirrored sunglasses, which parallels Sam observing Cady through one-way mirrored glass in the previous scene. Despite the mirrored glass, each party in these scenes is well aware that the other is watching him. Sam confronts Cady, who entices him to punch him in front of a street filled with witnesses. Cady later puts the moves on Lori, Sam's secretary, and ultimately lures her into bed, where he savagely assaults her, even going so far as to take a bite out of her cheek. Back at his home, Sam has just discovered that a wire is missing from his piano when Elgart telephones, informing Sam of Lori's assault. Elgart tells Sam that someone identified Cady's license plate but that Lori won't testify. Elgart then says that the law can't help Sam, insinuating that maybe he should take the law into his own hands.

Sam goes to a private investigator named Claude Kersek (Joe Don Baker), hiring him to keep tabs on Cady. We then see Sam explaining to his family that he feels completely relaxed regarding the situation now that he's hired Kersek. This claim, however, proves to be exaggerated when a ringing telephone breaks the conversation, causing Sam to jump and nearly fall out of his chair. The caller is Kersek, who relays a story he's just heard in which Cady apparently murdered a fellow inmate in prison. The air of distrust in the Bowden household thickens when Leigh later overhears Sam talking on the telephone with Lori. Despite Sam's insistence that he has no intimate ties with Lori, Leigh figures everything out. Leigh becomes enraged and begins punching Sam. We then learn through her dialogue that Sam has a history of marital infidelity. As Sam and Leigh fight in the next room, Danielle watches a Jane's Addiction music video ("Been Caught Stealing") in her bedroom. She calls her friend Nadine to vent.

The following day Kersek is sitting in a diner, observing Cady and pretending to read a newspaper. Cady knows he's being followed, however, and orders breakfast for the private investigator. Kersek then confronts Cady, threatening him and demanding that he leave town. Cady is not intimidated and correctly labels the private investigator as a former cop who wasn't "good enough to remain on the force." Cady makes it clear that he will not be leaving town anytime soon.

As Leigh steps out to the mailbox to get her mail, Cady pulls up in his Mustang. He holds out Benjamin's collar and asks her if it belongs to her. Cady insinuates that he's been watching her, and Leigh figures out who he is. The two of them spar verbally, but there's a strange and unmistakable sexual tension present between them. Cady causes Leigh to briefly reconsider her stance on him when he suggests that Sam has betrayed each of them. "Who knows? We might have been different people. We might have been happy, Leigh." This brief moment of reconsideration is disrupted, however, when Danielle emerges from the house.

Kersek goes to visit Sam in the parking lot of his law firm. Kersek explains that things are going to become expensive rather quickly if he continues to tail Cady. He then suggests an alternate plan; just as Elgart insinuated, Kersek wants to take the law into his own hands. He wants to hire some thugs to beat up Cady with two pieces of pipe and a bicycle chain. This suggestion offends Sam, who reminds Kersek that he's a lawyer and cannot operate outside the boundaries of the law.

Later that evening, Danielle receives a telephone call from Cady, who pretends to be her new drama teacher. As Cady attempts to convince Danielle that he's a caring friend who understands her problems, we see him hanging upside down from a pull-up bar as he talks. The camera then does a 180-degree turn, making Cady appear to be upright. He then plays Aretha Franklin's "Do Right Woman, Do Right Man" for Danielle. Cady tells her that she can trust him because he's a "do right man." By the time the conversation is over, Danielle is smitten with her new teacher, sight unseen.

The following day, Danielle is lured down into the darkened basement of her high school, where she is to meet her new drama teacher. There she finds Cady sitting inside a *Hansel and Gretel*–like prop house, smoking a joint. Singing Tommy James and the Shondells' "I Think We're Alone Now," Cady offers Danielle a hit from the joint. Danielle attempts to connect with Cady, telling him that the things he told her on the telephone the previous night made sense. They then discuss the works of Henry Miller, which leads to a penis reference, changing the tone of the conversation from merely flirtatious to something darker and more seductive. Cady tries to attain Danielle's confidence by telling her what she wants to hear—that her parents' restrictions are stifling her growth into adulthood. Danielle misinterprets Cady's manipulative behavior as his treating her like an adult, which she clearly enjoys. Danielle then figures out Cady's true identity, but Cady plays on her naïveté and still manages to seduce her. He puts his arm around her and presses his finger into her mouth suggestively, coaxing her to suck on it. Cady then leans in and kisses Danielle passionately. He then turns and walks off the stage without saying a word. Danielle suddenly becomes self-conscious and is overcome with feelings of guilt. She turns and runs.

After learning that Danielle had some sort of run-in with Cady, Sam telephones Kersek and agrees to have Cady attacked by thugs. Kersek tells him that the cost will be $1,000 for three men. Sam agrees to this. Sam then foolishly seeks out Cady, finding him reading in a restaurant. Sam threatens him, telling him that if he doesn't leave his family alone, he will be "hurtin' like you never dreamed." Cady tells Sam that he has no intentions of moving and that he's going to teach Sam the meaning of commitment.

Sam goes home that night and attempts to bond with Danielle, but she insinuates that something sexual may have happened between her and Cady, causing Sam to become enraged. He grabs her face and screams at her, pushing her further away emotionally (and perhaps closer to Cady).

Later that night, Sam hides and watches as three men wielding a bat, a chain, and a pipe attack Cady. Much to Sam's dismay, Cady brutally beats the three attackers. Sam becomes afraid and starts to flee but accidentally kicks a can, drawing attention to himself. In the film's most iconic scene, Cady calls to Sam, "Come out, come out, wherever you are!" Cady walks toward the dumpster behind which Sam is hiding but ultimately gives up his search and walks away.

The following day, Sam telephones a powerful attorney named Lee Heller (Gregory Peck) about helping him to get an injunction against Cady. However, Heller says he must end the conversation as he is already representing Cady. In court it is revealed that Cady taped Sam's threats. The judge (Martin Balsam) informs Sam that the court does not condone "feuds, vendettas, or vigilantism" and grants the restraining order—to Cady. Heller then informs the court that he has petitioned to have Sam disbarred so that he may never again practice law in the state of North Carolina. "The law considers me more of a loose cannon than Max Cady!" Sam will later lament.

Sam goes to Kersek's office to ask him for a gun. Kersek talks him out of this, explaining the multitude of dangers in Sam's carrying a gun. During the conversation, Sam informs Kersek that an emergency hearing is being held in Raleigh to determine whether or not he will be disbarred. Realizing that Sam will be expected to be at the hearing, Kersek comes up with a new plan. Kersek informs Sam that it would be legal to kill Cady should he be caught breaking into Sam's home. Kersek's plan entails Leigh dropping Sam off at the airport, Sam sneaking back home from the airport, and an armed Kersek camping out in the Bowden home.

Things seem to go as planned. Cady watches the Bowdens drop Sam off at the airport as Kersek sets up camp inside the Bowden's house. Danielle finds a copy of Henry Miller's *Sexus*, which Cady has hidden for her on the porch of the house. Instead of telling her parents, she sneaks it into the house. As night falls on the house, the score becomes more ominous and all of the characters appear on edge. Scorsese once again utilizes a negative image here as Sam imagines Cady standing over his bed. Sam turns to Leigh and tells her that he has the feeling that Cady is already inside the house. Downstairs things go terribly wrong as Cady—disguised as the maid—strangles Kersek with the missing piano wire and then forces him to shoot himself in the head. After hearing the gunshot, the Bowdens discover the bodies of Kersek and the maid. Sam rushes outside and begins firing wildly in the hopes of hitting Cady, but Cady is nowhere in sight.

The Bowdens take to the road, hoping to escape Cady by traveling to their houseboat docked at Cape Fear. Unbeknownst to the Bowdens, however, Cady is traveling with them; he is strapped to the undercarriage of the family Jeep Cherokee. Once the family is onboard the houseboat, they maneuver it down the river as a storm is brewing in the sky overhead. After dark Sam anchors the boat for the night. As the family eats dinner, a squall rocks the boat. Sam steps outside in the rain to make sure that the anchor is holding firmly. Once outside, Sam is attacked by Cady, who chokes him until he loses consciousness.

Cady steps into the houseboat, surprising the two female Bowdens. "Good evening, ladies," he says. Leigh warns him that her husband has a gun, but Cady silences her by producing the gun he's taken away from Sam. Cady asks Danielle where her copy of *Sexus* is. She informs him that it's at home, but she's memorized some passages for him. Cady tells her that she knows him pretty well, but she's going to get to know him much better. Danielle angrily grabs a pot of boiling water from the stove and flings it onto Cady, but he is virtually unaffected. He then demonstrates his toughness by lighting a flare, allowing it to melt in his hand. He explains that his "granddaddy" handled snakes in church and that his "granny" drank strychnine. "I guess you could say I had a leg up, genetically speaking," he concludes. Cady tells Danielle that he will forgive her for attempting to hurt him. He then orders her to climb into the hold. Once Danielle is locked away in the hold, Cady approaches Leigh, clearly planning to rape her. He asks her if she is ready to be born again. Danielle peers out from the hold, watching as Cady forces himself on her mother. We now see a subdued Sam watching his wife being raped through the window. In the hold, Danielle has discovered weapons: a cigarette lighter and kerosene.

Cady catches Leigh trying to grab the pistol from his waistline. This angers him. He then handcuffs her to a railing and drags the tied-up Sam inside the houseboat so that he can watch him rape Leigh and Danielle. Cady says that he wants to witness "a mama's true love of her daughter, if you know what I mean." He unlocks the hold and lets Danielle out, throwing her onto the table. Sam begins to plead with Cady to leave his family alone. This angers Cady, who begins kicking Sam in the face. Teary-eyed, Leigh attempts to seduce Cady and convince him that the two of them should have sex without Danielle. She attempts to reason with Cady, telling him that because of Sam they both know what it is to live a life of deprivation and that they both know about losing years. Because of this, she says, they have a sort of spiritual connection. Cady dismisses Leigh's attempts to seduce him and lights a cigar. When he does, Danielle sprays the kerosene onto the lit cigar, catching Cady's face on fire. He begins to scream and runs outside, jumping into the river.

As the storm tosses the houseboat around like a toy, Cady once again emerges from the river, pulling a gun on Sam and holding it to his head. Cady's face is now badly burned and looks quite gruesome. He beats Sam, forcing him to admit that he wronged him fourteen years earlier by burying evidence that could have set him free. Cady then begins ranting that he's going to sentence Sam to the Ninth Circle of Hell and make him learn about true loss. He turns and holds the gun on Danielle and Leigh, demanding that they remove all of their clothes and get down on their knees. Cady tells them that tonight they will learn to live and die like animals. The violent storm throws the boat around and all of the people inside are thrown to the floor. Cady is momentarily winded, and both Danielle and Leigh jump from the houseboat. Just as Sam is about to jump, he is grabbed by Cady. The two of them begin wrestling on the floor. As they wrestle, they are once again thrown around inside the houseboat by the storm. Cady rises to his feet, the gun once again in his hand. Sam manages to handcuff Cady's leg to a railing. Cady becomes angry and begins firing the pistol wildly, but does not hit Sam. The houseboat runs up on large jagged rocks and is completely destroyed. Sam jumps into the water and washes up on shore. He opens his eyes and sees Cady still attached to a sinking piece of the ship. He moves toward Cady and strikes him in the head with a large rock. A bloody and crazed Cady taunts, "Forget about that restraining order, counselor? You're well within 500 yards!" Sam then strikes him with the rock again, but Cady just cackles maniacally. Cady then returns the favor by striking Sam in the head with a rock. Sam moves toward Cady, attempting to smash his head with a giant rock that will surely kill him, but just as he goes to strike him with it, the current pulls Cady down the river. As the tiny piece of the houseboat that Cady is attached to starts to pull him underwater, Cady begins to speak in tongues. He then starts to sing "Bound for the Promised Land" as he is pulled underwater. For a brief moment, Cady's eyes stay just above the water, staring at Sam, until finally he sinks to the bottom of the river. In a scene reminiscent of *Macbeth*, Sam stares at his bloody hands, which were responsible for Cady's death. As he attempts to clean them in the river, a splash jars him, and he momentarily believes that Cady has once again returned.

In the wake of Cady's death the battered Bowdens are reunited on the shore. In a voice-over Danielle explains that none of them would ever speak of Cady again. Similar to the end of *Mean Streets*, the Bowdens remain alive to continue the unhappy lives they had known prior to Cady's arrival. As Scorsese has said, sometimes living is the hard part.

Notes

1. Biskind, Peter, "Slouching toward Hollywood," *Premiere*, November 1991, 73.

2. Biskind, "Slouching toward Hollywood," 73.

3. Bouzereau, Laurent, *The Making of "Cape Fear,"* documentary (Universal Pictures, 2001).

4. Baxter, John, *De Niro: A Biography* (New York: HarperCollins, 2002), 309.

5. Baxter, *De Niro*, 307.

6. Bouzereau, *The Making of "Cape Fear."*

7. Morgan, David, "A Remake That Can't Miss: *Cape Fear*," *American Cinematographer*, October 1991, 34.

8. Morgan, "A Remake That Can't Miss," 35.

9. Bouzereau, *The Making of "Cape Fear."*

10. Kelly, Mary Pat, *Martin Scorsese: A Journey* (New York: Thunder's Mouth Press, 1991), 288.

11. Sangster, Jim, *Scorsese* (London: Virgin Books, 2002), 222.

12. Douglas, Illeana, interview by the author, October 16, 2009.

13. Bouzereau, *The Making of "Cape Fear."*

14. Bouzereau, *The Making of "Cape Fear."*

15. Smith, Chris, "Fair Juliette," *New York*, November 25, 1991, 32.

16. Ebert, Roger, *Scorsese by Ebert* (Chicago: University of Chicago Press, 2008), 129.

17. Travers, Peter, "*Cape Fear*," *Rolling Stone*, November 28, 1991, 138.

18. David Ansen is quoted in Brode, Douglas, *The Films of Robert De Niro* (Secaucus, NJ: Citadel Press, 1996), 234.

19. Todd McCarthy is quoted in Brode, *The Films of Robert De Niro*, 234.

20. Ansen is quoted in Brode, *The Films of Robert De Niro*, 234.

21. LoBrutto, Vincent, *Martin Scorsese: A Biography* (Westport, CT: Praeger Publishers, 2008), 308.

CHAPTER EIGHT

Casino (1995)

This story has to be on a big canvas. There's no sense in my getting Bob De Niro and Joe Pesci and making a 90-minute picture about only one aspect of one story out of Vegas for the past 40 years. It has to be set in the context of time and place, it has to be about America. Otherwise, why make another mob story? I couldn't care less.

—Martin Scorsese

The Backstory

After finishing the screenplay for *GoodFellas*, Nicholas Pileggi turned his sights toward Las Vegas. This idea had come from a 1980 *Las Vegas Sun* article about a domestic dispute between a key casino figure and his wife on the couple's front lawn. The couple was Frank "Lefty" Rosenthal, a central figure in the management of the Stardust casino, and his wife, a former showgirl named Geri McGee. This story piqued Pileggi's interest, and the author soon learned that Rosenthal had risen from an unknown Midwest gambler to the unofficial manager of the Stardust in just over a decade. Rosenthal and a heavy named Tony Spilotro had been sent to Vegas by the Mafia to protect their interests in the casino. Rosenthal and the psychopathic Spilotro, ultimately charged with some thirty-five murders, had a falling out that eventually led to Rosenthal nearly being killed by a car bomb.

Pileggi took this idea to his friend Martin Scorsese, who showed immediate interest in the project. Scorsese had long wanted to make a Western film like those of his filmmaking heroes Howard Hawks and John Ford, and with *Casino* he felt he could make a sort of contemporary Western. Scorsese also liked the idea of revisiting the gangster genre he had explored in *GoodFellas*, but doing something more expansive; whereas *GoodFellas* had been the story of a single crew, *Casino* would be a film about organized crime on a national level. Pileggi suggested that the story be written first as a book and then adapted into a film second. Scorsese convinced him that they should write the screenplay and the book simultaneously.

Scorsese then talked to his frequent collaborator Robert De Niro about appearing in the film as the Rosenthal character (renamed Ace Rothstein in the film). De Niro jumped at the chance to collaborate with Scorsese again. "I'm very fortunate," De Niro explains. "I speak to other actors who say, 'I wish I had somebody I could work with all the time, could always rely on and go back to. . . .' It's considered that your work is special and I like that. I know that if he says it, it's going to be what he says. I also support him as a director. I'll do whatever he wants, [the same] way he would do whatever I want, even if he feels it's not right."[1] Working with Scorsese wasn't the only reason De Niro agreed to make the film; after playing a long series of showy, emotional roles, the actor was attracted to the idea of this repressed character whose sense of control was the very thing that defined him.

By the time De Niro agreed to appear in *Casino*, Pileggi had already been conducting interviews and researching the story. Many of the central figures in the story—including Rosenthal himself—were at first reluctant to cooperate with the author. Then news of the impending film got out and things changed. One day Pileggi received an unexpected telephone call from Rosenthal, quizzing him about the film, about Scorsese, and about Robert De Niro. Rosenthal, now very much interested in the idea of his story being told, informed Pileggi that he believed De Niro was the greatest actor of his generation. Rosenthal asked if he could meet De Niro, and Pileggi said yes. The author then contacted Scorsese, who in turn contacted De Niro, and soon the actor was onboard a plane, flying to Miami to meet with Rosenthal. Pileggi soon found many other doors being opened for him as a result of the film. Potential interview subjects who had previously hung up on him or slammed doors in his face began calling and asking to meet various principals from the film ranging from Scorsese to Sharon Stone.

Pileggi and Scorsese met frequently over the course of the five years it took for the author to complete his research. As Pileggi tinkered with the script, he noticed that Scorsese was "writing the music, he's writing the shots, the visuals, the tone. He was writing a movie as I was writing a script. . . . He would have notations for music on cards, he would draw pictures on cards of scenes. He was seeing the movie in its totality in his head."[2] Because the book for *Casino* was being written at the same time as the screenplay, the project presented different challenges than *GoodFellas* had. Without knowing all of what would eventually appear in the book, Scorsese could not know what the structure of his film would be. Scorsese's views of the film's themes and structure continued to change even after the cameras had begun rolling. As the script evolved as Scorsese worked, he confided to close friends that there would never be a true final draft of *Casino*.

Because *Casino* was based on a true story, its ever-evolving screenplay had to be constantly approved by Universal's legal department before even the tiniest of changes could be implemented. This led to numerous skirmishes with lawyers who knew little about what Scorsese was trying to accomplish with the project. The lawyers ultimately requested more than forty changes to the screenplay. "The lawyers are actually sending me script changes!" Scorsese would later write in *Premiere*. "They're saying, 'Maybe the scene could read like this,' and they're combining the dialogue of different characters and cutting people out. They're giving me 'guidelines' that I feel endanger the entire project. I won't go along with it. They'll cut away the guts of the movie. The fine interweaving we did of all the threads, the relationships of the different characters. If we start undoing the threads carelessly, we'll undo the entire structure of the movie!"[3]

Interestingly, one of the lawyers' biggest concerns was a monologue in which Nicky (the Spilotro character) explains that a man had an ice pick jammed into his testicles but still didn't tell them what they wanted to know. The lawyers, convinced that any man would give up the goods after such excruciating torture, commented condescendingly, "Gee, Pileggi, I thought you knew this."[4] Another suggestion was that ten seconds was too long for a character to be subjected to the business end of a cattle prod. "Where are you from, Nick?" the lawyers' notes quipped. "New York?"[5] Of the forty-plus changes suggested by the lawyers, Scorsese gave consideration to about five. The director stood his ground where he could, arguing here and compromising there, as countless memos flew back and forth between the filmmaker and the legal department. In the end, the legal department's suggestions led to the changes of the character's names and Chicago being simply referred to as "back home." They were also responsible for the film being billed as having been "adapted from a true story" rather than being "based on a true story."

Scorsese and Pileggi decided that the story would be structured around a narrative voice-over such as the one they had utilized in GoodFellas. They both believed that the voice-over was key but that it had to sound authentic. As Pileggi explains in the documentary "Casino": The Story, even the most talented of writers couldn't successfully mimic the way a real Chicago gangster spoke.[6] After conducting countless interviews, Pileggi had recorded hundreds of hours of gangsters speaking. Once they reviewed the wealth of colorful stories they had obtained from these interview subjects, both Scorsese and Pileggi agreed that they should use voice-overs by multiple characters. In order to make the story more cinematic, some minor changes involving the compression of time and events had to be made in the screenplay. Because Rosenthal had script approval, Universal was nervous that he might balk at the artistic license Scorsese and Pileggi had taken. However, Pileggi explained the reasoning behind each change and Rosenthal eventually gave his consent.

Just as he had done for GoodFellas, Scorsese hired technical advisors who had actually been involved with the events in the story. First he hired former gangster Joe Russo, who had been a member of Tony Spilotro's crew. Russo described Spilotro's home and offices for production designers and later pointed out faults that made some of the locations unrealistic. For instance, Russo questioned the use of a room with a large wall-sized window, explaining that Spilotro would never have used a room with such a window as he could have easily been shot through it. In another instance, Russo explained that there was too much stolen "swag" present in the house. Scorsese also hired Mark Caspar, a former FBI agent who had arrested Spilotro. When Caspar and Scorsese worked out the raid on Nicky's home, Russo was present. Scorsese was afraid there would be trouble between Russo and Caspar. "A little unnerving, but it turns out that they're old acquaintances," Scorsese would later reveal. "Mark used to tail him!"[7]

Another of Scorsese's technical advisors on the film was Frank Cullotta, a former chief lieutenant under Spilotro. Cullotta, who was the inspiration for Frank Vincent's character in the film, proved to be quite friendly. However, due to his having been in the witness protection program, the cast members were afraid to associate with him for fear that they might be caught in crossfire. "Cullotta would be on set and he would have his car there," Vincent recalls. "And usually when we finished shooting, they would take us back to the hotel in a van. A couple of times Cullotta said, 'Come on, I'll take you back to the hotel,' and we said, 'No, that's quite all right.' We would look under the car to make sure there were no bombs, and we'd look under the hood."[8]

Scorsese and De Niro both felt that Joe Pesci should play Nicky in the film. Not only was Pesci perfect for the role, but both of them had enjoyed working with him on *Raging Bull* and *GoodFellas*. De Niro even went so far as to call his relationship with Pesci a brotherly one. "I found it relaxing to work with [De Niro], the way he works," Pesci explains. "Maybe that's what Marty sees. And also, when we talk about projects and what we're doing, maybe the input that I give Marty is also a lot of the same input that Bob gives. And we like Marty's ideas the same way, and we take direction from him. We really get enthusiastic. So it's a good working trio."[9]

Scorsese was interested in Sharon Stone for the role of Ginger (based on Geri McGee). Scorsese scheduled a meeting with Stone but had to back out at the last minute due to other obligations. Then, when a second meeting was scheduled, Scorsese missed that meeting because his Amtrak train from Las Vegas broke down. Stone didn't believe the train story and thought she was being blown off. She was having dinner in an Italian restaurant in Los Angeles when she received a telephone call from producers wanting to set up a third meeting. This time she refused. Moments later, Scorsese arrived at the restaurant and begged the actress for another chance. The two of them talked for more than an hour about Stone's previous roles and performances, and Scorsese ultimately convinced her to fly to New York for an audition. The scene in the audition called for Stone's character to beat up on De Niro's character. Afraid she might go too far and actually hurt De Niro, Stone held back in the audition, resulting in an unconvincing performance.

Scorsese soon began auditioning other actresses for the role. These included Nicole Kidman, Madonna, Michelle Pfeiffer, Melanie Griffith, Sean Young, and even former porn star Traci Lords. Many of the actresses expressed displeasure in having to read for the part, but Scorsese would have it no other way. "Whoever wants the part has to read," he later wrote in *Premiere*. "I know they can act, it's not about that. It's about the character. I need to know what those words are going to sound like coming out of that vessel, that particular actor. Plus, they need to really let loose—not hold back. Then there's the issue of looks: a Vegas look, but also a look close to that of the person the character's based on. I need someone who can deliver on both."[10] In the end, Scorsese ultimately settled on Stone—provided that she promise not to restrain herself when they filmed the actual scene between her and De Niro.

To round out the rest of the ensemble Scorsese cast such diverse talents as Kevin Pollak, Frank Vincent, Alan King, Don Rickles, James Woods, film critic Joe Bob Briggs, and TV star Dick Smothers. Although they weren't officially auditioned, many of these actors were called in for separate preliminary meetings with De Niro and Scorsese. "The two meetings could not have been more different." Pollak explains. "Marty's a talker; Bob is not."[11] When Pollak met with De Niro in a bungalow at the Bel-Air Hotel, he found the meeting unnerving. According to Pollak, the meeting with De Niro went as follows:

"How you doin'?" De Niro asked.
Pollak replied, "Good."
"Good, good. I just wanted to say hello. . . . How you doin'?"
"Still good."
"Good, good. Can I get you anything?"
"I'm fine."
"I just wanted to say hello. Are you sure you don't want anything?"
"No, I'm fine."
"Okay, well, thanks for coming by."[12]

When Pollak left the meeting, he was convinced that he had blown his chance to appear in a Martin Scorsese film. He believed De Niro was rushing him out of the meeting because he didn't like him. Then, a few days later, Pollak met with Scorsese. "That meeting was quite different," Pollak explains. "I said three words and Marty spoke for forty-five minutes."[13]

Pollak wasn't the only actor who was baffled by the casting process. Upon meeting with Scorsese, Dick Smothers questioned why he had been chosen for the role of a senator who headed the Nevada Gaming Commission. "I said, 'Why would you want *me* in a movie?'" Smothers explains. "I'm not really known for any acting, but Scorsese said he was watching *The Smothers Brothers Comedy Hour* on the E! Channel. [My brother] Tommy and I had bookended those and filmed new wrap-around segments to put those into context. And somehow I reminded him of Senator Harry Reid, who was the basis for the character."[14]

As the studio pushed for a September 1994 start for shooting, Scorsese secretly wondered if he would be ready. As September crept closer and closer, Scorsese and Pileggi continued to hone the film's dialogue. One scene that bothered the two screenwriters was Ace's marriage proposal to Ginger. "We feel we need more subtle dialogue," Scorsese would later write. "What we have now is like an outline, not real communication between people—too broad. Almost like a business deal being proposed to her. He has to make her understand that if she marries him she'll never have to worry about money again, and still be charming and show her that he loves her without being crude about it. But we must also be careful not to drop the 'deal' aspect of their relationship; otherwise, we may lose the drama when, later on, she feels betrayed [and] constantly talks about wanting her money."[15] In order to humanize the dialogue, Scorsese rehearsed the scene with De Niro and Stone, allowing them to improvise slightly. Once he heard the words that felt right for the scene, Scorsese incorporated them into the screenplay.

The selection of music for *Casino* was extremely important to Scorsese. He wanted the music to be like a character unto itself. He diligently sought tunes that would comment on the action taking place on the screen without being too literal a commentary. He decided that the music he selected for each scene should be from the time in which the scene took place and should, in some way, capture the feeling of Las Vegas. He would ultimately use music from the likes of the Rolling Stones, whose music had featured heavily in *GoodFellas*; Johann Sebastian Bach; Louis Prima; and the theme from the film *Picnic*. Scorsese also used the music to add depth to his characters. He believed that the music a character listens to makes an important statement about who he or she is as a person. The final result was a 177-minute film with only two brief scenes without musical accompaniment.

Robert De Niro and Nicholas Pileggi were not the only ones who met with Rosenthal for the film. Rita Ryack and John Dunn, in charge of wardrobe for the production, also met with Rosenthal, borrowing much of his wardrobe from which they would then design De Niro's outfits for the film. For the look of Ginger, Ryack and Sharon Stone worked closely, designing their own look for the character. Each day before shooting Scorsese would personally handpick the suits, shirts, and ties to be worn by De Niro and other male characters in the film. De Niro ultimately had fifty-two changes of clothes in the film, Stone would have forty, and Pesci would have twenty-five.

Filming for *Casino* began on September 14, 1994. To commemorate the event Pesci presented Scorsese a bullet with his name inscribed on it. "Everyone should have one of these with their name on it," Pesci's accompanying card read. "Here's yours! Good start! Joe."[16] Scorsese's agents also presented him with a gift to mark the occasion: a Contax automatic camera with Zeiss/Ikon lens engraved with the title of the film and the starting date.

The then-closed Landmark casino stood in for external shots of the fictional Tangiers casino. Scenes taking place inside the casino were filmed inside the Riviera over a six-week period. Shooting in a real casino provided benefits that a soundstage could not have, such as the depth of the casino, as well as hundreds of real extras in the background. Scorsese also believed that shooting in a real casino would allow him to capture the feel of Las Vegas. Scorsese's camera would stay tight on the foreground, which was filled with paid extras clad in seventies attire. Then, as Scorsese explains, the background with the real casino patrons would "sort of fall off."[17] The downside to filming in a casino, as Scorsese would soon learn, was the perpetual sound of slot machines, which made capturing the audio somewhat of a nightmare.

Most of the scenes in the Riviera were filmed in the wee hours of the night, during the casino's slower periods. Although the Riviera claimed they didn't want their business to be affected by the shoot, they posted a banner outside proclaiming, "Robert De Niro, Sharon Stone, and Joe Pesci Filming the New Movie *Casino* Inside!" in an effort to draw in more customers. During one late-night shoot, Scorsese was filming a scene in which Nicky abuses a blackjack dealer. A real blackjack dealer was used for this scene. "The dealer went through the whole scene with Joe, who was improvising, throwing cards at him and saying the worst possible things," Scorsese recalls. "Halfway through the scene, the dealer leaned over to me and said, 'You know, the real guy was much tougher with me—he really was uncontrollable.' That happened a number of times during the shoot. It was comforting to know we were on the right track."[18]

But not everything about the shoot went so smoothly. In locating the house that would serve as Ace's home in the film, Scorsese and crew had searched diligently for a house that had been built in the late fifties or early sixties, which was very rare in Las Vegas. They had also wanted a house that sat on a golf course. After a lengthy search, they had at last found the perfect home for Ace. After Scorsese had laid all his shots there and used the home for rehearsals, they were informed that they could no longer use the house. This initially upset Scorsese, but he eventually found a home with the same specifications in what he felt was an even better location.

Another incident occurred when the crew was filming the scene in which Melissa Prophet's character is carrying smuggled diamonds in her beehive hairdo. After shooting of the scene had already stretched on for far longer than anyone had anticipated, the heat from the lights set off the sprinkler system, soaking the crew and equipment. "The sprinklers just went nuts," Prophet recalls. "It was one of those situations where everything got crazy. We all started laughing. It was really funny."[19] Refusing to let this incident slow him down, Scorsese decided to shoot the scene in extreme close-up so that no one would notice that the actors' clothes were still wet.

Scorsese continued to utilize improvisation based upon the screenplay throughout the shoot. "Robert De Niro and Joe Pesci would have the script down," Dick Smothers explains. "But not word for word, really. They let the physical set-up of the scene, and then working

Scorsese and his mother Catherine on the set of Casino.

together, shape the final scene. It was really fun to watch."[20] Kevin Pollak recalls that actors had "100 percent freedom to improvise and do whatever they wanted within the boundaries of the composition."[21] One scene that Scorsese believed was improved greatly by improvisation was a scene in which Ginger lies to Ace, telling him that she spent $25,000 on suits for her ex-boyfriend. "I'm not a john," De Niro said through improvisation. "I know you think I am, but I'm not." Scorsese believed that these improvised lines were important because they hit upon Ace's primary weakness, which was his pride. These lines also said more about Ace and Ginger's relationship than any other in the film. This improvisation also strengthened Sharon Stone's reaction to De Niro's dialogue. "You could see the reaction from Sharon Stone," Scorsese says. "She's really something in that [scene]."[22] Using the same technique he had used with Pesci on *Raging Bull* and Jerry Lewis on *The King of Comedy*, De Niro angered Dick Smothers in their scene together, eliciting a realistic reaction from him. "I don't know if he thought I needed help, and I didn't care," Smothers recalls. "I had a fairly long scene and he was right next to the camera. Anyone could have fed me those lines, but he did it himself. He called me names to get me going. He called me everything. Then he said, 'That was good. Your nostrils flared a bit!'"[23]

But this time, De Niro wasn't the only one shouting at actors and giving them a difficult time. At some point during the production, Don Rickles learned that De Niro was a huge fan of his. So, in typical Don Rickles fashion, the sometimes mean-spirited comic would unload on De Niro during shooting, hurling insults at him. De Niro would be in the middle of a scene, delivering a monologue, and Rickles would tease, "*That's* how you're gonna do that? I guess you know what you're doing since you've won all these awards, but that's not how I would do it." The first few times this occurred, other actors and crew stood in silent shock. De Niro, however, got the joke and would cackle with laughter each time Rickles dressed him down. "My favorite part of the entire experience was watching Rickles go after De Niro," Kevin Pollak explains. "It was really something to see."[24] Rickles also chided other actors. "Rickles was constantly tearing into the actors," Melissa Prophet recalls.[25] However, not everyone took the ribbing as well as De Niro. Although he said nothing to Rickles, Joe Pesci eventually became quite irritated by the constant barrage of height jokes that Rickles hurled in his direction.

Interestingly, De Niro no longer stayed in character when he was off-screen as he had during previous shoots. However, this is not to say that his moods weren't affected by the moods of his character. "When Bob is shooting a scene where his character is playful and having fun, that's exactly how he shows up on set," Melissa Prophet explains. "And when he's shooting a scene where he's more menacing, he'll stand there with his arms crossed, looking straight ahead. You can just see the differences in his mood shifts depending on what scene he's filming."[26]

It wasn't until he was working with editor Thelma Schoonmaker in postproduction that Scorsese finally decided on the final structure of the film. Once the film was cut, it then had to be recut to appease the Motion Picture Association of America and avoid an NC-17 rating. The primary scene trimmed in the recut was a scene in which a man's head is crushed in a vise until his eyeballs pop out.

Casino was released on November 22, 1995. At that time, Pileggi boasted that Scorsese's trilogy—*Mean Streets*, *GoodFellas*, and *Casino*—would one day be widely seen as having the importance of John Ford's cavalry trilogy or Francis Ford Coppola's *Godfather* trilogy.

While aspects of the film, such as Scorsese's direction and the individual performances—particularly that of Sharon Stone—would receive praise, most film critics agreed that *Casino* was unbalanced, meandering, too long, and featured too many unlikable characters. "*Casino* is about as weak a film as can be imagined from the team of Martin Scorsese and actors Robert De Niro and Joe Pesci," wrote Mick LaSalle of the *San Francisco Chronicle*, who went on to dub the film "a bad hand."[27]

Variety's Todd McCarthy praised the film's direction in no uncertain terms: "Scorsese's technique here is dense, assured and utterly exhilarating. Lensed entirely at the Riviera Hotel casino and on other real locations, the film possesses a stylistic boldness and verisimilitude that is virtually matchless."[28] Critics also loved De Niro's restraint in the film. "*Casino* is worth seeing for De Niro's powerful performance alone," raved Tom Gliatto of *People*.[29] Joseph Morgenstern of the *Wall Street Journal* asserted that "no single performance in Mr. De Niro's long career can match this one for ineffable authority. It's as if he had never heard of Robert De Niro; all his mannerisms have fallen away. He has even reduced his famous impassivity—gimlet stare, mouth turned down ever so slightly at the corners—to an absence of response, as opposed to a subtle display of unresponsiveness."[30]

Scorsese and Sharon Stone were nominated for Golden Globe Awards. Scorsese ultimately lost his to Mel Gibson for *Braveheart*, but Stone won the award for Best Actress over the likes of Emma Thompson and Meryl Streep. Stone also received an Oscar nomination, but lost to *Dead Man Walking*'s Susan Sarandon, whom Stone had defeated in her Golden Globe run.

"We always have a good time working together," De Niro would later say of his eighth collaboration with Scorsese. "No matter how well the film turns out or how it's received it will always be a special experience."[31]

The Film

White letters against a black screen inform us that the film has been adapted from a true story. We are then told that the year is

1983. The first image in the film is Sam "Ace" Rothstein (Robert De Niro) approaching his 1981 Cadillac Eldorado. As he approaches the automobile, Ace explains in a voice-over that there can be no love without trust. With that trust, Ace says, you must "give them the key to everything that's yours." Ace then climbs into the Caddy and attempts to the start the car, setting off a car bomb that propels him from the vehicle. Just as he did previously with *GoodFellas*, Martin Scorsese has begun *Casino* with a slightly different version of a scene that will appear later in the film. As Bach's "Saint Matthew's Passion" fills the soundtrack, the screen erupts into a fiery credit sequence designed by Saul and Elaine Bass. Ace tumbles through the air against a backdrop of symbolic hellfire. "I guess for me the Bach is essential to the sense of something grand that's been lost," Scorsese says of the sequence. "Whether we agree with the morality of it is another matter—I'm not asking you to agree with the morality—but there was the sense of an empire being lost, and it needed music worthy of that. It needed music which would be provocative. The destruction of [Las Vegas] has to have the grandeur of Lucifer being expelled from Heaven for being too proud."[32] The fiery backdrop is then replaced by images of neon lights. At the conclusion of the sequence, the flames reemerge, symbolically enveloping both the glitz of Las Vegas and Ace himself.

As the credit sequence ends, Bach continues to play and Scorsese treats us to the iconic image of Ace standing tall against the interior of the Tangiers casino. In a voice-over, Ace explains that he was a handicapper back home and that he made so much money for the Mafia that the bosses gave him "Paradise on Earth"—control of the Tangiers hotel and casino in Las Vegas. Nicky Santoro (Joe Pesci), a heavy, is then introduced through his own voice-over. Santoro also introduces Ginger (Sharon Stone) and explains that the three of them once had it made, but they ultimately screwed everything up and lost the slice of paradise they had been given. This would be the last time, Santoro explains, that "street guys" would be given control over anything as valuable as the Tangiers.

In her book *The Scorsese Psyche on Screen*, author Maria T. Miliora asserts that the theme of "Mafia-as-church" that appears in *GoodFellas* is once again employed here. "The casino and its system of control, ex-ercised by the mob bosses from the Midwest, is an ecclesiastical system of sorts," she writes.

> Its sacraments include skims to the mob bosses and payoffs to the right politicians in Nevada. Keeping the church stable requires the right balance of give-and-take among the bosses, the workers, the police, and the politicians. Paradise or heaven on earth, as defined by getting unlimited amounts of money from the suckers who come to the casino to gamble, is lost as the demigods—Rothstein and Santoro—become hungrier and hungrier for the forbidden fruit, greedier and greedier for unrestrained power and megalomaniacal control. Inevitably, the greed breeds violence, which once unleashed, spins out of control. In the nar-rative, Nicky relates that they "fucked it up," and, ultimately, destroyed their paradise on earth.[33]

The film's fractured time line now moves backward to a time when the casino was thriving. Ace explains through voice-over that any-where else in the world he was seen only as a bookie, but in Las Vegas, he was legitimate; he ran a casino. He introduces us to Billy Sherbert (Don Rickles), his casino manager. "For guys like me," he explains, "Las Vegas washes away your sins. It's like a morality car wash. It does for us what Lourdes does for humpbacks and cripples." He then informs us that Las Vegas was extremely lucrative for the Mafia. As "Moonglow" plays over the soundtrack, we see Mafia errand boy John Nance (Bill Allison) allowed into the counting room, where all the money the casino takes in goes. The casino employees look the other way as Nance skims a suitcase filled with hundred-dollar bills. This monthly payment is then carried out of the casino and flown to Kansas City, which is as close as the Mafia bosses can go to Las Vegas without being arrested. Mafia chieftains from all over the country meet once a month in the back of the San Marino Italian Grocery in Kansas City to pick up their share. In a voice-over Nicky explains that these Mafia chieftains were the men who secretly controlled Las Vegas through the Teamsters Union.

Andy Stone (Alan King), head of the Teamsters Pension Fund, is shown presenting a loan of $62,700,000 to Phillip Green (Kevin Pol-lak), the Mafia's front man for the Tangiers. Nicky explains through voice-over that Green is the perfect stooge; he knows very little about what goes on, and he asks no questions. According to Nicky, Green wants to believe the Teamsters loaned him the money because he's smart. Chairman Green, Nicky explains, was an Arizona real estate hustler who barely had enough money to pay for the gas to come and pick up the check from the Teamsters. Although Green is the face of the Tangiers, it is secretly Andy Stone who pulls his strings.

In the next scene, Stone asks Ace to run the Tangiers. Ace balks, explaining that the gaming commission will never give him a license to run the casino as he has numerous gambling arrests on his record. Stone explains that he doesn't need a license to work in a casino; under the law, a person could work at a casino as long as they've turned in an application for a license. Because of the ten-year backlog of requests the commission has to consider, it will be years before they get to Ace's request. In the meantime, Stone says that Ace could work in the casino under different nondescript titles, such as food and beverage chairman. Stone believes that if Ace changes job titles with some regularity, the commission will move his application back to the bottom of the pile each time. To this Ace says that should he decide to run the casino, he would have to be able to do things his way with absolutely no outside interference. Stone agrees to this demand, and Ace is made unofficial boss of the casino. His official title will be public relations director.

Through another voice-over, Nicky tells Ace's backstory. As a gambler, Ace was said to be the only sure thing. Unlike other gamblers, Ace didn't have any fun gambling, and he left nothing to chance. Relying on solid information regarding the drug habits of quarterbacks, the effect of wind velocity on kickers, and the types of bounces footballs made on different types of turf, Ace perfected his gambling techniques. Over the years Ace made a lot of money for the Mafia leaders, such as boss-of-bosses Remo Gaggi (Pasquale Cajano). Nicky explains that Ace made more money for the bosses in a weekend's worth of bets than he himself could earn pulling heists for a year. Because Ace made them so much money, the bosses didn't want anything to happen to him. So Nicky, the enforcer, was instructed to accompany Ace to Las Vegas and protect him. The next scene, in which Nicky repeatedly stabs a man in the throat with an ink pen and then beats him severely for being disrespectful to Ace, illustrates this point.

Ace explains that he had to play politics and grease the wheels in order to keep things at the casino running smoothly. He has a brief encounter with Don Ward (John Bloom), an incompetent casino worker who is employed because he's related to a local official. Ace explains that he must also pay off dozens of politicians with complimentary rooms and women. A senator (Dick Smothers) who is also the head of the gaming commission is shown receiving such treatment. In contrast to the "cheap" politicians is K. K. Ichikawa (Nobu Matsuhisa), a Japanese high roller who gambles with enough money at stake to shut down a casino. Ace explains that Ichikawa had cleaned out two casinos in the Cayman Islands the previous year. After Ichikawa wins $2 million from the casino, Ace instructs his pilot to lie to him, telling him that the plane isn't working and that he must stay in Las Vegas for another night. Ichikawa ultimately loses his $2 million winnings (plus an additional $1 million of his own) back to the Tangiers, and order is once again restored in Ace's world. Here Ace explains that the cardinal rule in a casino is to keep people playing; the longer a person plays, the better the house's chances of winning.

In an effort to eliminate dishonesty, everyone who works or plays in the casino is watched closely. The dealers watch the players. The box men watch the dealers. The floor men watch the box men. The pit bosses watch the floor men. The shift bosses watch the pit bosses. The casino manager watches the shift bosses. Ace himself watches the casino manager. All the while, ceiling-mounted cameras watch everyone. Ace explains that a team of former gambling cheats works around the clock, analyzing the monitors and watching for cheaters.

Ace sees high-priced call girl and all-around hustler Ginger at the casino for the first time. Ginger is accompanying a gambler who's on a hot streak at the craps table. Believing herself to be the man's source of good luck, Ginger helps herself to handfuls of his chips when he's not looking. Eventually he calls her on this, angering her. Ginger's response is to toss all of the man's winnings into the crowd. For Ace, this is an instance of love at first sight. In a montage set to the Rolling Stones' "Heart of Stone," we see that Ace and Ginger have begun dating.

Ace explains in a voice-over that Ginger has the "hustler's code" down; in true Las Vegas fashion, she takes care of people in return for their taking care of her. We then see Ginger paying off dealers, floor managers, pit bosses, and the valet parkers, who, according to Ace, make it possible for Ginger to hustle. Ginger takes care of the valet parkers because they take care of the security guards who take care of the cops who, in turn, allow her to continue working without hassle. Ace explains that the position of valet parker is so lucrative that people have to pay off the hotel manager in order to land it in the first place. Despite appearing to have everything in her life under control, Ginger cannot control her feelings for her former pimp and boyfriend Lester Diamond (James Woods). In what is surely one of many instances, Ginger is shown lending a large sum of money to him.

We see Nicky back home in Chicago. His bags are being searched by customs agents, but they find nothing. Ace explains that the police believe Nicky is connected to a diamond heist, but they cannot prove his involvement. We then see Nicky, Frank Marino (Frank Vincent), and Nicky's wife, Jennifer (Melissa Prophet), shake the diamonds from a bun in Jennifer's hair. Ace explains that Nicky loves being a gangster, which is what worries him about the probability of Nicky relocating to Las Vegas. As Ray Charles and Betty Carter sing "Takes Two to Tango" over the soundtrack, Ace shows Nicky and Jennifer his penthouse apartment and introduces them to Ginger. Then Ace and Nicky go for a ride to talk, and Nicky introduces the idea of his moving to Las Vegas. Ace is momentarily stunned but says nothing. He explains to Nicky that Las Vegas is different from Chicago; in Vegas, wiseguys have to keep a low profile as the police dislike them. Ace explains that he himself has already been arrested twice and that any misdeeds by Nicky could jeopardize his "legit" business at the Tangiers. However, Nicky vows that he won't do anything that will affect Ace.

Nicky soon goes to work in Vegas, shaking down bookies, pimps, and drug dealers. He then devises a nonscientific method of betting: when he wins, he collects; when he loses, he forces the bookies to pay him anyway. "What were they gonna do? Muscle Nicky? Nicky was the muscle." Nicky also protects the bosses' interests at the Tangiers by keeping other crews from cheating the casino. Members of other crews receive one warning without repercussion, but outsiders receive punishment immediately. (First assistant director Joseph Reidy makes a cameo here as a goon who is given a warning by Nicky.)

Ace asks Ginger to marry him, but she informs him that she doesn't love him. He tells her that this doesn't matter. As a realist, he expects only a mutual respect. In what is more a business pitch than a marriage proposal, Ace promises that Ginger will be heavily compensated whether or not the marriage works. Knowing a good thing when she sees it, Ginger eventually relents and agrees to marry Ace. Immediately after the wedding, we see Lester Diamond snorting cocaine and begging Ginger for money over the telephone. Ace walks into the room and catches Ginger on the telephone, and she quickly excuses herself and hangs up. She tells Ace that she just wanted to say good-bye to Lester and promises that this part of her life is over.

Ace purchases a lavish home filled with jewelry and gifts for Ginger, but he tells her that none of it means anything if they don't have trust. To show her how much he trusts her, he gives her the only key to a safety deposit box in Los Angeles containing $2 million reserved for shakedowns and kidnappings.

Nicky is soon back to his old tricks. Nicky begins loan sharking to the dealers at the Tangiers, and he soon has most of them in his pocket. He then brings in teams of "mechanics," or card sharks, to cheat the casino. Nicky doesn't think anyone knows what he's doing, but Ace does—and so do gaming agents. Ace admits in a voice-over that he wishes Nicky's entire crew would disappear, but he's stuck. There's nothing Ace can do. If he goes back and complains to the bosses about Nicky, a made man, a war will ensue. Ace tries to warn Nicky to play a little more cautiously, but Nicky doesn't listen. Predictably, Nicky is soon added to the government's "black book" and banned from every casino in Las Vegas. As a result, Ace cannot be seen speaking to Nicky anywhere near Las Vegas.

Forced to find a new way to make money, Nicky gathers a crew of professional thieves from Chicago and begins pulling heists around Las Vegas. With the aid of tipsters from around the city, Nicky is once again making a substantial amount of money. However, these actions are against the rules. Because the Mafia bosses are making so much money with the Tangiers, they don't want any of their people doing anything to bring attention to them. Because of this, Nicky doesn't have to give the bosses a cut of the stolen booty; instead, he pockets it all. Nicky soon uses his ill-gotten gains to purchase a jewelry store and a swanky restaurant. Now a local celebrity, Nicky uses his newfound stature to bed showgirls. To stay in the good graces of the Mafia bosses, Nicky continues carrying out jobs for them. In one instance, Nicky squeezes a man's head in a vise until his eyes pop out and sticks ice picks into his testicles—to "send a message" not to rob Remo's establishments.

When Ace senses foul play at the casino, he fires the slot machine manager, Don Ward, for incompetence after three slots each pay out $15,000 jackpots within a fifteen-minute period. Phillip Green tries to convince Ace to rehire Ward, informing him that his brother-in-law is County Commissioner Pat Webb (L. Q. Jones). However, Ace refuses.

Ace experiences trouble at home when Ginger asks him for $25,000. Ace doesn't refuse her the money, but he does ask her why she needs the money. This angers Ginger, who refuses to provide him with a reason. Ace has Ginger followed by Nicky and learns that Ginger has removed $25,000 from their safety deposit box. When Ginger meets Lester at a seedy diner, they are both surprised to see Ace show up. Lester is looking over the $25,000 when Ace sits down at the table and shakes his hand. As Ace becomes angry, Lester looks around the room and sees two goons standing by the door. Ace warns him that if he comes after his money again, he had better bring a pistol with him so he will have a fighting chance. He then asks him to leave so he can be alone with his wife. Ace reprimands Ginger and then escorts her out to the parking lot to watch his goons beat Lester.

Set against the melodic sounds of the Moody Blues' "Nights in White Satin," Nicky and Ginger talk about her relationship problems with Ace. Nicky appears to be a good friend, defending Ace. Nicky provides Ginger a shoulder to cry on. Ginger then begins to kiss Nicky, signaling trouble in Ace's future. Compounding Ace's problems, County Commissioner Webb pays him a visit. Webb has come to speak on behalf of Don Ward. Despite his request that Ace rehire Webb as a personal favor to him, Ace refuses to consider such a thing. Webb makes reference to Ace's friendship to Nicky and threatens to have the gaming commission investigate his record, but Ace refuses to budge on the matter.

After discovering that Ginger has taken nearly all of his painkillers, Ace confronts her about her drug use and alcoholism. The two of them embrace, and Ginger agrees to seek help for her problems.

Nicky explains in a voice-over that the Mafia bosses have become concerned that their skim money is coming up light. "What's the point of skimming if we're being skimmed?" one of them asks. So the bosses then assign incompetent Kansas City underboss Artie Piscano (Vinny Vella) to watch over the skim. Things start to sour at the Tangiers when Phillip Green's secret partner, Anna Scott (Ffolliott Le Coque), comes forward and demands money. When Scott takes Green to court, the judge orders him to open up the books and disclose exactly where financing for the Tangiers came from. The Mafia bosses decide to "settle the case out of court" by sending Nicky to murder Anna Scott. The murder brings unwanted attention to Green. The local media then uncovers the truth behind the Tangiers: that Ace is the real boss. Webb uses the newspaper report to convince the gaming commission to investigate Ace. The media then uncovers Ace's ties to Nicky.

Nicky comes to Ace's home to confront a bank executive. After Nicky threatens the banker's life, Ace becomes irritated. When Ace tries to explain to Nicky that threatening non-Mafia people will cause trouble, Nicky becomes angry and lectures Ace about his marital problems with Ginger. When Ace learns that Ginger has been talking about their problems with Nicky, he asks Nicky to stay away from his wife and mind his own business.

In a voice-over, Ace explains that Nicky wants to take over Las Vegas from the bosses back home. Ace doesn't want to be involved with this. Ace also explains that Nicky has stopped asking the bosses for permission to do things. In addition to this, Nicky has been the primary suspect in at least two dozen murder investigations. However, the police have been unable to make anything stick as there are never any witnesses. The bosses are beginning to irritate Nicky by complaining that things aren't running as smoothly as they would like. As Nicky explains in a voice-over, things don't run smoothly in his line of work. As a result of all the FBI scrutiny, Nicky is forced to have his meetings with his crew at a crowded bus stop. Nicky and his men must also cover their mouths so that lip-reading experts with binoculars won't know what they're saying. Ace laments that his job is on the line with his license hearing looming in the near future, and meanwhile Nicky is having the time of his life playing golf.

Back in Kansas City, Piscano is overheard by FBI bugging equipment complaining about his frequent trips to the Tangiers to oversee the skim. According to Ace, Piscano "basically sunk the whole world." As a result of what they have heard Piscano say on tape, the FBI is now paying close attention to the Tangiers and the Mafia bosses. Making matters worse, Ace's application is denied by the gaming commission, and he is denied the opportunity to defend himself. Pat Webb's presence in the courtroom signals his involvement in the application denial. When Ace angrily accuses gaming officials of corruption and hypocrisy, he once again makes the news. The Mafia bosses decide to allow Ace to continue running things under a different title. Boss-of-bosses Remo Gaggi insists that Ace be given a position that is "quiet." Against Remo's wishes, entertainment director Ace winds up hosting *Aces High*, a local television variety program from the Tangiers. Unconvinced that Ace is no longer running the Tangiers, Webb and gaming commission officials continue to watch his activities. When Ace sues the gaming commission and accuses Webb of hypocrisy on his television show, the Mafia bosses become agitated. Remo then sends Andy Stone to lean on Ace and convince him to drop his lawsuit. During his conversation with Stone, Ace complains about

Nicky. Nicky soon learns that Ace has been complaining about him, and as a result, Nicky wants to meet Ace in the desert. Ace is worried that Nicky is going to murder him and bury him in the sand, but Nicky only berates him and warns him never to go behind his back again.

Devo's "Whip It" used as source music informs us that time has passed and the year is now 1980. Ace and Nicky sit at separate tables in a nightclub, and Nicky is lamenting to his crew that Ace acts like he doesn't know him. Nicky explains that the bosses have instructed them to avoid each other, but Nicky is still aggravated by Ace's ignoring him. Later, Billy telephones Ace in the middle of the night, waking him. Billy explains that Nicky is inside the casino. Nicky insists on a $50,000 marker, but Billy (under orders from Ace) won't allow it. Finally Ace arrives at the casino and tries to talk sense into Nicky. When Ace says he will only give him a $10,000 marker, Nicky becomes angry and beats Billy with a telephone.

Ace and Ginger meet with Ace's lawyer to discuss Ginger's desire to divorce. Ace assures her that not only will she never get the jewels and alimony that he'd promised her, but she will also never get custody of their daughter. Ginger and Ace then decide to take some time off away from each other. Ace soon learns that Ginger is up to her old tricks again, this time having an affair with Lester in Beverly Hills with their daughter, Amy (Erika von Tagen), in tow. Ace uses his Mafia connections to obtain a phone number and address where Ginger and Lester are staying. Ace telephones Lester and asks to speak to his wife. Ginger is busy cutting cocaine in front of Amy, and Lester asks if she can call him back. Lester hangs up the telephone and attempts to convince Ginger to run away with him to Europe with Ace's $2 million and get plastic surgery. Lester also expresses interest in kidnapping Amy and holding her for ransom. A frightened Ginger then calls Nicky and tells him that she's afraid Ace will have her killed. Nicky meets with Ace and facilitates a safe return home for Ginger and Amy. After quizzing Ginger about what she spent his missing $25,000 on, an angry Ace chastises her, telling her that if she hadn't come home he would have had her and Lester killed.

Ace overhears Ginger talking on the telephone to someone (Nicky) and saying that she wants him killed. This enrages Ace, and he fills a shoebox with cash and demands that she leave the house. Ginger tells him that she's going to the bank to take out her jewelry the following morning, and Ace agrees to let her take it. Ginger later returns and climbs into bed with him as though nothing has happened. In a voice-over Ace explains that he still loves Ginger and that he doesn't want to give her the money because he knows he'll never see her again if he does. After Ace explains to Ginger that she must now carry an electronic pager with her at all times so that he can reach her whenever he needs her, she meets with Nicky. As B. B. King's "The Thrill Is Gone" plays, Ginger attempts to convince Nicky to assist her in stealing Ace's money. Nicky promises to protect Ginger from Ace, and she then performs oral sex on him. FBI agents photograph Ginger and Nicky kissing outside. In a scene reminiscent of Jake LaMotta's grilling of his wife Vickie in *Raging Bull*, Ace interrogates Ginger about where she's been, even going so far as to ask her what she ate. When Ace attempts to telephone Ginger's friend to ask what she had for dinner, she admits that she was "with someone." She then confesses that she has been having an affair with Nicky. Ginger agrees to end it with Nicky, but we then see them having sex in the next scene. Nicky explains to Ginger that their affair could cause real trouble with the bosses back home.

Remo asks Frank if Nicky is sleeping with Ginger, adding that if he is, "it's a problem." In a voice-over Frank explains that a wrong answer here could get Nicky, Ginger, and Ace all killed because the old-time Mafioso do not approve of sleeping with other men's wives because it's bad for business. So Frank lies, insisting that there's nothing between Nicky and Ginger. Remo then asks Frank to watch Nicky. Later, Frank tells Nicky that Remo has asked him for a second time if he's having an affair with Ginger. Nicky explains to Frank that he doesn't trust Ace and is afraid that he will start a war. He then instructs Frank to dig a hole in the desert in case he decides to have Ace whacked.

When Ace cannot reach Ginger, he goes home and discovers that she has tied Amy to her bed and left her alone. Meanwhile, Ginger is having dinner with Nicky at his restaurant. Nicky telephones Ace to tell him that Ginger is with him, and Ace says he will be there soon. Nicky meets Ace at the door and tries to cover for Ginger, saying that Ginger only wanted to talk to him about her marriage. Ace confronts his wife, warning her that if she ever touches Amy again he will have her killed. Ginger offers to hand over custody of Amy in exchange for the key to a safety deposit box containing her jewelry. Ace refuses. When Ace sees Nicky motioning to Ginger that she can leave, he becomes enraged and grabs her. In return, Ginger threatens his life. When Ace and Ginger arrive at their home, the two of them argue and Ginger storms out of the house. Ace then telephones Billy and asks him to bring over a gun for his protection. Ginger goes to Nicky and asks him to kill Ace. The two of them get into an argument and Nicky has Ginger tossed into the alley. She then threatens to go to the FBI and tell them what she knows.

Ace locks up all the doors in his house in a scene that is similar to Sam Bowden's locking of the doors and windows in *Cape Fear*. He and Billy then sit up and wait for Nicky, but Nicky never shows. Instead, Ginger arrives and rams her car into the back of Ace's car. The two of them get into a heated argument on the front lawn, and Ginger admits that she's still sleeping with Nicky. Soon the police arrive, and the irate Ginger screams at them, as well. Meanwhile, the FBI photographs the entire incident. Ace tells her that she cannot enter the house to get her belongings, but the police convince him to allow her inside for five minutes. While Ace is outside talking with a police officer, Ginger ransacks his desk in search of the key to the deposit box. Once she has located and stolen the key, she leaves the property. When Ace realizes that Ginger has the key to the safety deposit box, he and Billy leave for the bank. However, the police stop Ace and allow Ginger to leave with the money. A block or so down the street, Ginger is apprehended by the FBI, but she tells them nothing. Even without Ginger's help, the FBI now have all the information they need to bring down the Mafia's entire operation at the Tangiers. Numerous arrests are made, and all of Ace's money is seized.

FBI agents eventually bring photographs of Nicky and Ginger to Ace, and ask him to testify against his old friend. Ace refuses. As the Animals' "The House of the Rising Sun" plays, we see the Mafia's Las Vegas empire crumble before our eyes. The Mafia bosses are shown sitting in the courtroom during their trial. After the arraignment, they hold a secret meeting in the courthouse and order the executions of several key players. Andy Stone is shot six times outside a diner. The Mafia then tracks down John Nance, who is hiding in Costa Rica.

Three more murders are then shown. Although Ginger isn't killed by the Mafia, she soon overdoses in the hallway of a seedy hotel. As the song concludes, Ace climbs into his 1981 Cadillac and turns the key. The car explodes.

Because Nicky blew up Ace's car, lied to the bosses, and went behind their backs, he is executed next. Nicky and his brother Dominic (Philip Suriano) are beaten to a pulp with a baseball bat by Nicky's own crew and buried alive in a cornfield.

We are then shown the destruction of Ace's car for the third time. This time we learn that he escapes with minor injuries due to a metal plate beneath the driver's seat. The explosion of Ace's Cadillac then transitions into footage of a building symbolically collapsing. At the end of the film, Ace laments that Las Vegas has transformed into a family vacation spot à la Disneyland. Because of Ace's ability to pick winners, the Mafia keeps him alive to continue earning for them.

Notes

1. Brode, Douglas, *The Films of Robert De Niro* (Secaucus, NJ: Citadel Press, 1996), 271.

2. Brode, *The Films of Robert De Niro*, 267.

3. Scorsese, Martin, and Wilson, Michael Henry, "Living Las Vegas: *Casino* Diary," *Premiere*, February 1996, 52.

4. Scorsese and Wilson, "Living Las Vegas," 52.

5. Scorsese and Wilson, "Living Las Vegas," 52.

6. Bouzereau, Laurent, *"Casino": The Story*, documentary (Universal Pictures, 2005).

7. Scorsese and Wilson, "Living Las Vegas," 50.

8. Vincent, Frank, interview by the author, September 30, 2009.

9. Bouzereau, Laurent, *"Casino": The Cast and Characters*, documentary (Universal Pictures, 2005).

10. Scorsese and Wilson, "Living Las Vegas," 49.

11. Pollak, Kevin, interview by the author, September 29, 2009.

12. Pollak, interview.

13. Pollak, interview.

14. Smothers, Dick, interview by the author, January 3, 2007.

15. Scorsese and Wilson, "Living Las Vegas," 51.

16. Scorsese and Wilson, "Living Las Vegas," 51.

17. Thompson, David, and Christie, Ian, eds., *Scorsese on Scorsese* (Boston: Faber and Faber, 1989), 204.

18. Thompson and Christie, *Scorsese on Scorsese*, 205.

19. Prophet, Melissa, interview by the author, September 30, 2009.

20. Smothers, interview.

21. Pollak, interview.

22. Ebert, Roger, *Scorsese by Ebert* (Chicago: University of Chicago Press, 2008), 152.

23. Smothers, interview.

24. Pollak, interview.

25. Prophet, interview.

26. Prophet, interview.

27. LaSalle, Mick, "Scorsese's *Casino* Comes Up Broke," *San Francisco Chronicle*, November 22, 1995, 32.

28. McCarthy, Todd, "*Casino*," *Variety*, November 17, 1995, 122.

29. Tom Gliatto is quoted in Brode, *The Films of Robert De Niro*, 270.

30. Joseph Morgenstern is quoted in Brode, *The Films of Robert De Niro*, 270.

31. Dougan, Andy, *Untouchable: A Biography of Robert De Niro* (New York: Thunder's Mouth Press, 1996), 273.

32. Thompson and Christie, *Scorsese on Scorsese*, 106.

33. Miliora, Maria T., *The Scorsese Psyche on Screen* (Jefferson, NC: McFarland, 2004), 63.

Epilogue

When gearing up to film *Gangs of New York*, a dream project he'd been contemplating since the mid-1970s, Martin Scorsese turned to his old friend and frequent collaborator Robert De Niro. Scorsese wanted De Niro to appear as William "Bill the Butcher" Cutting. De Niro was interested in the role but was ultimately forced to decline due to prior obligations. The role then went to Daniel Day-Lewis, who received an Academy Award nomination for his performance. The film itself received an impressive ten Oscar nominations, including Best Picture and Best Director. However, these nominations failed to yield a single award.

It is rumored that Scorsese initially wanted De Niro to appear in *The Departed* as Francis "Frank" Costello, a role that eventually went to Jack Nicholson. If this rumor is true, it is unclear why this ninth Scorsese/De Niro collaboration did not occur. The film went on to receive five Oscar nominations, winning four statuettes. These included Best Picture, Best Adapted Screenplay, Best Editing, and a long-overdue Best Director award for Scorsese.

In 2008, Scorsese optioned Charles Brandt's book *I Heard You Paint Houses*. It was then announced that the ensuing film—based on the life of Irish mobster Frank Sheeran—would be written by *Gangs of New York* scribe Steven Zaillian and would star De Niro. Shortly after this announcement, De Niro told reporters that he and Scorsese would also be making a tenth film together. The untitled film, which would be shot simultaneously with *I Heard You Paint Houses*, was described as a "film-within-a-film." As of October 1, 2009, there has been no visible movement on either project.

Collaborative Filmography

Mean Streets (1973)

35mm, color, 110 minutes
Director: Martin Scorsese
Production company: Warner Bros.
Executive producer: E. Lee Perry
Producer: Jonathan T. Taplin
Writers: Martin Scorsese, Mardik Martin
Cinematographer: Kent Wakeford
Editor: Sid Levin
Cast: Harvey Keitel (Charlie), Robert De Niro (Johnny Boy), David
    Proval (Tony), Amy Robinson (Teresa), Richard Romanus (Mi-
    chael)

Taxi Driver (1976)

35mm, color, 114 minutes
Director: Martin Scorsese
Production company: Columbia Pictures
Producers: Michael Phillips, Julia Phillips
Writer: Paul Schrader
Cinematographer: Michael Chapman

Editors: Marcia Lucas, Tom Rolf, Melvin Shapiro
Cast: Robert De Niro (Travis Bickle), Jodie Foster (Iris), Cybill Shepherd (Betsy), Harvey Keitel (Sport), Peter Boyle (Wizard)

New York, New York (1977)

35mm, color, 153 minutes
Director: Martin Scorsese
Production company: United Artists
Producers: Irwin Winkler, Robert Chartoff
Writers: Earl Mac Rauch, Mardik Martin
Cinematographer: Laszlo Kovacs
Editors: Irving Lerner, Marcia Lucas
Cast: Robert De Niro (Jimmy Doyle), Liza Minnelli (Francine Evans), Lionel Stander (Tony Harwell), Barry Primus (Paul Wilson), Mary Kay Place (Bernice Bennett)

Raging Bull (1980)

35mm, black and white, 129 minutes
Director: Martin Scorsese
Production company: United Artists
Producers: Irwin Winkler, Robert Chartoff
Writers: Paul Schrader, Mardik Martin
Cinematographer: Michael Chapman
Editor: Thelma Schoonmaker
Cast: Robert De Niro (Jake La Motta), Cathy Moriarty (Vickie La Motta), Joe Pesci (Joey La Motta), Frank Vincent (Salvy), Theresa Saldana (Lenore)

The King of Comedy (1983)

35mm, color, 108 minutes
Director: Martin Scorsese
Production company: Twentieth Century Fox
Executive producer: Robert Greenhut
Producer: Arnon Milchan
Writer: Paul Zimmerman

Cinematographer: Fred Shuler
Editor: Thelma Schoonmaker
Cast: Robert De Niro (Rupert Pupkin), Jerry Lewis (Jerry Langford), Dial11111e Abbott (Rita), Sandra Bernhard (Masha), Shelley Hack (Cathy Long)

GoodFellas (1990)

35mm, color, 146 minutes
Director: Martin Scorsese
Production company: Warner Bros.
Executive producer: Barbara De Fina
Producer: Irwin Winkler
Writers: Nicholas Pileggi, Martin Scorsese
Cinematographer: Martin Ballhaus
Editor: Thelma Schoonmaker
Cast: Robert De Niro (Jimmy Conway), Ray Liotta (Henry Hill), Joe Pesci (Tommy DeVito), Paul Sorvino (Paul Cicero), Lorraine Bracco (Karen Hill)

Cape Fear (1991)

35mm, color, 128 minutes
Director: Martin Scorsese
Production company: Universal Pictures
Producer: Barbara De Fina
Executive producers: Kathleen Kennedy, Frank Marshall
Writers: Wesley Strick, James R. Webb
Cinematographer: Freddie Francis
Editor: Thelma Schoonmaker
Cast: Robert De Niro (Max Cady), Nick Nolte (Sam Bowden), Jessica Lange (Leigh Bowden), Juliette Lewis (Danielle Bowden), Joe Don Baker (Kersek)

Guilty by Suspicion (1991)

35mm, color, 105 minutes
Director: Irwin Winkler

Production company: Twentieth Century Fox
Producer: Arnon Milchan
Executive producer: Steven Reuther
Writer: Irwin Winkler
Cinematographer: Michael Ballhaus
Editor: Priscilla Nedd
Cast: Robert De Niro (David Merrill), Annette Bening (Ruth Merrill), George Wendt (Bunny Baxter), Patricia Wettig (Dorothy Nolan), Martin Scorsese (Joe Lesser)

Mad Dog and Glory (1993)

35mm, color, 97 minutes
Director: John McNaughton
Production company: Universal Pictures
Producers: Barbara De Fina, Martin Scorsese
Writer: Richard Price
Cinematographer: Robby Muller
Editors: Elena Maganini, Craig McKay
Cast: Robert De Niro (Wayne "Mad Dog" Dobie), Uma Thurman (Glory), Bill Murray (Frank Milo), David Caruso (Mike), Mike Starr (Harold)

Casino (1995)

35mm, color, 171 minutes
Director: Martin Scorsese
Production company: Universal Pictures
Producer: Barbara De Fina
Writers: Nicholas Pileggi, Martin Scorsese
Cinematographer: Robert Richardson
Editor: Thelma Schoonmaker
Cast: Robert De Niro (Sam "Ace" Rothstein), Sharon Stone (Ginger), Joe Pesci (Nicky Santoro), James Woods (Lester Diamond), Frank Vincent (Frank Marino)

Shark Tale (2004)

35mm, color, 90 minutes
Directors: Bibo Bergeron, Vicky Jenson, Rob Letterman
Production company: DreamWorks Animation
Producers: Bob Damaschke, Janet Healy, Allison Lyon Segan
Writers: Michael J. Wilson, Rob Letterman
Editors: Peter Lonsdale, John Venzon
Cast: Will Smith (Oscar), Robert De Niro (Don Lino), Renee Zellweger (Angie), Jack Black (Lenny), Martin Scorsese (Sykes)

Mr. Warmth: The Don Rickles Project (2007)

35mm, color, 89 minutes
Director: John Landis
Production company: Dark Horse Indie
Producers: Robert Engleman, John Landis, Mike Richardson, Larry Rickles
Writer: John Landis
Cinematographer: Tom Clancey
Editor: Mark L. Levine
Cast: Harry Dean Stanton (himself), Don Rickles (himself), Clint Eastwood (himself), Robert De Niro (himself), Martin Scorsese (himself)

Bibliography

Print Materials

Agan, Patrick. *Robert De Niro: The Man, the Myth, and the Movies*. London: Robert Hale, 1989.

Ansen, David. "A Hollywood Crime Wave." *Newsweek*, September 17, 1990.

Baxter, John. *De Niro: A Biography*. New York: HarperCollins, 2002.

Bishop, Kathy. "Ray Liotta." *Rolling Stone*, November 1, 1990, 62.

Biskind, Peter. *Easy Riders, Raging Bulls*. New York: Simon & Schuster, 1998.

———. "Slouching toward Hollywood." *Premiere*, November 1991, 70–73.

Bracco, Lorraine. *On the Couch*. New York: Berkley Books, 2006.

Brode, Douglas. *The Films of Robert De Niro*. Secaucus, NJ: Citadel Press, 1996.

Cameron, Julia. "Devoted to Betrayal." *American Film*, October 1989.

Cameron-Wilson, James. *The Cinema of Robert De Niro*. London: Zomba Books, 1986.

Casillo, Robert. *Gangster Priest: The Italian American Cinema of Martin Scorsese*. Toronto: University of Toronto Press, 2007.

Christie, Ian. "Martin Scorsese's Testament." *Sight & Sound*, January 1996.

Colley, Iain. *GoodFellas*. York, UK: York Press, 2001.

De Curtis, Anthony. "The Martin Scorsese *Rolling Stone* Interview." *Rolling Stone*, November 1, 1990.

———. "What the Streets Mean." *South Atlantic Quarterly*, Spring 1992.

Denby, David. "Time on the Cross." *New York*, August 29, 1988, 50.

"Dialogue on Film: Robert De Niro." *American Film*, March 1981, 39–48.

Dougan, Andy. *Martin Scorsese: Close Up*. New York: Thunder's Mouth Press, 1998.

———. *Untouchable: A Biography of Robert De Niro*. New York: Thunder's Mouth Press, 1996.

Duncan, Paul. *Martin Scorsese*. Manchester, UK: Pocket Essentials, 2004.

Ebert, Roger. *Scorsese by Ebert*. Chicago: University of Chicago Press, 2008.

Ebert, Roger, and Siskel, Gene. *The Future of the Movies*. Kansas City, MO: Andrews and McMeel, 1991.

Ehrenstein, David. *The Scorsese Picture: The Art and Life of Martin Scorsese*. New York: Birch Lane Press, 1992.

Evans, Mike. *The Making of "Raging Bull."* London: Unanimous, 2006.

Farber, Manny, and Patterson, Patricia. *"Taxi Driver." Film Comment*, May/June 1998.

Fine, Marshall. *Harvey Keitel: The Art of Darkness*. New York: Fromm International, 1997.

Flatley, Guy. "He Has Often Walked Mean Streets." *New York Times*, December 16, 1973.

———. "Martin Scorsese's Gamble," *New York Times*, February 8, 1976, 56.

Foster, Buddy, and Wagener, Leon. *Foster Child: A Biography of Jodie Foster*. New York: Dutton, 1997.

Fox, Terry Curtis. "Martin Scorsese's Elegy for a Big-Time Band." *Village Voice*, May 1978.

Friedman, Lawrence S. *The Cinema of Martin Scorsese*. New York: Continuum Publishing, 1997.

Fuller, Graham. "The Inner Scorsese." *Interview*, January 1998.

Gatrell, Alex. *The Unofficial and Unauthorized Biography of Robert De Niro*. London: Kandour, 2004.

Goldstein, Richard, and Jacobson, Mark. "Martin Scorsese Tells All." *Village Voice*, April 1976.

Goodman, Mark. "Tripping with Martin Scorsese." *Penthouse*, May 1977, 69–78.

Hayes, Kevin J. *Martin Scorsese's "Raging Bull."* Cambridge: Cambridge University Press, 2005.

Henry, Michael. *"Raging Bull." Positif*, April 1981, 87.

Hermann, Rick. "Rules of the Game." *Cinemonkey*, Fall 1978.

Hickenlooper, George. *Reel Conversations: Candid Interviews with Film's Foremost Directors and Critics*. New York: Citadel Press, 1991.

Hodenfield, Chris. "Martin Scorsese's Back-Lot Sonata." *Rolling Stone*, June 16, 1977, 42.

————. "You've Got to Love Something Enough to Kill It." *American Film*, March 1989.

Jackson, Kevin. *Schrader on Schrader*. Boston: Faber and Faber, 1990.

Jacobson, Mark. "Pictures of Marty." *Rolling Stone*, April 14, 1983, 108.

Kael, Pauline. "The Current Cinema." *New Yorker*, October 8, 1973, 157.

Kakutani, Michiko. "Scorsese's Past Colors His New Film." *New York Times*, February 13, 1983.

Kaplan, Jonathan. "Taxi Dancer." *Film Comment*, July/August 1977.

Kauffmann, Stanley. "Stanley Kauffmann on Films: Young Americans." *New Republic*, October 27, 1973, 22.

Kellman, Steven G. *Perspectives on "Raging Bull."* New York: G. K. Hall, 1994.

Kelly, Mary Pat. *Martin Scorsese: A Journey*. New York: Thunder's Mouth Press, 1991.

Keyser, Les. *Martin Scorsese*. New York: Twayne Publishers, 1992.

Kouvaros, George. *Paul Schrader*. Urbana: University of Illinois Press, 2008.

Kroll, Jack. "De Niro: A Star for the '70s." *Newsweek*, May 16, 1977, 82.

————. "Hackie in Hell." *Newsweek*, March 1, 1976, 82.

————. "Marty Scorsese: The Movie Brat." *Newsweek*, May 16, 1977.

LaSalle, Mick. "Scorsese's *Casino* Comes Up Broke," *San Francisco Chronicle*, November 22, 1995, 32.

Levy, Shawn. *King of Comedy: The Life and Art of Jerry Lewis*. New York: St. Martin's Griffin, 1996.

LoBrutto, Vincent. *Martin Scorsese: A Biography*. Westport, CT: Praeger Publishers, 2008.

Maltin, Leonard. *Leonard Maltin's TV Movies, 1981–1982*. New York: Signet, 1980.

Martin, Richard. *Mean Streets and Raging Bulls: The Legacy of Film Noir in Contemporary American Cinema*. Lanham, MD: Scarecrow Press, 1997.

McCarthy, Todd. "Casino." *Variety*, November 17, 1995, 122.

McKay, Keith. *Robert De Niro: The Hero behind the Masks*. New York: Ultra Communications, 1986.

Miliora, Maria T. *The Scorsese Psyche on Screen*. Jefferson, NC: McFarland, 2004.

Morgan, David. "A Remake That Can't Miss: *Cape Fear*." *American Cinematographer*, October 1991.

Murphy, Kathleen. "GoodFellas." *Film Comment*, May/June 1998.

Nicholls, Mark. *Scorsese's Men: Melancholia and the Mob*. London: Pluto Press, 2004.

Nyce, Ben. *Scorsese Up Close: A Study of the Films*. Lanham, MD: Scarecrow Press, 2004.

Paris, Barry. "Maximum Expression." *American Film*, October 1989, 36.

Parker, John. *De Niro*. London: Victor Gollancz, 1995.

Phillips, Julia. *You'll Never Eat Lunch in This Town Again*. New York: Random House, 1991.

Powell, Elfreda. *The Unofficial Robert De Niro*. Bristol: Parragon Books, 1996.

Randall, Stephen, and the editors of *Playboy* magazine, eds. *The Playboy Interviews: The Directors*. Milwaukie, OR: M Press, 2006.

Rausch, Andrew J. *Fifty Filmmakers: Conversations with Directors from Roger Avary to Steven Zaillian*. Jefferson, NC: McFarland, 2007.

Sangster, Jim. *Scorsese*. London: Virgin Books, 2002.

Scorsese, Martin. *Martin Scorsese: Interviews*. Edited by Peter Brunette. Jackson: University Press of Mississippi, 1999.

Scorsese, Martin, and Wilson, Michael Henry. "Living Las Vegas: *Casino* Diary." *Premiere*, February 1996, 49–54.

———. "On Color Preservation." *Film Comment*, May/June 1998.

———. *A Personal Journey with Martin Scorsese through American Movies*. Boston: Faber and Faber, 1997.

Scorsese, Martin, Wilson, Michael Henry, and Pileggi, Nicholas. *GoodFellas*. Boston: Faber and Faber, 1990.

Shepherd, Cybill. *Cybill Disobedience*. New York: HarperCollins, 2000.

Smith, Chris. "Fair Juliette." *New York*, November 25, 1991.

Smith, Gavin. "Martin Scorsese Interviewed." *Film Comment*, September/October 1990.

———. "Martin Scorsese Interviewed." *Film Comment*, November/December 1993.

———. "Street Smart." *Film Comment*, May/June 1998.

Stern, Lesley. *The Scorsese Connection*. London: British Film Institute, 1995.

Taubin, Amy. "Martin Scorsese's Cinema of Obsessions." *Village Voice*, September 18, 1990.

———. *Taxi Driver*. London: British Film Institute, 2000.

Thomson, David. "*Raging Bull*." *Film Comment*, May/June 1998.

Thompson, David, and Christie, Ian, eds. *Scorsese on Scorsese*. Boston: Faber and Faber, 1989.

Travers, Peter. "*Cape Fear*." *Rolling Stone*, November 28, 1991, 138.

Wiener, Thomas. "Martin Scorsese Fights Back." *American Film*, November 1980, 34.

———. "*Raging Bull*'s Secret Punch." *American Film*, November 1980, 20–35.

Woods, Paul A., ed. *Scorsese: A Journey through the American Psyche*. London: Plexus Publishing, 2005.

Yakir, Dan. "Two Sticklers and a Slugger." *After Dark*, November 1980, 29.

Films/Documentaries

Altobello, Stephen. *Getting Made: The Making of "GoodFellas."* Documentary. Warner Bros., 2004.

———. *A Shot at the Top: The Making of "The King of Comedy."* Documentary. Twentieth Century Fox, 2002.

Apple, Wendy. *The Cutting Edge*. Documentary. Warner Bros., 2004.

Bouzereau, Laurent. *After the Fight*. Documentary. Metro-Goldwyn-Mayer, 2004.

———. *"Casino": After the Filming*. Documentary. Universal Pictures, 2005.

———. *"Casino": The Cast and Characters*. Documentary. Universal Pictures, 2005.

———. *"Casino": The Look*. Documentary. Universal Pictures, 2005.

———. *"Casino": The Story*. Documentary. Universal Pictures, 2005.

———. *Inside the Ring*. Documentary. Metro-Goldwyn-Mayer, 2004.

———. *Made Men: The "GoodFellas" Legacy*. Documentary. Warner Bros., 2004.

———. *The Making of "Cape Fear."* Documentary. Universal Pictures, 2001.

———. *Making "Taxi Driver."* Documentary. Columbia Pictures, 1999.

———. *Outside the Ring*. Documentary. Metro-Goldwyn-Mayer, 2004.

———. *"Raging Bull": Before the Fight*. Documentary. Metro-Goldwyn-Mayer, 2004.

———. *The Workaday Gangster*. Documentary. Warner Bros., 2004.

Carson, Greg. *God's Lonely Man*. Documentary. Columbia Pictures, 2007.

———. *Influence and Appreciation: "Taxi Driver."* Documentary. Columbia Pictures, 2007.

———. *Liza on "New York, New York."* Documentary. Metro-Goldwyn-Mayer, 2005.

———. *Martin Scorsese on "Taxi Driver."* Documentary. Columbia Pictures, 2007.

———. *The "New York, New York" Stories*. Documentary. Metro-Goldwyn-Mayer, 2005.

———. *Producing "Taxi Driver."* Documentary. Columbia Pictures, 2007.

———. *"Taxi Driver" Stories*. Documentary. Columbia Pictures, 2007.

Emery, Robert J. *The Directors: Martin Scorsese*. Documentary. AFI, 2000.

Geisinger, Elliott. *Martin Scorsese: Back on the Block*. Documentary. Warner Bros., 1973.

Schickel, Richard. *Scorsese on Scorsese*. Documentary. TCM, 2004.

Scorsese, Martin. *Cape Fear*. Universal Pictures, 2001.

———. *Casino*. Universal Pictures, 1995.

———. *GoodFellas*. Warner Bros., 1990.

———. *The King of Comedy*. Twentieth Century Fox, 1983.

———. *Mean Streets*. Warner Bros., 1973.

———. *New York, New York*. Metro-Goldwyn-Mayer, 1977.

———. *Raging Bull*. Metro-Goldwyn-Mayer, 1980.

———. *Taxi Driver*. Columbia Pictures, 1976.

Wurtz, Jeff. *Inside the Actors Studio: Martin Scorsese*. Documentary. Bravo, 2002.

———. *Inside the Actors Studio: Robert De Niro*. Documentary. Bravo, 1998.

Original Interviews

DiLeo, Frank, October 1, 2009.

Douglas, Illeana, October 16, 2009.

Martin, Mardik, October 10, 2008.

Pollak, Kevin, September 29, 2009.

Prophet, Melissa, September 30, 2009.

Satlof, Ron, October 20, 2008.

Smothers, Dick, January 3, 2007.

Taplin, Jonathan, January 11, 2007.

Vincent, Frank, September 30, 2009.

Wertheim, Allan, March 20, 2009.

Index

About the Author

Andrew J. Rausch is a freelance journalist whose essays, critical reviews, and celebrity interviews have appeared in numerous publications. He is the resident film critic for the *Parsons Sun* in Parsons, Kansas. He has worked on a handful of motion pictures in a variety of capacities, including producer, screenwriter, actor, cinematographer, and composer. Rausch is also the author of numerous books on the subject of cinema, including *Turning Points in Film History, Fifty Filmmakers: Conversations with Directors from Roger Avary to Steven Zaillian, Reflections on Blaxploitation* (with David Walker and Chris Watson), and *Making Movies with Orson Welles* (with Gary Graver). *The Films of Martin Scorsese and Robert De Niro* is his ninth book.